Praise for *Baseball: The Movie*

"Like a wise catcher who sees the whole field, Noah Gittell brings a keen eye and sharp perspective to two national pastimes that work as perfect companions: baseball and the movies. The summer game and the silver screen have evolved together through the decades, and Gittell traces their twin histories in rich detail, with riveting behind-the-scenes stories that make you appreciate the ballpark and the box office like never before."

—Tyler Kepner
Senior writer, *The Athletic*, author of
K: A History of Baseball in Ten Pitchers

"There are baseball fans, baseball aficionados, baseball fanatics—and then there is Noah Gittell. *Baseball: The Movie* is at once literate, scholarly, and passionate. Most of all, it understands that the sport's depiction in the movies is as revealing a narrative history of America as it is of our 'national pastime.' Imagine reading Franklin Foer's classic *How Soccer Explains The World* in one hand while clutching a hot dog and a beer in the other. Move over, Bart Giamatti and Bill James, here's a new one to add to the canon."

—Edward Zwick
Cubs fan and director
of *Blood Diamond* and *The Last Samurai*

"Despite scant mention of the absolutely atrocious Grover Cleveland Alexander drama *The Winning Team*, Noah does a wonderful job of celebrating baseball and the movies and, mostly, baseball at the movies. Now if you will excuse me, I must go watch *A League of Their Own* for the 293rd time."

—Joe Posnanski
Author of *The Baseball 100* and
Why We Love Baseball: A History in 50 Moments

"If baseball explains America, Noah Gittell explains how movies about America's pastime teach us about ourselves. Gittell deftly chronicles the arc of the baseball movie the way a fan follows their favorite team—with careful attention, fanatical but rigorous understanding, and a world-weary optimism. As fans, we don't always win, but we always come back for more."

—**Sean Fennessey**
Co-host *The Big Picture* podcast

"Absolutely fantastic. *Baseball: The Movie* is much, much more than a list, a ranking, or a mere remembrance of some beloved baseball movies. It's a truly great work of cultural history."

–**Craig Calcaterra**
Author of *Rethinking Fandom: How to Beat the Sports-Industrial Complex at Its Own Game*

"Finally, someone takes baseball movies seriously! *Baseball: The Movie* blends the passion of a fan with the rigorous analysis of a film critic to create a persuasive argument that the baseball movie matters—to baseball, to Hollywood, even to America."

—**Ben Mankiewicz**
Host, Turner Classic Movies

"Just as you can always tell an actor who's held a bat and ball before being fitted for a uniform, you can always tell an author who has a feel for the sport. Fortunately, Noah Gittell's baseball mastery is more Costner or Sheen than Cooper or Perkins. To paraphrase Jacques Barzun, whoever wants to know the heart and mind of America had better learn baseball movies, and *Baseball: The Movie* is the best possible primer: a perceptive, persuasive, and comprehensive account of a quintessentially American movie genre. This union of subject and writer is a match made in heaven—or Iowa, anyway. Here's hoping Hollywood busts baseball movies out of their slump and gives Noah enough material for a sequel someday."

—**Ben Lindbergh**
Co-author of *The Only Rule Is It Has to Work* and *The MVP Machine*

"Noah Gittell has written an insightful book that falls right smack into this baseball and movie fan's sweet spot. He examines how baseball and movies about the game have reflected the culture of America through the years. What does the Lou Gehrig story, *Pride of the Yankees*, say about our need for heroes during and after World War II? What does *The Jackie Robinson Story* say about America's attitude toward race? What does *Bull Durham* say about women and sexual mores? Which actors who played baseball players knew how to hit the ball and which stars had to be replaced by stunt doubles in action scenes? Through fascinating interviews with filmmakers and careful study of a full slate of films, Gittell gives readers a true treat—a unique look at the favorite pastimes of millions around the world. Trust me: if you love baseball and movies about it, you'll treasure this book."

—**Jane Heller**
New York Times bestselling author
of *Confessions of a She-Fan* and *The Club*

"A thoughtful exploration of why baseball movies have entranced viewers for generations—and what those films tell us about the shifting priorities and temperament of this country. Rightly or wrongly, the beauty of baseball has long been synonymous with the beauty of America, and Gittell takes a close look at both, dissecting the mythologizing and questioning assumptions one film at a time."

—**Tim Grierson**
Film critic and author of *This Is How You Make a Movie*

"I'm a lifelong baseball fan and, at best, a career minor leaguer steadily working his way toward an equivalent literacy in film. I share this to magnify what makes Noah Gittell's work so impressive. Sure, I learned plenty about the history of film's long obsession with baseball, but the greatest compliment I can give *Baseball: The Movie* is that through Noah's writing on baseball's inherent cinematic brilliance and explanatory power, I grew fonder of my favorite sport."

—**Bradford William Davis**
Reporter and cultural critic

"*Baseball: The Movie* is, like the best baseball movies, fun, engaging, and illuminating. Noah Gittell tackles films both popular (*A League of Their Own* and *Bull Durham*) and obscure (*The Stratton Story* and *Fear Strikes Out*), digging deep on the numerous ways that baseball movies have always revealed larger societal trends."

—**Luke Epplin**
Author of *Our Team: The Epic Story of Four Men and the World Series That Changed Baseball*

"If you're a fan of baseball or movies, you'll gain a deeper appreciation of both after reading Noah Gittell's engaging book about these two great American pastimes—and when you're done you'll have a whole list of films to watch during the next off-season."

—**Matt Singer**
Author of *Opposable Thumbs: How Siskel & Ebert Changed Movies Forever*

"The greatest baseball moments can feel like they're happening in a movie: Human drama on an epic scale, one combatant pitted against each other, with everything on the line. Noah Gittell's *Baseball: The Movie* understands the inextricable connection between the sport and the silver screen. It's hard to get baseball right. It's hard to get movies right. This book gets them both right."

—**Will Leitch**
Film critic, sportswriter, and author of *How Lucky* and *The Time Has Come*

"For most of my life, I've been waiting for a great book about baseball movies, because for nearly all my life I've been obsessed with both baseball and movies. Thanks to Noah Gittell, it's been worth the wait. Gittell doesn't just write brilliantly about baseball movies; he also places them in the context of American culture and society over the better part of a century. This book is a bravura, Oscar-worthy achievement."

—**Rob Neyer**
Author of *Power Ball: Anatomy of a Modern Game*

"There's analysis and there's storytelling. In my professional life, I practice them in the booth all season long. Noah Gittell not only masters each skill in *Baseball: The Movie*, but intertwines them seamlessly with humor, depth, and a personal perspective that makes it a must-read for any movie lover, baseball fan, or curious observer of American culture."

—**Ron Darling**
Author, baseball analyst, and former MLB pitcher

"Reading Noah Gittell's book is as satisfying as watching Ray Kinsella have a twilight catch with his father or Dottie Hinson snatch a hardball with her bare hand. With a fan's passion and a critic's clear eyes, Gittell pays excellent tribute to America's pastime and the beloved films staged among its diamonds and sandlots. Nostalgic, smart, and entertaining all at once."

—**Erin Carlson**
Author of *No Crying in Baseball:*
The Inside Story of A League of Their Own

"Noah Gittell conveys the magic of baseball and cinema, and he helps us to understand the relationship of both to American life. This is a book with brains and heart."

—**Andy Martino**
Author of *The Yankee Way* and *Cheated*

Baseball
· THE MOVIE ·

Noah Gittell

TRIUMPH
BOOKS

Library of Congress Cataloging-in-Publication Data available upon request.

This book is available in quantity at special discounts for your group or organization. For further information, contact:

Triumph Books LLC
814 North Franklin Street
Chicago, Illinois 60610
(312) 337-0747
www.triumphbooks.com

Printed in U.S.A.
ISBN: 978-1-63727-264-0
Design by Patricia Frey

For Breanna, of course

Contents

Foreword

THIS IS A BOOK BY A FAN, A FAN BOTH OF BASEBALL AND OF THE MOVIES, and he begins by explaining why the two seem to go together so well. I think only boxing has been used more frequently as a sports setting for film, and boxing's appeal is that it is the polar opposite of a team effort— one battler alone with an opponent in the ring and there's nobody else to blame. One of the eternal dramas of any professional team is that athletes who live and work and play together are often competing for the same job. That kid you gave so many veteran batting pointers to might just be the one who pushes you out of the game for good. Baseball is unique in that it has so many drumroll confrontations—time *stops,* people meet on the mound, a new pitcher or pinch-hitter is brought in, the combatants get to stare at each other for a moment—you can even add a few foul balls to increase the tension. A foul shot in basketball or field goal in football can carry the same game-ending stakes, but there it's up to one man to deliver (why no teammate talks to or even likes to *look* at the kicker until the ball goes between the goalposts).

A baseball game is full of *story,* as well as backstory (scoreboards now flash the batter's statistics when they step to the plate) and legend. You don't have to call a time-out for somebody to have a conversation. Weak hitters occasionally guess right against terrific pitchers, and pitchers can have an awful day (how does one "scatter" 13 hits?) and muddle through with a shutout because all those screaming line drives were hit straight at a fielder. The players don't wear helmets so you can see their faces, and the play-by-play announcers provide running narration and context to the on-field action, as well as providing a ubiquitous and useful cutaway. A game tailored for cinema.

Noah Gittell has also thought hard about what these movies, and the sport itself, has meant to Americans over the various decades—why they got made, how they were received, whether the message and tone of the movies were underscoring or challenging the zeitgeist of the moment. My favorite, *The Bad News Bears*, is included here, a terrific movie that probably could only have gotten made by a Hollywood studio within a five- or six-year period—a kind of *glasnost* moment where an honest look at ourselves was permitted and sometimes even financed. The quality of the baseball itself is commented upon—Tony Perkins is a two-sport disaster in *Fear Strikes Out* and *Tall Story*—but Gittell properly considers the tone of the movie in question. If angels are influencing the flight of the ball, we're not talking about documentary realism.

We did a charity event with *Eight Men Out* for an organization called BATS, formed by major leaguers to help financially stressed former colleagues who played before a pension was offered. After the screening, I asked the attendees, who included former stars like Warren Spahn and Enos Slaughter, what they thought of the movie. Almost to a man they said, "I wish I could have hit against that pitching." Even with us chopping frames to speed the ball up, our 85–90 mph fastballs looked to them like batting-practice tosses. Our actors and extras did a manful job catching sizzlers with the tiny gloves used in 1919, and otherwise acquitted themselves well, but modern sports movies have long-lens and even drone coverage of real games to compete with, a very tough act to follow.

So dip into *Baseball: The Movie*, and try to check out the films you haven't seen. These are movies that tell you as much about the people who made them and the American audience they were aimed at as about the sport itself. Baseball, as Noah Gittell reminds us, has as complicated and contentious a history as the movies themselves.

—John Sayles
Writer/director of *Eight Men Out* and
two-time Academy Award nominee for Best Original Screenplay

Introduction

Warm-Up

THERE ARE CERTAIN THINGS THAT CAN ONLY HAPPEN IN A BASEBALL GAME or a movie. One of them occurred when I was six. It was 1986, and the New York Mets were about to lose the World Series, an unthinkable scenario to a boy who had only fallen in love with baseball earlier that year and assumed that his favorite team would surely win it all. Sadly, it seemed not to be. The Red Sox, up three games to two in the series and 5–3 in the game, were preparing to pop the champagne. The Mets were down to their final out. Then Gary Carter, my favorite player, stepped to the plate and singled to left. Kevin Mitchell followed with another single. Ray Knight fought off an inside fastball and blooped it over the second baseman's head. A run scored. The Mets were within one.

That's when the movie began. Sox reliever Bob Stanley threw a wild pitch. The game was tied. As Knight danced off of second base, Mookie Wilson fouled off a couple of tough pitches, then hit a dribbler down the first-base line. Bill Buckner, the usually sure-handed first baseman, was hobbled by a bad ankle, and as he moved to his left and put his glove down, the ball somehow slipped through his legs. "Behind the bag! It gets through Buckner!" exclaimed play-by-play announcer Vin Scully, his voice rising in excitement. "Here comes Knight, and the Mets win it!"

I've been searching for that feeling ever since, and the only place I've ever found it is in baseball movies. Hollywood exists to provide the glorious catharsis life rarely does, but the baseball movie, a collision of two dreams, is a little different. It returns us to a heaven we've already glimpsed. Watching Roy Hobbs round the bases with sparks flying down on him at the end of *The Natural*, or the Indians winning a play-in game in the bottom of the ninth in *Major League*, brings me back to that night in 1986, when the unbelievable actually happened. Buckner blamed his error on a "loose glove." Baseball fans know the truth. It was magic.

Magic is the chain that links baseball history together, keeping silly fans like me on the edge of their seats through the dog days of summer, when their team's playoff chances are dropping faster than a Shohei Ohtani splitter. It's all worth it. Once a week, you see something in a game you've never seen before. A few times a year you'll see something you can barely wrap your mind around, and when it happens in a big spot, there's nothing better in sports. "I don't believe what I just saw!" shouted Scully, when Kirk Gibson, with a bad knee in one leg and a bad hamstring in the other, limped to the plate in Game 1 of the 1988 World Series and hit a game-winning, pinch-hit home run against Dennis Eckersley, the game's greatest reliever. We could say the same thing about Babe Ruth calling his shot in the '32 World Series, Bobby Thomson winning the pennant with the "Shot Heard 'Round the World" in '51, or Joe Carter hitting a walk-off homer to win the '93 World Series for the Blue Jays. Baseball is largely a game spent waiting for these moments.

It's the most cinematic of all sports, and watching it triggers our primal need for drama, suspense, and even a Hollywood ending. The other sports—basketball, football, hockey, soccer—only move left to right on your television, or right to left. They make great video games. But baseball exists in three dimensions, with the ball zipping in one direction and then another in the same play. It's the only sport where the points are scored away from the ball. It's a game of dramatic confrontation, telling its story through faces rather than bodies. The pitcher peers in at the catcher, and the batter stares down the pitcher, like an armed standoff in a classic western or a Tarantino flick. It's rich with perspective and thick with drama. Better still, there is time—even with the newly-introduced pitch clock—to contemplate the meaning of these images. Football is war, and basketball is a dance, but baseball, in which a single moment can seemingly stretch toward the infinite, is cinema.

Because of its focus on individual matchups, baseball lends itself to heroes and villains, often in the same game. The guy who made the crucial error in the top of the ninth inning can win it in the bottom. Cardinals pitcher Rick Ankiel can lose his composure on the biggest possible stage by throwing five wild pitches in a playoff game, leave baseball for three years, then return as an outfielder and hit 25 home runs in a season. In baseball, a pitcher who has only the full use of one of his arms— Jim Abbott—can not only get to the major leagues but actually throw a no-hitter. Does this happen in other sports? Not really, but I can't tell you why, except for the fact that baseball is cinema, and different rules apply. Redemption stories abound, and suspension of your disbelief is rewarded.

Growing up in the '80s and '90s, I enjoyed a full roster of baseball films to support my burgeoning baseball obsession and teach me to believe in the impossible. I was too young to see *Bull Durham* and *Major League* when they first came out, although they became VHS staples a few years later. I didn't understand everything about *Field of Dreams* or *Eight Men Out*, but their recreations of early baseball fascinated me all the same. Once the kids' baseball movie boom started, I devoured *Rookie of the Year, Little Big League, The Sandlot,* and *Angels in the Outfield*. As a young baseball fanatic with virtually no athletic ability, these films and their uncoordinated protagonists lodged permanently in my heart.

Baseball movies are important. They develop fans of the game by drawing out its drama and revealing its humanity. Let's be honest: Baseball players aren't always so forthcoming about their inner lives, their hopes, and their fears. The league doesn't help us get to know them; particularly in recent years, it has been terrible about marketing its stars. We need the movies to show us what it feels like to be on a hot streak or stuck in a slump, to take those long bus trips between minor league stadiums, or to scream in an umpire's face after a blown call. When we watch a catcher get tossed after a nose-to-nose confrontation at home plate, we wonder if he used the same word that got Crash Davis ejected in *Bull Durham*. Each time a player hits a walk-off home run, the theme from *Moneyball* echoes in our ears. In many ways, real-world baseball still aspires to the baseball movie.

The cynics will always disagree. They'll shake their heads and say baseball movies are cheesy and unrealistic. They'll scoff at the end of *The Natural*, when Roy Hobbs hits a home run to win the pennant while bleeding from an old wound in his gut. They'll point out that in the book Roy Hobbs actually strikes out in his climactic at-bat and tell you that it's a much better ending for a game built on loss and disappointment. They'll gleefully remind you that the best hitter in baseball makes an out seven out of every 10 times. Pay them no mind. These people misunderstand baseball, as well as the baseball movie. The disappointment is real, but so is the magic. If we believe in Kirk Gibson, we must believe in Roy Hobbs.

Believe in them both, since baseball and cinema have walked together in lockstep throughout history. They weren't invented at the same time; baseball, from what we can gather, was first played in the early 1840s, while film as a commercial enterprise was coined in the 1890s. But they both became popular American entertainments over the first few decades of the 20th century, when immigrants and rural Americans alike were flocking to urban areas and found themselves in desperate need of amusement. Baseball, with its wide-open spaces, reminded them of home. The movies took them to places they'd never been.

In the years following World War I, both film and baseball became enmeshed—corrupted, to some—in the culture of sin and excess, and each industry was forced to take drastic steps to ensure its continued existence. In baseball, the owners created the office of the Commissioner of Baseball to guarantee the game would be played cleanly and without the influence of gamblers. The movie studios created the self-censoring Production Code, which outlawed the depiction of challenging or subversive material, including everything from adultery to interracial marriage, in a successful attempt to keep crusading moralists like the Catholic League off their back. Belief in the impossible was too wild and powerful to go unregulated.

Nearly a century later, baseball and cinema once again find themselves on a shared precipice. As the digital revolution has dramatically restructured the way humans entertain themselves, both baseball and the movies have fallen from their shared perch atop American culture. Baseball has been leapfrogged by football and basketball in popularity and resorted to a series of new rules intended to quicken the game's pace and attract the attention of younger fans. Robot umpires, they tell us, are coming next. Meanwhile, the advent of streaming services and prestige television have made movie executives just as desperate, and they've determined that the best way to get butts in the seats is to turn viewers into something akin to sports fans. They work to create franchise allegiance and rivalries between studios; the Marvel fans hate DC like the Red Sox hate the Yankees, and they have the ticket stubs to prove it.

Any institution that's around for a century and a quarter will have to reinvent itself a few times to remain relevant. That's the story of cinema and baseball. They're not dying. They're just in flux, as they always have been. Is their future a bit more uncertain than it was, say, at the turn of the 21st century? Probably. But there is a long, complex series of events that need to occur for either one to actually end. We're not close to that happening, and the fact that both have survived numerous threats before—the Catholic League, the National Football League, television, VHS, and steroids—should give nervous fans some confidence. We're dealing with sturdy things here.

The baseball film, however, is far more intricate. As a synthesis of two national pastimes, it is uniquely positioned to explain America. It's as efficient a propaganda machine as you could dream up—rippling with optimism and overstuffed with Americana—but its popularity is dependent on the mood of the nation. On the surface, the baseball film may only concern itself with platitudes like teamwork and self-fulfillment, but it also wrestles admirably with race, gender, labor, war, and religion. Look closely at the baseball film and you'll see the American experience in microcosm; an institution grappling with its own values, wrestling its contradictions into a reasonable facsimile of what the Founding Fathers called "a more perfect union." In their way, the best baseball movies contribute to the ongoing debate over the soul of America.

Those are the ones I explore in this book, which brings us to a crucial disclaimer: As you look over the table of contents, you might get annoyed that your favorite baseball film—be it *For Love of the Game*, *Fever Pitch*, or *Mr. 3000*—did not merit a chapter. I understand your frustration, but to be perfectly clear, it's not that those films aren't worthy entries in the canon. I love *Fever Pitch* with my whole heart, and I think *Mr. 3000* is underrated. *For Love of the Game* is half a great movie (the baseball stuff is stellar, the love story not so much). I refer to each of them—as well as *Mr. Baseball*, *Hardball*, and *61**—in these pages, but to give every baseball movie a full excavation would disrupt the story I'm trying to tell. This is a book about how baseball cinema explains America, and those films just don't contribute meaningfully to that narrative.

They're still worth loving, though. All baseball movies are, even the bad ones. Even *The Benchwarmers*. Offscreen, athletes come and go, and only a precious few will stay on your favorite team for their whole career. Even fewer will go into the Hall of Fame with your team's logo on their cap. Baseball is a game of letting go, but a baseball movie doesn't require that of us. It lives in an eternal present, where Jake Taylor is still hanging on to his major league career, Roy Hobbs is forever rounding those bases, and Dottie Hinson never went back to Oregon to have kids. Watching these films transports me back to 1986, before I knew about free agency, labor agreements, steroids, or ulnar collateral ligament damage, when the game was just magic.

As a film critic and lifelong fan of the game, I wrote this book to spend time with my two great loves and deepen my understanding of their union. I wanted to share their secrets. I wanted to confirm the brilliance of old classics and discover new classics that had been overlooked. I wanted to spend time thinking about how they were made and figure out why they have endured. As I investigate and celebrate the baseball movie, I hope to illuminate how it reflects the ever-changing landscape of American culture. I'd also be happy if it made you just love baseball and movies a little bit more. It did for me.

· PART I ·

How the Baseball Film Built the American Dream

Chapter 1

Pride of the Yankees (1942) and The Stratton Story (1949)

"IT'S BOX-OFFICE POISON. IF PEOPLE WANT BASEBALL, THEY GO TO THE ballpark." Those were the words reportedly spoken by legendary Hollywood producer Samuel Goldwyn about baseball films—just before he made the most successful one his industry had ever produced.

In 1939, the movie rights to the life story of Lou Gehrig, whose name Goldwyn surely knew but whose place in the hearts of baseball fans he couldn't possibly understand, were dropped on the great producer's desk. Goldwyn was famously ignorant of the national pastime. He didn't know the number of outs in an inning or innings in a game. He was simply not a fan of the sport, and he couldn't understand why anyone would want to see a movie about it.

The receipts bore his position out. "No baseball film has ever been successful at the box office," read the *New York Times* in a January 1942 story announcing the start of production of *The Pride of the Yankees*. On the other hand, a serious attempt had never been made. *The Pride of the Yankees* would eventually be nominated for 11 Academy Awards, winning one for Best Editing, but no previous baseball movie had even aspired to one. Upon the film's release, the *New York Herald Tribune*

3

took stock of the genre: "We don't remember that the movies ever before tried seriously to portray the life, character, hopes and tragedies of a ball player. Such former baseball pictures we remember were comedies, or far-fetched melodramas, or intricately worked-out stories of how somebody managed to murder somebody else while a baseball game was going on." Babe Ruth had starred in a pair of goofy silent features, 1920's *Headin' Home* and 1927's *Babe Comes Home*. Both were trounced by critics and roundly defeated at the box office. Wallace Beery, a silent film star who made a successful jump to talkies, starred in 1927's *Casey at the Bat*, which built up a flimsy comic narrative around Ernest Thayer's famous Mudville-set poem. It underperformed and was swiftly forgotten. Baseball films continued to be made—often as shorts that preceded feature-length films in cinemas—but like a hot young prospect who had never been able to adjust to big-league pitching, they were on the verge of forced retirement.

The story of Lou Gehrig, however, had rare potential, even if it took Goldwyn a minute to see it. *The Pride of the Yankees* was never going to be just a baseball film. At its core, it's a drama, a romance, and a tear-jerker. Gehrig's accomplishments on the field were unimpeachable, but it was his character—that unearthly combination of courage, integrity, and decency—and his untimely death that elevated his story into the great commercial cinema. His life was a structurally sound narrative that even the most hackneyed screenwriter couldn't screw up. There was the promising start in which the talented young ballplayer embarks on a career so that he can take care of his immigrant parents; the happy middle that finds Gehrig dominating his sport and falling in love; and the tragic, heroic end in which the legend crumbles before our eyes, maintaining his dignity to the last, and in his final public appearance, inspiring untold millions with his off-the-cuff oration at Yankee Stadium. They wouldn't need a dialogue-polisher; the climactic speech was already written.

In fact, it was this speech that finally convinced Goldwyn that Gehrig's story was worthy of the cinematic treatment. He watched the newsreel in his private screening room; when it was over, he watched it again.

Gary Cooper's recitation of Gehrig's famous words is one of the most indelible moments in American cinema, the speech to which all orations from real-life athletes are compared. It's the moment that turns the movie from a first-rate weepie into a classic. In a sense, it's a good thing Goldwyn wasn't a baseball man. If he were, he might have included far more action in it. *The Pride of the Yankees* might have just been another failed baseball picture instead of a smash hit with audiences and critics, and eight decades of baseball cinema might never have happened. With its underdog narrative, central romance, and unabashed patriotism, *The Pride of the Yankees* is the template on which all future baseball films are based. They either emulate it, subvert it, or retrofit it to a new era or setting, but the core metaphor of the sport as a vessel for America's virtues remains fundamental.

So what exactly did Goldwyn see in that newsreel footage that compelled him to invest in this story? We can't know for sure. The actual footage has been lost to history, and the speech written for *The Pride of the Yankees* was at least slightly altered. Historians have been able to cobble together a reasonable guess at Gehrig's full remarks from reports at the time. I have a strong suspicion these are the lines that alerted Goldwyn to the potential of the story:

> *When you have a wonderful mother-in-law who takes sides with you in squabbles with her own daughter—that's something. When you have a father and a mother who work all their lives so you can have an education and build your body—it's a blessing. When you have a wife who has been a tower of strength and shown more courage than you dreamed existed—that's the finest I know.*

It's an oration befitting a president: eloquent and incisive, with a touch of down-home charm. You can see why Goldwyn went for it. In Gehrig, he saw a man of humble origins who made good and never lost sight of everything that mattered in life. Someone to whom audiences could both relate and aspire. That's the stuff of blockbusters.

Goldwyn may not have known baseball, but he was uniquely qualified to recognize an effective tear-jerker. Since branching out from MGM to start his own company, the still-operating Samuel Goldwyn Company, Goldwyn had made his mark with melodramas and women's pictures. His first major success was 1937's *Stella Dallas*, starring Barbara Stanwyck as a poverty-born woman who suffers tragically in her efforts to rise above her station and provide for her daughter. Then came 1939's *Wuthering Heights*, a hit romance based on the novel by Emily Brontë that was nominated for eight Oscars, including Best Picture. While he was planning *Pride of the Yankees*, he was also producing *The Little Foxes*, a Bette Davis melodrama, and *Ball of Fire*, starring Cooper and Stanwyck. Whatever you want to call them—melodramas, women's pictures, movies for sad boys—Goldwyn was the best at making them.

In its final version, *The Pride of the Yankees* is a romance as much as a baseball movie, and according to all accounts, Goldwyn insisted on this from the beginning. The first draft delivered to him had too much baseball in it and was immediately re-written. Publicly, he was clear about his intentions. "First of all, *The Pride of the Yankees* is not to be, in a strict sense, a 'baseball picture,'" he said at the time. "I have not been motivated, for example, by the fact that baseball is America's greatest sport, that no ambitious motion picture has ever been made with big-league baseball as its background or that 1941 was baseball's greatest year." That last sentence should have raised an eyebrow or two—Goldwyn hardly knew enough about baseball to make such a claim. He must have checked with some actual baseball fans who knew that 1941 was the year Ted Williams hit .406 and Joe DiMaggio had a 56-game hitting streak. Goldwyn took every opportunity to market the movie as something more than a baseball film, but he also understood that he couldn't afford to alienate the sport's fans. Fifty-five years later, another film tried it with football. It was called *Jerry Maguire*, and like *The Pride of the Yankees*, it featured on-field action, locker room scenes, and a breathtaking romance. It worked. Both films were acclaimed by critics, adored by fans, and recognized at the Oscars.

To chalk up the film's success to either its baseball, its romance, or some combination of the two, however, is to miss the real reason it resonated so deeply with audiences. *The Pride of the Yankees* was also a war movie, a story about what it means to be an American at a time when Americans were thinking about little else. It spells out its metaphor right at the top. The film opens with onscreen text penned by famed sportswriter Damon Runyan: "This is the story of a hero of the peaceful paths of everyday life. It is the story of a gentle young man who, in the full flower of his great fame, was a lesson in simplicity and modesty to the youth of America. He faced death with that same valor and fortitude that has been displayed by thousands of young Americans on far-flung fields of battle. He left behind him a memory of courage and devotion that will ever be an inspiration to all men. This is the story of Lou Gehrig."

When Goldwyn greenlit *Pride of the Yankees*, the United States had not yet entered World War II, so there was no way for him to know how Gehrig's life and death—a shining example of an American hero cut down in his prime—would serve as a symbol of the more than 400,000 young American men who would die in the next few years. He couldn't possibly have understood what *The Pride of the Yankees* would mean to many Americans who feared for the lives of their sons and brothers. There is no record of Goldwyn or anyone else involved in the making of the film even thinking about this. Maybe it would have been uncouth to discuss it during production. A bit too much like war profiteering. And yet they must have had an inkling, as the calls for the U.S. to join the war were growing stronger throughout 1941, when the film was in preproduction. In fact, one film that beat it to theaters, *Woman of the Year*, helped to lay the groundwork for this intermingling of baseball and war on the big screen.

The first collaboration between Spencer Tracy and Katharine Hepburn, 1942's *Woman of the Year* is the story of two newspaper columnists who fall in love. For our purposes, it's most notable for an early scene in which Tracy, after Hepburn casually suggests putting baseball on hiatus until the war is over, steadfastly defends the importance of the game in trying times: "We're concerned with a threat to what we like to call our American way of life. Baseball and the things it represents are part of that way of life. What's the sense in abolishing the thing you're trying to protect?" In these succinct lines, *Woman of the Year* sets up baseball as a fundamental symbol of American freedom. Just watch. From this point on, every baseball film will in some way be a film about America, its ideals and virtues, its myths and its illusions.

As Gehrig, Gary Cooper ably embodies American righteousness, but he wasn't the only cast member contributing to the film's stirring war subtext. Let's consider the character of Mom Gehrig, as she's identified in the credits, played by Elsa Janssen. To establish baseball as the great American game, and one worth fighting a war on foreign soil to save, the screenwriters focused on Janssen as a proxy for the baseball skeptics in the audience. Mom Gehrig starts out as resistant to the idea of her son playing baseball for a living, even if he is doing it only to help take care of his parents financially. "That's what we came to America for?" she asks him, when he reveals that he has signed with the Yankees. "A wonderful country where everybody has an equal chance? That's why you studied, why you went to Columbia, so that you could play baseball?" At her first game, she shows her ignorance when the guy selling her a scorecard says he's never heard of her son. "Substitute?" he asks. "No, Yankee," she replies. It establishes Mom Gehrig as an entry point to the game for the baseball-averse, and her transformation into a baseball fanatic left skeptics with little recourse but to become fans themselves. By the final game, Mom Gehrig is analyzing the games with the eye of an expert. "He should wait him out," she says, anxiously, as she watches her son bat. "The pitcher has been missing the corner since the sixth inning." It's delightful to see her become a superfan in real time, but the politics of her transformation cannot be ignored. Turning a German immigrant who finds the sport frivolous and unworthy into a baseball lifer powerfully contextualizes the sport in the politics of World War II. To be American, it says, is to love baseball.

The whole cast is excellent, especially Teresa Wright, who shines as Gehrig's devoted, mischievous wife, Eleanor, a woman who likes to eat "hot dogs and champagne" for dinner, enjoys tricking sportswriters into thinking Gehrig is cheating on her, and can take a practical joke—like when Cooper pulls out her chair for her, leaving Wright to fall on her fanny. Out of the many young actresses who could have played Eleanor, Wright possessed a perhaps unique combination of courage and wit, making her perfect for a character who is Gehrig's equal. Consider the famous clause in her contract with MGM:

> *The aforementioned Teresa Wright shall not be required to pose for photographs in a bathing suit unless she is in the water. Neither may she be photographed running on the beach with her hair flying in the wind. Nor may she pose in any of the following situations: In shorts, playing with a cocker spaniel; digging in a garden; whipping up a meal; attired in firecrackers and holding skyrockets for the Fourth of July; looking insinuatingly at a turkey for Thanksgiving; wearing a bunny cap with long ears for Easter; twinkling on prop snow in a skiing outfit while a fan blows her scarf; assuming an athletic stance while pretending to hit something with a bow and arrow.*

It's hard to overstate how rare it was for a young actress to refuse to do this kind of promotional work. The *Pride of the Yankees* was only Wright's third movie, and she was 24 when she signed. She got away with it because her talent couldn't be denied. She was particularly adept at displaying realistic emotion. William Wyler, nominated for a record 12 Best Director Academy Awards, described her as "the best cryer in business," a skill that she crucially displays in the final reel of *Pride*. After learning of her husband's diagnosis, she does her best to keep his spirits up. Then, finally, before his special day at Yankee Stadium, she lets down her guard and sobs in his arms. "I've got a right to cry a little," she tells him. "It's such a beautiful thing." If Gehrig is a stand-in for young American soldiers risking their lives overseas, Eleanor represents their mourners. Much as Cooper showed young men how to be stoic in the face of injury or death, Wright provided a model for how their loved ones might suffer a devastating loss with courage and vulnerability.

Still, *Pride of the Yankees* belongs to Cooper, an ascendant star in a role that would define his legacy. In 1942, when *Pride* began shooting, there were few hotter actors in Hollywood. In the prior year, he'd made three standout films that worked in perfect concert to prepare audiences to accept him as Gehrig. First was *Ball of Fire*, the whimsical and eccentric romantic comedy that solidified him as a romantic lead. In the same year, he made *Sergeant York*, a biopic about one of the most decorated soldiers of World War I. Cooper won the Best Actor Oscar for playing York, as the film resonated with a public that was gearing up for another righteous war.

Rounding out Cooper's 1941 was *Meet John Doe*, the Frank Capra fable in which Cooper plays a minor league pitcher who, having fallen on hard times, agrees to play the role of the fictitious John Doe, a character invented by a desperate journalist and used by the paper's scheming publisher to advance his political aspirations. It's a complicated idea made gloriously simple by Capra, known for broadly appealing films such as *It's a Wonderful Life* and *Mr. Smith Goes to Washington*. It's not quite a baseball movie—there's no actual baseball action in it—but the choice to make Cooper's character a ballplayer signifies how filmmakers were already keying into the cinematic possibilities of baseball as shorthand for patriotism. "A baseball player," says Barbara Stanwyck in the film, dreaming of how Doe's story could enchant her readers. "What could be more American?"

His role in *Meet John Doe* also surely helped viewers buy Cooper as a professional ballplayer, which, considering his total ineptitude with a bat and glove, was no small feat. Cooper was a good athlete—especially on a horse—but much like Goldwyn, baseball was never his game. At least Cooper had an excuse: he lived in England between the ages of seven and 11. His parents eventually settled back in Montana, but by then it was too late. "The other kids were so far ahead of me at playing ball," he explained, "I just never got started and stuck to football and track instead." The good news for Cooper was that he didn't need to play the game like a pro. Total authenticity in baseball films was not yet a prerequisite. Since only 5,000 American homes had a television in 1942, baseball fans had few onscreen visual references to which they would compare the film. Still, he couldn't look like a total doofus out there while playing a great American hero who would inspire millions. In order for his physical deterioration to resonate, we had to first buy him as a legendary athlete, at least in short snippets. To learn the basics, Cooper spent six weeks training with Lefty O'Doul, a former ballplayer and manager of the San Francisco Seals, who played in the Pacific Coast League, a regional professional league that kept California baseball fans busy until the Dodgers and Giants moved there in the 1950s.

O'Doul wasn't impressed with Cooper's skills. "You throw a ball like an old woman tossing a hot biscuit," he told the star. Over time, Cooper made progress. O'Doul taught him to compare the swinging of a baseball bat to that of an ax, an activity Cooper was well familiar with from his time in Montana. The training made for a fun story for the press. As he worked on his game, critics and sportswriters scoffed at his chances of winning them over with his baseball skills. "BASEBALL FILM BAFFLES GARY," read a headline in the *Oakland Tribune* on the Sunday before shooting began, reporting Cooper was working hard at the game but was still not up to snuff. Some have suggested that stories like these were planted by Goldwyn's publicity team. It's a good theory, as they certainly added a level of intrigue to the film. Some baseball fans might have shown up just to watch Cooper embarrass himself.

Through his work with O'Doul, Cooper did improve but not enough that he didn't need some filmmaking chicanery to smooth over his rough edges. In the finished film, Cooper is often seen swinging the bat, running the bases, and fielding, but precise cutting allows the filmmakers to swap in stunt doubles and archival footage to create a seamless final product. In Richard Sandomir's book *The Pride of the Yankees: Lou Gehrig, Gary Cooper, and the Making of a Classic*, he demonstrates that "[w]hen batting, Cooper appears to cleanly line one pitch but is framed in such a tight close-up on the next shot that it is impossible to know if he hit the ball, save for the accompanying sound effect. His throws are also cropped so severely that their strength and accuracy cannot be determined." If you want to see other examples of this technique, put on pretty much any other baseball movie ever made. *Pride of the Yankees* invented the visual grammar of the baseball film, discovering and employing editing techniques to turn a movie star with little baseball experience into a reasonable facsimile of one of the most talented players of all time. In later years, these techniques were used to make actors as disparate as John Cusack (*Eight Men Out*), Rosie O'Donnell (*A League of Their Own*), and Bernie Mac (*Mr. 3000*) look like they're zinging line drives all over the field.

There were other falsehoods in the film, contrivances that retrofitted Gehrig's story to the contours of effective film drama. The film shows Lou and Eleanor meeting on the day his consecutive-games streak began. They actually met several years later. He was not knocked nearly unconscious by a ball thrown in a double-play on that day, so of course no one uttered the ironic words, "What do we have to do, kill you to get you out of the line-up?" Gehrig didn't hit a homer the day he and Eleanor were married. He actually went hitless but did drive in two runs with a walk and a sac fly. Later, he mentions that he won a batting championship the year they were married. Nope. They got married in 1933, and he won the batting title in 1934. Finally, Yankee fanatics will note that the Yankees didn't wear numbers on their uniforms until 1929, but the film shows one on Gehrig's back when he makes his debut in 1923.

One of the film's dramatic liberties would be obvious to any baseball fan today, even if they were unfamiliar with Gehrig's story. When Gehrig can no longer deny the toll his illness has taken on his baseball skills, and chooses to end his consecutive-games streak, he does so by taking himself out of a game in the middle of it. It's a poignant moment, but as any baseball fan knows, that would still count as a game played, and his streak would live to see another day. He'd have to miss an entire game to end it, which is of course what occurred in real life.

To fault the film for these mistakes, however, is to misunderstand how baseball films were judged at the time. These days, moviegoers expect total authenticity from their biopics, and mimicry from their stars. Rami Malek won an Oscar for wearing fake teeth and lip-syncing to Freddie Mercury in 2018's *Bohemian Rhapsody*, and while he didn't really look much like him, the effort alone was considered award worthy. In 1942, failures of verisimilitude were easily overlooked if the story moved viewers. *The Pride of the Yankees* certainly did that. It grossed $4.2 million dollars, a pittance by today's standards, but enough to make it the ninth-highest grosser of the year. Not bad for a baseball film. It was certainly enough to persuade studio executives that the genre was not box-office poison.

Its reception with critics was a little more muted. Bosley Crowther, the famed critic for the *New York Times*, initially gave *Pride* a mixed review, writing that it "inclines to monotony" in its lack of baseball action. "Sports fans will protest," he continued. Although he bemoaned the quantity of baseball, he acknowledged that "what is shown is accurate." Hardly a ringing endorsement, but his true feelings actually ran deeper. After sitting with it for a week, he felt compelled to expound upon his frustrations:

> *The Great American Pastime is still waiting to be brought to life upon the screen! Yet here, in the ball parks of this nation, is the rich and pungent flavor of our life, the surge of ebullient spirit and the mammoth cohesion of the crowd. When is somebody going to capture on film the dramatic entity of a Summer afternoon at Yankee Stadium or any other park throughout the land—the ululation of the grandstands, the hot sun beating down on the green outfield, the cry of the vendors, the click of telegraph instruments, the echoing roar of the announcers, the thud of the catcher's mitt, the crack of bats, that first hit, a runner racing madly around third base and tearing down on home, the dust around the plate, the crowded dugout when the players come trooping in, the*

suspense of a long foul and the afternoon shadows ever lengthening across the playing field! Who says there isn't color and drama in an American baseball game? Who says that it couldn't be put into a film?

Crowther isn't critiquing *The Pride of the Yankees*. He's asking for more transcendent baseball films to be made, ones that properly capture the majesty of the game. In essence, he's confirming that Goldwyn accomplished his goal of making *The Pride of the Yankees* into something other than a baseball movie. And in part because Goldwyn's formula proved so successful, Crowther's plea to the Hollywood gods to make a more dynamic baseball film would go unheeded for quite some time. For years, *The Pride of the Yankees*, a story with more romance than baseball, would be the template.

In the meantime, the film found yet another audience overseas with U.S. service members. Like many stars of his generation, Cooper did not serve in the war and instead did his part by making propaganda films (like *Sergeant York* and *The Pride of the Yankees*) and embarking on USO tours to entertain the troops. On one tour stop in 1943, he had just finished his routine, which involved some basic vaudeville and a romantic scene with B-movie actress Phyllis Brooks, when a soldier shouted out a request that he recite the Gehrig speech. Cooper had recently recreated the speech on a radio program, so it wasn't far from his mind. He took a minute to refresh his memory and delivered it for the troops. Writing about that moment 13 years later for *The Saturday Evening Post*, he said, "They were the words of a brave American who had only a short time to live, and they meant something to those kids in the Pacific." Word spread of his recitation, and he performed the speech at several other stops in the South Pacific.

That's why *The Pride of the Yankees* endures. Yes, it invented the modern baseball movie, shaping its tropes and solidifying its use of sport as a metaphor for democracy, but it also spoke with great power and specificity to this crucial moment in history, when young, able-bodied men were asked to sacrifice their bodies to preserve a way of life. It validated the national pastime as a fundamental symbol of American greatness. At that moment, and due to the efforts of all involved in making *Pride of the Yankees*, it was even something worth dying for.

Unlike Gary Cooper, Jimmy Stewart served in World War II, and he did so enthusiastically. At the time the U.S. entered the war, Stewart was a star on the rise. In 1938, the 30-year-old burst onto the screen with a celebrated role in *You Can't Take It With You,* an Oscar-winning comedy based on a Pulitzer-Prize winning play. A year later, he starred in *Mr. Smith Goes to Washington,* and the year after that, he won a Best Actor Oscar for holding his own against Cary Grant and Katharine Hepburn in *The Philadelphia Story.* There was no hotter actor in Hollywood.

So no one would have criticized Stewart for opting out of military service and putting his talents to use entertaining Americans on the home front. After all, that's exactly what many film stars did, including Cary Grant, John Wayne, and, of course, Gary Cooper. But for Stewart, military service was an ancestral duty. Going back to the American Revolution, every male Stewart had volunteered and served in the military. In fact, Stewart's strained relationship with his own father, who served in both the Spanish-American War and World War I, was, according to some biographers, compounded by Stewart's own lack of service up until that point. Acting is a noble profession to some, but perhaps not in a military family.

Much like Theodore Roosevelt and Ernest Hemingway, Stewart seemed to see war as a means to achieving an authentic manhood, but even after he was drafted, the chance for self-actualization eluded him. First, he was rejected at his physical examination for being too skinny. He packed on the pounds in between filming scenes of 1941's *Ziegfield Girl* and was eventually accepted by the military thanks only to the help of a friendly doctor who, according to Stewart, "looked the other way" on his weight. Once accepted, Stewart's frustrations with the realities of his service only grew. After spending a few dull days in camp, some of which were spent literally peeling potatoes, he pulled a few strings for a transfer to the Air

Corps, where he was more likely to see real action. Once again, however, Stewart's dreams of military glory were thwarted. He spent most of 1942 doing public appearances, using his celebrity status to build support for the war effort at home. He even attended the Oscars in full uniform and presented the Best Actor award to, wait for it, Gary Cooper for playing a military hero in *Sergeant York*. The irony might have been too much for Stewart to bear. After fulfilling his immediate duties by acting in two propaganda films produced by the U.S. military, Stewart demanded a more consequential role. His superiors finally acquiesced. He was placed in command of a dozen B-24 bombers and 350 soldiers and pilots. In a sense, this was all Stewart needed; the night before he left for Europe, he received a note from his father that concluded with the words, "I love you." It was the first time he'd ever told his son that.

Like many young men eager to prove their manhood on the battlefield, Stewart got everything he wanted but wasn't prepared for what he got. He led numerous missions, with his squadron taking heavy fire from enemy aircraft on more than one occasion. His first mission was described by those who were there as a "blazing dogfight." The longer Stewart was at war, the more his nerves began to fray. On one mission, Stewart suffered a direct hit. The fuselage cracked open, and he barely made it back to base, crash-landing on the runway. He became afflicted by insomnia and panic attacks. He began avoiding the press. He lost more weight and became even skinnier than when he joined up. "I got the fear," he explained.

The effect of the war on Stewart was succinctly described by his biographer Marc Eliot, who wrote that it "deepened, darkened, and complicated everything about him." Upon Stewart's return stateside, he refused to discuss his missions or how they affected him. His hair had turned gray, but when asked about it he only said, "It got pretty rough overseas at times." In other words, "the fear" had left a mark, and it changed the way he looked at his film career. He told MGM, where he was under exclusive contact, he would not play soldiers in combat in any future films, and that he would not allow them to publicize his service.

Privately, he told friends he would never fly again. The war would always be with him, but he began to seek something resembling a normal life.

All of which made him the perfect choice to play Monty Stratton, a major league pitcher who lost his leg in a hunting accident and fought through adversity to return to the mound. *The Stratton Story* is something of a spiritual sequel to *The Pride of the Yankees*. It's another film about a young talented player who rises to the top of his sport, falls in love, and is tested by a physical ailment. But where Gehrig's illness and death is a metaphor for the loss of American men fighting the war, Stratton's amputation and subsequent depression is a clear emblem of the physical and mental disorders that afflicted so many veterans struggling to adjust to life on the home front.

Surprisingly, Stewart wasn't even the first choice to play Monty Stratton. The director, Sam Wood, who also helmed *Pride of the Yankees*, wanted Van Johnson, a young actor who had coincidentally just played an Air Force pilot in 1944's *Thirty Seconds Over Tokyo*, but the real-life Stratton, who served as a consultant on the film, rejected him after seeing the actor meekly throw a ball around. Stratton wanted Stewart. Everyone has fantasized about which movie stars would play them in a film. Stratton is one of the few who actually got to have his way.

Strange as it might seem, Stewart badly needed the role. He left for the war as one of Hollywood's biggest stars, but the industry wasn't as hospitable to him when he returned. He had not yet had a hit in his postwar career, even though it included 1946's *It's a Wonderful Life*—which we'll talk about in a minute—and 1948's *Rope*, directed by Alfred Hitchcock. Both films are considered classics today, but they flopped at the box office. *The Stratton Story*, on the other hand, was the sixth highest-grossing film of the year, and Stewart received fantastic reviews for his performance, restoring him to the upper echelon of A-list stars.

Although it hits many of the same beats as *The Pride of the Yankees*, *The Stratton Story* sets itself apart from its predecessor right from the start. It opens with Stratton playing baseball as a side job in the small Texas town where he and his mother run the family farm, and in this very first scene it makes clear that Jimmy Stewart is doing his own baseball playing. In one continuous shot, we see him on the mound receiving the ball from the catcher, turning around to face the camera, and then going into his wind-up and throwing a strike. *The Stratton Story* would not rely on excessive newsreel footage or nifty editing to show us professional baseball on the silver screen. Stewart was no Gary Cooper. Or rather, Cooper was no Stewart. This actor could really play.

Several classic baseball films open with scenes like this one, showing the sport being played not in cavernous urban stadiums but in sandlots all over the country. In *The Pride of St. Louis* (1952), a scout discovers future Hall of Famer Dizzy Dean while playing as an amateur in the Ozarks. *The Pride of the Yankees* opens with Gehrig as a child, worming his way into a sandlot game by trading baseball cards. These scenes are crucial to cinema's fusing of baseball with America itself, as they imply that at any given time, baseball is being played somewhere—or everywhere—in the country, from the cities to the small towns, from the mountains to the prairies. This trope also perpetuates a very specific but very common version of the American Dream: the fantasy that lives in the back of every man's mind that one day his favorite team might knock on his door and offer him a contract. If you have never once dreamt about that, you're not a baseball fan.

That's essentially what happens to Stratton. An old, washed-up scout stumbles off a train, sees Stratton pitch, and convinces him to come to spring training in California, where he has promised Stratton a try-out with the Chicago White Sox. The scout, played by Frank Morgan (who also played the Wizard in *The Wizard of Oz*), is emblematic of many men who lost everything during the Great Depression. When we first meet him, he's a vagabond riding the rails; Stratton is kind enough to offer him a place to stay during the winter. Later, when they arrive at the try-out, we learn through another character that the scout once had a serious drinking problem. Right up front, *The Stratton Story* imbues its characters with the traumas and anxieties of the American people.

Those anxieties bloom when Stratton, after marrying and having a child, and becoming the most dominant right-handed pitcher in the league, accidentally shoots himself in the leg while out hunting rabbits. With Stratton unconscious, his wife makes the decision to save his life by having his leg amputated, seemingly ending his baseball career. Bitter at his loss, he sulks in his farmhouse for months. He refuses to read the hundreds of letters of support his fans have sent. He snaps at his wife and mother. In a harrowing scene, he refuses to show joy when his son takes his first steps. "He's got two legs, doesn't he?" he snarls.

The performance brings to mind one of the most gut-wrenching scenes from *It's a Wonderful Life*, in which George Bailey, played by Stewart, returns home after making the crucial error of losing several thousand dollars of his bank's money just as a bank examiner has launched an investigation. Bailey storms around the house, angrily rebuking his wife, children, and even his house. When his son mentions their neighbor's new car, he barks, "What's wrong with our car? It's not good enough for you?" Later in the kitchen, he snaps at his wife: "Why do we have to have all these kids?" While Bailey never went to war, he nonetheless expresses the anger, detachment, and disillusionment that was common to returning veterans. It's a side of Stewart that didn't exist in *The Philadelphia Story* or *Mr. Smith Goes to Washington*, a deep well of pain and trauma that Stewart brought back with him and drew from in the greatest performances of his career.

When Stewart brings that darkness to the home-front scenes in *The Stratton Story*, he is validating the emotional struggles of millions of Americans. Amputation and post-traumatic stress disorder were both common maladies for returning veterans that made it exceedingly difficult to return to their lives as they were. Both conditions were memorably portrayed in the 1946 film, *The Best Years of Our Lives*, a better film than *The Stratton Story* but one that sadly features no baseball. *The Stratton Story* addresses its true subject obliquely, blending the wish-fulfillment arc of a regular guy who becomes a star player with the tragedy of amputation to construct a story that resonates widely and deeply. When he musters the courage to put on his prosthetic leg and walk down the driveway with his son, he is showing them how to survive.

Unlike *The Pride of the Yankees*, this baseball film actually ends with a baseball game. Monty tells his wife that he'd like to attend the All-Star Game—placed with dramatic license at the end of the season, not when the "midsummer classic" was actually played—but he has secretly arranged to pitch in it. "I keep saying to myself that I'm just the same as everyone else," he tells Ethel in the tunnel between the clubhouse and the field, recalling a similarly staged moment between Lou and Eleanor just before his climactic speech in *The Pride of the Yankees*. "But I wanted to prove it."

Once on the mound, Monty gets beaten up in the first inning but pitches out of a jam and puts up zeroes for the next eight innings. Other aspects of the game prove more challenging. His first trip to the batter's box ends in humiliation when he falls on his face trying to run to first. In his next at-bat in the top of the ninth, he provides a key hit and actually makes it to first base. To believe what happens next, however, baseball fans would have to turn off their brains: Stratton is taken out for a pinch-runner but allowed to return to the mound in the bottom of the ninth. That's when the opposing team, down by a run, finally decides to take advantage of his disability. The leadoff hitter bunts and Stratton can't reach the ball in time. Same thing happens with the next hitter. But on the third hitter, Stratton gets off the mound quicker this time and slings the ball to first for an out.

Now with the tying run on third and the winning run on second, Stratton bears down and strikes out the next batter, before securing the final out of the game by snagging a hard liner back to the mound. In finishing the game, Stratton has proved to himself and the world that life's challenges were made to be overcome.

The game action that concludes *The Stratton Story* is a huge part of its legacy. *The Pride of the Yankees* didn't end with baseball. It concluded with an unfinished game. *The Stratton Story* innovated the convention of ending a baseball movie with a climactic game rich with personal stakes. In *The Bad News Bears, The Natural,* and *A League of Their Own,* the screenwriters would figure out that it works even better if the team's season is on the line, too, but there's something special about *The Stratton Story* setting its climax in an exhibition, which isolates the emotional stakes for Stratton and creates profound human drama in its final moments. It's not the tension you feel when your team is in the World Series, where the mood of a fandom the size of a small country rests on the outcome. It feels closer to the poignancy of watching one of your favorite players approach an individual milestone after a long journey you have closely followed.

In the end, it's impossible to separate the success of *The Stratton Story* as a pure baseball film from its postwar mythmaking, in part because it integrates them so well. But the film also makes sure to drive home its message. Just before it ends, a narrator we've never heard before starts to speak: "Monty Stratton has not won just a ballgame. He's won a greater victory. If he goes on pitching, winning, living a rich, full life, he stands as an inspiration to all of us. Living proof of what a man can do when he has the courage and determination to refuse to admit defeat." This dialogue serves the same purpose as the opening text in *The Pride of the Yankees,* linking the story we've just seen to the soldiers who fought in the recent war. It's less explicit here but the connection is unmistakable. It appeals to the audience's pride and patriotism. They won the war, so why should they admit defeat at home?

It's only a slight variation on the truth, but fealty to the facts wasn't the priority. This All-Star game never took place, but the real-life Stratton did take part in a game at Comiskey Park designed to raise funds for his care. He pitched well enough to launch a professional comeback that stalled out in the minor leagues, although he was fairly effective, pitching in his first year to an 18–8 record and a 4.17 ERA. He never made it back to the majors. The apex of his career came a few years later, when Hollywood immortalized him on the silver screen. There is no happier ending than having a hit movie made about your life—for Stratton, for Hollywood, and for baseball. With America's most popular cultural institutions working together to immortalize the sport's most inspirational figures, the country was in good hands.

Chapter 2

The Jackie Robinson Story (1950)

IF YOU WANT THE TRUTH ABOUT JACKIE ROBINSON, DON'T GO TO THE movies. Read the books instead. Start with *I Never Had It Made*, which Robinson wrote himself, and then move on to the excellent biography, *Jackie Robinson: A Biography* by Arnold Rampersad. Every other artistic work about the man who broke baseball's color line in 1947 is mythology at best and propaganda at worst, with lots in between. Robinson has been the subject of a Ken Burns documentary, a TV movie chronicling his time in the U.S. Army, and a pair of TV after-school specials. On stage, he was the subject of *The First*, a Broadway musical that sang of his groundbreaking career; it closed after 34 performances. There's even a 1949 song, "Did You See Jackie Robinson Hit That Ball?" by Count Basie and His Orchestra, as well as a jazz suite about the baseball legend, entitled "Stealin' Home," written by Bobby Bradford and first performed in 2019.

Some of these works are more factual than others, while others aren't concerned with the facts at all. That's okay. Their very existence is the point. Robinson is the most covered, most mythologized man in baseball history because he tells a story about baseball that fans want to hear, and a story about America that Americans want to hear. The arc of his life, as framed in these narratives, justifies the game's reputation as the national pastime. It's a story of democracy in action, of a great wrong righted, an injustice overcome, and a nation becoming more perfect. It doesn't hide America's ugly realities; all tales about Robinson deal in part with the harassment and abuse he faced in his first year as a Brooklyn Dodger. Its persistent focus, however, on how he rose above that abuse through quiet strength and preternatural restraint, and how White people overcame their own prejudices to find him worthy of their respect, concludes the story on a reassuring note. If you wanted to persuade Americans that their racial problems were behind them, you couldn't dream up a story as effective as the life of Jackie Robinson.

The Robinson narrative does more than simply convey his achievements. It also reinforces them. Robinson's success in the majors was revolutionary, but so was the idea of telling his story to mainstream audiences. There were no Black movie stars in Hollywood in 1947, and no major films centering Black experiences. Hattie McDaniel won an Oscar in 1940 for playing Mammy in *Gone with the Wind*, and acted in over 20 films after that, but she never had a lead role. One could argue that baseball was ahead of the movie industry, for at least they had one Black star. But even before *The Jackie Robinson Story* was made in 1950, Robinson was the first Black figure in America to play a lead role in his own story, doing so in articles, newsreels, and public appearances. According to president Barack Obama, Robinson "laid the foundation for America to see its Black citizens as subjects and not just objects." In this way, telling and retelling Robinson's tale does more than just enshrine his memory. It codifies the progress he achieved by making Blackness a subject, over and over and over again.

The first myth about Robinson was written while he was still playing. *The Jackie Robinson Story* was released in 1950, just three years into his major league career, when only five of the 16 Major League Baseball teams had been integrated. Like Jackie himself, the film makes no waves. It doesn't fight back. It fits in with the other baseball biopics as much as possible. After *Pride of the Yankees* set the template for a baseball story about a real-life team enlivened by the presence of a young, tragically fated star, Hollywood producers jumped on the bandwagon. They made *The*

Winning Team, in which Ronald Reagan plays Grover Cleveland Alexander, a pitcher who suffers from another PTSD, epilepsy, and alcoholism; *The Pride of St. Louis*, about hayseed-turned-All-Star Dizzy Dean; and one of the worst films ever made, *The Babe Ruth Story*. *The Jackie Robinson Story* fits the mold. It starts in Robinson's childhood, then tracks his maturation into a gifted young adult who is plucked from obscurity and thrust into the national spotlight, suffers setbacks, and eventually overcomes them, and in the process turns his team into a winner.

Of course, *The Jackie Robinson Story* is inherently more complicated than any of those films. While the film fictionalizes elements of Robinson's life—and whitewashes others—it feels more factual than other Hollywood biopics if only because it stars Robinson in the lead role. When we watch the real person enact his life's events, speaking dialogue written by two White screenwriters, we receive it as his endorsement that this was the way it happened. We're not watching an actor imitating Robinson and wondering if that's what he was really like. Since it carries this inherent force of truth, *The Jackie Robinson Story* is the foundational text of the Robinson myth and no future Jackie Robinson story would veer too far from the trail it blazes.

The Jackie Robinson Story was not even supposed to be the first film about the great athlete's life. In 1947, before Robinson's rookie campaign with the Dodgers was even over, he signed a contract with Jack Goldberg, a producer known to be interested in "race films." The deal was orchestrated by Robinson's lawyer, Martin Stone, who had been placed in charge of shopping Robinson's story around. The film, which was to be called *Courage*, fizzled out before production began, and Robinson ended up suing Goldberg over it and winning. After the *Courage* debacle, Stone and screenwriter Lawrence Taylor spent two years looking for a producer to take the project on, with no takers. According to Robinson biographer Arnold Rampersad, "The biggest obstacle to finding a buyer was a predictable one. The major studios were hesitant to release a motion picture in which the hero was a Black man. They didn't think it would sell in the 'heartland.' One studio proposed a doctored version of the story, rewritten to make it more palatable to Whites. This incarnation had a blatantly pandering subplot, which claimed Jackie owed all his athletic prowess to a factional White coach."

Egregious as that may sound, the final product panders only slightly less to White audiences. The film sees racial progress as something that must be gifted by White saviors and continuously earned through the self-restraint and graciousness of Black people. It paints Robinson as a unicorn, a gifted athlete whose opportunities come from the benevolence of White people in power. An early scene shows Robinson as a child proving his worth to a team of White youngsters by catching hard hit grounders without a glove. The White coach is so impressed he gives Robinson a free mitt. It's so ratty and broken that it was likely headed for the dumpster, but Robinson is delighted with it all the same, and his mother gleefully offers to stitch it up for him. The coach may not teach Robinson how to play as he did in that early draft, but the film makes clear that if it weren't for his kindness, none of Robinson's achievements would have been possible.

The concept of a White savior film, which portrays racial progress by centering benevolent White people, had not been identified in 1950, and it was unlikely White audiences found anything problematic in the portrayal of a Black child being gifted his opportunities by nice, reasonable White people. But throughout *The Jackie Robinson Story*, the generosity of Whites in helping Robinson break the color line is underlined, while tangible contributions by people of color are ignored. The goal was clearly to make the film more palatable to White audiences, but like all White savior movies, it ends up inadvertently reinforcing existing power structures more than challenging them.

Racial politics aside, a clearer view of reality would have made *The Jackie Robinson Story* a richer, more rewarding film. As it stands, it opens with Robinson as a child in California, ignoring his early life in Georgia, where his sharecropper father left his wife and children to be a bachelor in the big city; and where his mother fought their landowner for a larger income and won, but eventually left for California to escape the dangers and indignities of Jim Crow laws. It also ignores the racism Robinson suffered as a child in Pasadena, where White neighbors routinely harassed the only Black family on their block, yelling at the young Robinson children for playing in their front yard. A cross was once burned on their lawn. The film revises the story of Robinson's brother Mack, who won a silver medal in the 1936 Olympics, finishing second only to Jesse Owens, but could only get a job as a street sweeper when he returned to the U.S. In the film, Mack, played by Joel Fluellen, is happy with his steady employment. "I got a good, steady job!" he boasts. In reality, Mack wore his Olympic jacket while he swept as a bitter reminder of his talents on the track and his limited options off it.

The film also notably omits Jackie's involvement with the Pepper Street Gang, a group of Black, Asian, and Latino youths in Pasadena who threw dirt clods at cars and occasionally stole from fruit carts. It was strictly kids' stuff that might only merit a call to the parents of White children, but Jackie and his friends became frequent targets of the police. One day, Robinson was marched at gunpoint to the police station as punishment for swimming illegally in a reservoir. In another incident, he was detained after a confrontation with a police officer who took offense to Robinson singing a vaguely anti-police song, "Flat Foot Floogie." These incidents played a major role in shaping Robinson's identity as a Black man, but they were left out of the film presumably to hide the realities of race in America, and to make Robinson seem like a saint for whom racial anger was an impossibility.

The biggest Robinson-related omission in the film regards his time in the U.S. Army, which is absurdly condensed to a single scene. Despite starring as a three-sport athlete at UCLA, Robinson can't find a coaching job in his post-collegiate life, but the Army wants his services. The film never shows Robinson in the Army, although it does give us an image of him looking sharp in his uniform when he returns to his family. What it leaves out is his tumultuous experience at Fort Hood, where Jim Crow laws were still in effect despite being a violation of official Pentagon policy. It was there that Robinson became friends with boxer

Joe Louis, the world heavyweight champion who was a fierce opponent of segregation. Robinson's anger at the Army's segregation grew, and it boiled over in two separate incidents. The first came when Robinson called the provost marshal to complain about the lack of seats for Black personnel at the post exchange, where soldiers bought personal supplies and often socialized. The provost was unaware the man on the other end of the line was Black, and as the conversation escalated, he used racial epithets to make his point. "Pure rage took over," Robinson later wrote about the incident. "I was shouting at the top of my voice. Every typewriter in headquarters stopped. The clerks were frozen in disbelief." But it worked. Robinson filed a report about the incident, and additional seats were made available for Black soldiers. It would have made a great scene in a movie willing to reckon with Robinson's racial anger.

The details of his court-martial are more widely known. One evening on an Army bus, Robinson was chatting with the wife of a friend when he was ordered by the driver to move to the back seat. Army buses were not segregated at this time, and Robinson refused to move. His exchanges with the bus driver grew more and more heated, and Robinson eventually cursed and threatened him with a beating, which prompted the driver to call the MPs and have Robinson detained. A full court-martial followed, at which Robinson was acquitted. The incident would eventually be the subject of a stellar 1990 TV film, *The Court-Martial of Jackie Robinson*, but it was completely left out of *The Jackie Robinson Story*. Why gloss over such an important incident in Robinson's life? To maintain the myth that Robinson had spent his whole life as a friendly, peaceful man for whom racial resentments rolled off his back. Instead of showing the series of complex events that determine a person's identity, every second of *The Jackie Robinson Story* is dedicated to the idea that Robinson was born fully formed. As an advertisement for integration, this approach could be justified—at that exact time, maybe baseball thought it needed heroes more than three-dimensional humans—but it came at a cost. It sends a message to both Black and White Americans that anger as a response to racism is unjustified and unproductive.

Instead, the Robinson myth upholds passivity as the only strategy for social change. If there is a core moment in the Robinson myth, it takes place when he is first summoned to the office of Dodgers owner Branch Rickey to be given his assignment. At first, Robinson misunderstands the purpose of the meeting. He thinks that Rickey is interested in him for his Negro League team the Brooklyn Brown Dodgers, but Rickey quickly shuts that down. He tells him that he wants Robinson to play on the actual Dodgers, and he tells him why. "I want to win pennants." Rickey's motivations don't receive much scrutiny in the film, but in real life they were fascinatingly complex. He was a staunch advocate for racial progress and even hung a portrait of Abraham Lincoln in his office, but he was also a devout capitalist and knew that the first owner to embrace integration would hold a distinct advantage over the rest of the league. It's true that Ricky played a crucial role in breaking baseball's color line, but he did so by putting the Negro Leagues, which was formed by Black owners, out of business. When he signed Robinson, he took advantage of the fact that Negro League players didn't have binding contracts. He took Robinson without compensation, a practice that was soon imitated by his peers, initiating a severe talent drain on the Negro League teams that wiped them out within a decade.

In reality, racial progress is a crooked line, but *The Jackie Robinson Story* doesn't have time to meander. Instead, it portrays Rickey as a wise, benevolent White man clearing a path to equality. The famous office scene is just a venue for the screenwriters' pontifications about the fairness of baseball. It sounds tin-eared to today's ears but must have been catnip for postwar Americans. "A box score is really democratic," Rickey tells Robinson. "It doesn't say how big you are, or how your father voted in the last election, or what church you attend. It just tells you what kind of ballplayer you were that day.... It's all that oughta count, and maybe someday, it's all that will count." Astute observers of Major League Baseball over the years will note that the box score has never been all that counts, and there is a subtle but undeniable demand embedded in this ideal that baseball players not advocate for themselves, their community, or others in need. Shut up and play, in other words.

Rickey's admittedly well-scripted words about baseball and America, however, do not comprise the most enduring moment from this scene. Instead, it's in the exchange between Rickey and Robinson, where Rickey explains that he must resist the urge to respond to racial taunts. "You want a ballplayer without the guts to fight back?" Robinson asks him, incredulously. "I want a ballplayer with guts enough not to fight back," Rickey barks in response. Rickey was surely correct that segregationists would use any hint of aggression from Robinson as evidence that Black men were not civilized enough to play America's game, but it's telling that *this* is the exchange that made it into every subsequent telling of Robinson's story. Not any one of Robinson's actual exploits on the field. Not his flashes of anger at the racism he endured. And certainly not his post-baseball activism, which showed a fascinating political complexity and independence of thought—after all, this is a man who endorsed Richard Nixon in the 1960 presidential election over John F. Kennedy. Instead, it's the scene in which a rich, powerful White man instructs his poor, Black employee not to fight back against harassment and abuse that endured.

Even at the time, this framing was noticed and called out by the Black press, most notably by the *New York Amsterdam News*, which published a mixed review of *The Jackie Robinson Story* including these words of caution: "There are two ways to look at this movie—through the eyes of a Negro and through the eyes of a White man. In both cases you get different impressions. As a Negro, one is likely to think that too much emphasis is placed on the 'don't fight back' attitude which Jackie sells. How is the Negro ever to get any place without fighting—mostly, fighting back? There are only a few Jackie Robinsons among our group who can gain by 'not fighting back.' This philosophy is likely to be misinterpreted." While many in the Black press were simply happy that a film centering Robinson was being made at all, this editorial shows there were always more critical voices within the Black community who applied scrutiny to the manner in which Black characters were portrayed.

In accounting for his inner experience, *The Jackie Robinson Story* spends a significant amount of its runtime detailing the abuse Robinson endured, although most of it is portrayed as pretty harmless. The opposing team conspicuously eats watermelon while Robinson is at the plate. A black cat is thrown onto the field—in real life, Robinson admitted this one made him laugh. There's also the matter of the "Welcoming Committee," a small gang of racists that confronts Robinson after a game and threatens him with violence. Robinson is saved by his White teammates, and it's later revealed that the thugs are Ku Klux Klan members, but they feel more like cartoonish gangsters who wandered out of a James Cagney movie. All in all, Robinson's fight against racism feels flat. There's no real sense of danger because that would implicate White audiences too much. It doesn't help that Robinson, an unskilled actor, does little to convey his own torturous experience.

It's a portrayal of racial progress whose timidity has several authors. For starters, the Civil Rights Era had not begun in earnest—Brown vs. Board of Education was still four years away—and the notion of Black activists fighting back against racism would have been seen as radical. Hollywood would want nothing to do with a film like that in 1950. But *The Jackie Robinson Story* was shaped with an even more specific beneficiary in mind: Rickey himself. During the production, the creative process was co-opted by Arthur Mann, Rickey's chief publicist, who co-wrote the screenplay. He is also listed in the credits as the film's technical advisor, which is all he was supposed to be before he finagled a larger role for himself. According to his own account published in *The Sporting News*, he began his work on the film with a straightforward task: "I went out to Los Angeles in mid-January with the picture in my pocket. This was in the form of a directive wherein the Brooklyn club and Branch Rickey were protected against misuse or abuse of the situation. This was necessary because never before had a baseball club extended the right to film such a player-situation, added to which was the right to portray the part of Branch Rickey."

Somehow his job to protect Rickey from potential slander got expanded. Maybe Mann caught the Hollywood bug and wanted a larger role, or perhaps his dedication to his former boss was so great that he jumped at the opportunity to lionize him. Mann spent the first two weeks rewriting the story with the co-screenwriter Lawrence Taylor. After finishing the script, Mann then spent 18 days and six nights with director Al Green. "I was at his side constantly," he wrote, "in his air, and often on his toes." Mann stuck around throughout production to make sure the script was followed and the speeches were read as intended. After the shooting, he supervised the editing and scoring. In the end, he was proud to have created a film that showed how, according to Mann, "Jackie had lived up to the letter of Rickey's teachings."

In holding up Rickey as the sole champion of baseball integration, *The Jackie Robinson Story* errs by ignoring the Black activists who were among the first to push for the erasure of baseball's color line. Black sportswriters such as Wendell Smith and Sam Lacy wrote on the topic often, and organized boycotts and picketing. The Communist press was also on the beat, starting petitions and penning editorials in their newspaper *The Daily Worker*. When their movement finally reached a critical mass, the mainstream press jumped on the bandwagon. Journalists from the *Chicago Tribune*, *Washington Post*, and the *New York Daily News* all editorialized in favor of integration. The *Boston Record* even printed a piece registering "disgust at the thought that Negro athletes, solely because of their color, are barred from playing baseball." All of this was done before Rickey called Robinson up to the big leagues.

Lacy in particular deserves extra attention. The journalist, who had both African and Native American heritage, began arguing in favor of integration in the *Washington Tribune* as early as 1935. Two years later, he presented his case against desegregation directly to Clark Griffith and William Richardson, owners of the Washington Senators, only to be told that the climate wasn't right for it. "The climate will never be right if you don't test it," he responded. He became the face of the desegregation movement and was eventually seen as a villain by many Negro League players who found themselves out of a job after integration. Lacy, who viewed the Negro Leagues as the most high-profile symbol of segregation, was undeterred in his convictions.

He was also one of the sharpest critics of *The Jackie Robinson Story*. Years later, Lacy slammed the film for turning away from the totality of Robinson's suffering: "Omitted for some reason—probably because of the pressure of time—were legitimate shots, which, quite plausibly, could have been worked into the flicker," he wrote. "Like having to live in the third-class Los Angeles hotel in Havana while his White teammates were being put up at the Academia Militare during spring training in 1947... like having to search from one end of the Cuban capital to the other, hoping to find a decent place to eat. And like being forced to ride taxi cabs 22 miles each day to and from his hotel to the training grounds.... These things and countless others might well have been included."

The great sportswriter also found fault in Robinson's on-screen performance. He felt Robinson focused too much on his line readings and not enough on the physical aspects of his performance, perhaps because he took his athletic skills for granted. Lacy argued that in the film Robinson "acts better than he plays...the way he fields and the manner in which he goes down to avoid 'dust off' pitches would make one think that Jackie had never gotten in or out of the way of a ball in his life.... Those of us who know Robinson as a nimble guy so light on his feet that he could skate on a feather, the clumsy, bulbous figure of the movie is hardly recognizable." Other critics agreed. "The theme of *The Jackie Robinson Story* weaves around Jackie as a Negro in baseball's higher classification," wrote Cal Jacox in Virginia's *New Journal and Guide*. "Its producers could have made it a better movie by stressing his worth as an all-around player who could hit, run, and steal bases." In this way, *The Jackie Robinson Story* robs viewers of seeing Robinson at his most liberated, at the plate and on the basepaths, where he could give all of himself to the game within the relative safety of the baseball diamond.

Perhaps it was unavoidable that this film would paint an incomplete portrait of Robinson. After all, his life was just beginning. He was only 30 years old when *The Jackie Robinson Story* was made, and the fascinatingly complex man who would later sit on the board of the NAACP, support Martin Luther King Jr, clash with Malcolm X, and appear at many civil rights rallies, including the 1963 Peace March and the March on Selma in 1965, was still gestating. As was the Civil Rights Movement and America's ongoing effort to reckon with its racial crimes. In his 1972 biography *I Never Had It Made*, Robinson looked back on his career in baseball with mixed feelings, writing: "I must tell you that it was Mr. Rickey's drama and that I was only a principal actor. As I write this twenty years later, I cannot stand and sing the anthem. I cannot salute the flag. I know that I am a Black man in a White world. In 1972, in 1947, and at my birth in 1919, I know I never had it made." Reading these words is a reminder that there's less space between him and Colin Kaepernick, the NFL player who ignited a culture war in 2016 when he kneeled during the National Anthem to protest state violence against Blacks, than many would think. You would never know it from *The Jackie Robinson Story*.

The final, perhaps most unforgivable omission from the film is the great joy that permeated Robinson's life. Breaking the color line was beyond challenging for Robinson, but he also considered it a great gift that supplied him moments of pure elation. Consider the unfilmed incident when Robinson, after winning the minor league World Series with the Kansas City Monarchs, was carried off the field like a hero. In the locker room, his manager Clay Hopper, a Southerner whose hard resentment and eventual acceptance of Robinson would make a neat arc for a feature film, shook his hand and told him, "You're a great ballplayer and a fine gentleman. It's been wonderful having you on the team." When Robinson finally left the stadium, the crowd was still waiting for him. "They stormed around him, eager to touch him," Dink Carroll of the *Montreal Gazette* reported. They serenaded him with a French-Canadian celebration song and "almost ripped the clothes from his back." Another journalist wrote: "It was probably the only day in history that a Black man ran from a White mob with love instead of lynching on its mind." It would have made a great scene, but the film's scope is too narrow to allow it, and its understanding of Robinson's plight too clouded with patriotic purpose.

There is, however, one area in which *The Jackie Robinson Story* shows some creativity and genuine innovation: in the baseball itself. In the film's climactic game, with the pennant in the balance, Robinson comes up in the bottom of the ninth with the tying run on second base. The first two pitches are shown in the film's established visual language, with the camera unnaturally placed a few feet up the first-base line, showing the batter, catcher, and umpire in a single shot. After a ball and a strike, however, it cuts to a new shot from behind the catcher's left shoulder, where we can see the pitcher in the distance and Robinson in the foreground taking up the left part of the screen. It looks like a modern-day video game. For the first time in a baseball film, we can feel the speed of the ball as it whizzes into the catcher's glove. It puts the viewer in Robinson's shoes, bringing a much-needed visual dynamism to the baseball film and finally allowing the viewer to experience the intensity of the game, which, with televised baseball only in its infancy, would have felt truly novel at the time. For one fleeting moment, the viewer understands what it feels like to be Jackie Robinson, at least on the field. For baseball and for the movies, that's a major step forward, even if the rest of the story feels more like a dive back to first.

Chapter 3

The Babe Ruth Story (1948) and Angels in the Outfield (1951)

IN *THE JACKIE ROBINSON STORY*, JUST BEFORE JACKIE ROBINSON ACCEPTS Branch Rickey's offer to join the Brooklyn Dodgers, he calls his mother for advice. "They must have churches in New York," she counsels him. "Anytime you have a real problem, listen to God for a while." In real life, Robinson was a devout Methodist who often turned to prayer during his ordeal, but strangely, the fictionalized conversation he has with Reverend Carter, played by veteran actor Laurence Criner, has little to do with religion. Carter never quotes scripture, and the two men don't pray together. God doesn't even come up. Instead, the reverend imparts to Robinson how many people of color there are whose lives will be improved if he accepts Rickey's offer. Social justice moves Robinson; God is just the conduit.

It's never a surprise when religion finds its way into a baseball movie. Baseball was first called the "national pastime" in 1856, but it was always treated more like a secular religion. From the beginning, Americans worshiped the game with a holy fervor. F. Scott Fitzgerald called it "the faith of fifty million people." Ballparks are cathedrals, and fans are believers. When something strange happens that tips a game in a team's favor (or, more often, against them), fans chalk it up to the work of "the baseball gods." Later in this book, we will discuss a movie that opens with a monologue on "the church of baseball" and another that hinges on the question, asked on a baseball field, "Is this heaven?" Yeah, sort of. Baseball has long been adjacent to God.

So has America, especially in the postwar era. The years directly after World War II, when *The Jackie Robinson Story* and a host of other inspirational baseball films were made, were particularly rejuvenating for religion in America. By the mid-1950s, almost half of all Americans were attending church—the highest percentage in U.S. history. Over the decade church membership grew at a faster rate than the population, from 57 percent of the U.S. population in 1950 to 63.3 percent in 1960. At a time of acute national anxieties—from the Red Scare to the threat of nuclear war—many of America's citizens desired real spiritual guidance. At the same time, church attendance became an accelerating social trend, a signal of respectability for those who wanted to get ahead or simply fit in with their neighbors.

Either way, Hollywood was no place for piety. There's an old witticism of unknown origin that says the movie industry is "a Jewish-owned business selling Catholic theology to Protestant America." It's true that all the original studio owners were Jewish, and their content was greatly influenced by the Legion of Decency, the Catholic group that staged boycotts of films they deemed immoral. The studios saw religiosity as a way to appease their censors and appeal to the masses. It was also increasingly seen as a national duty. In 1950, a young U.S. Senator from Wisconsin gave a speech that set the stage for one of the darkest chapters in the 20th century, leading with these words: "Today we are engaged in a final, all-out battle between communistic atheism and Christianity. The modern champions of communism have selected this as the time. And, ladies, and gentleman, the chips are down—they are truly down." Evoking the spirit of a coach rallying his team to win an important game, Sen. Joseph McCarthy, a devout Catholic, wielded religion to cement America's moral superiority over the Soviet Union. His efforts, and the efforts of others who spread religion and religiosity in this era, had an immeasurable impact. Americans had long valued the clear separation of church and state, but the line became blurred in the 1950s. The words "under God" were added to the pledge of allegiance in 1954, and in 1957 "In God We Trust" first appeared on U.S. currency.

Broadly put, religion in postwar America wasn't so much about the divine. It was instead seen as a vital stitch in the fabric of society, a building block of the American Dream. Naturally, the baseball films of this era incorporated religious imagery and themes into their stories, both with the intent to please the religious masses and as a natural extension of their melding of baseball with patriotism. McCarthy, who despised the perceived immorality of Hollywood, surely appreciated baseball movies for their wholesome portrait of American exceptionalism. In cinema, baseball was America's game, and America was good because it was godly.

He would have been especially pleased with 1948's *The Babe Ruth Story*, a hagiography of the great Yankees slugger who boosted the game's popularity in the 1920s with his unprecedented home run power and voracious personality, and was rewarded with a biopic framing him as the second coming of Jesus Christ. Considered by many to be the worst baseball movie ever made, its reputation was tarnished right from the start. After its premiere in 1948, the *New York Times* wrote, "It is hard to accept the presentation of a great, mawkish, noble-spirited buffoon… in this picture as a reasonable facsimile of the Babe. Ruth was a great one with the kid fans, but it smacks of sheer artifice to show his bulbous counterfeit in this movie maundering over pathos-coated tots." The film is deserving of sharp criticism, but watching it now, it's hard to see it as a total disaster. It's a competent film made by competent people, especially its cast. William Bendix, who plays the Babe, earned an Oscar nomination a few years earlier for the war drama *Wake Island*. Claire Trevor, playing the Babe's second wife, Claire, actually won an Oscar the same year that *The Babe Ruth Story* was released, albeit for a different film, the noir classic *Key Largo*. William Frawley, better known as Fred Mertz on *I Love Lucy*, plays the manager. Helmed by journeyman director Roy Del Ruth (no relation), *The Babe Ruth Story* looks and feels like a real movie, and its womb-to-tomb narrative, which follows the Babe from his rough-and-tumble childhood through his years on the field before culminating in his tragic death, is broadly similar to other baseball movies of this era.

The problem with *The Babe Ruth Story* is that it reveres its subject too much. While *The Pride of the Yankees* and *The Stratton Story* operated subtextually as films about Americans' experience in World War II, and *The Jackie Robinson Story* is obviously a story about racism and civil rights, *The Babe Ruth Story* is only about Babe Ruth. And not even the real, flawed person we know Ruth was. Instead, it paints the Babe as a hero as virtuous as Gehrig. There were many rough edges that need to be sanded down for that to happen—Ruth was a drinker and a womanizer for long periods of his life—so the film simply abandons all sense of realism and instead turns him into a saint who could heal the weak and, in the end, died so that others could live. No joke.

The thread of religiosity starts in the very first scenes that find young George Herman Ruth suffering under the tyranny of his abusive father, who puts the young lad to work in his bar where he is insulted and abused by the patrons. Ruth is rescued by Brother Matthias (Charles Bickford) and taken to St. Mary's Industrial School, which, it is noted in the film, is most definitely not a reform school (the connotations associated with reform schools at the time would have tarnished Ruth's legacy). At first, Ruth doesn't like it there. He even runs away twice. But the third time's a charm, and Ruth eventually thrives under Christian tutelage, growing into a fine young man and the world's greatest ballplayer.

At 19 years old, Ruth is still at St. Mary's, although he is now ludicrously played by the 42-year-old Bendix. Ruth gets signed by the Baltimore Orioles, and as his major league career begins, he casts off his mortal shell and approaches the supernatural. At spring training, he exercises the ministry of healing. A man and his disabled son, who we're told is a huge fan of the Babe, are watching the team practice, when Ruth walks by and offhandedly greets the boy, "Hiya kid." As if touched by God, the boy stands up on his own, miraculously cured of his condition. Later, Ruth would do one better. During Game 3 of the 1932 World

Series, he receives a call from another distressed father, this one with a child dying of an unnamed disease. Babe promises to hit a home run for him, and just so he knows it was for him, he even promises to "call his shot" first. It's a clever bit of movie conflagration; Ruth called his shot in the 1932 World Series, but it was in the 1926 World Series that he promised to hit a home run for Johnny Sylvester, a boy who had been kicked in the head by a horse and suffered a subsequent infection of the skull. Sylvester did survive his injuries, going on to graduate from Princeton and become a Lieutenant in the U.S. Navy. He lived until the age of 74 and was survived by his son and three grandchildren. Naturally, there is no evidence that it was Ruth's homer that saved his life, but in baseball and in film, the myth matters more than the facts.

Still, it's a neat bookend to the scene in *The Pride of the Yankees* in which Ruth (playing himself) promises to hit a home run for a hospitalized boy, while a gaggle of reporters takes notes and snaps photos. After Ruth leaves, Cooper's Gehrig sneaks in and, with no reporters in sight, earnestly pledges to hit two for him. The scene is a study in contrasts, implying that Ruth did it for the glory, and Gehrig did it for the boy. It's not true; Gehrig never promised any dying kid anything, and in fact the entire sequence is ripped from Ruth's real-life experience with Sylvester. But it's a testament to the urgency of telling Gehrig's story at a time when America needed its hero that Ruth allowed himself to look so foolish, and then allowed a different film to cast off those flaws and ludicrously turn him into a Christ figure just a few years later—when the war was over.

For Ruth, it was later than late; it was near the end. Battling cancer while the film was being made, he was so sick by the premiere date that he had to leave the screening halfway through to return to the hospital. In the film, Ruth gets sick and accepts an experimental serum to try to stave off his illness. This bit is rooted in fact; Ruth was one of the first patients to receive chemotherapy for cancer, and some researchers say he was the very first to get chemo and radiation concurrently. The film suggests that Ruth became a willing test subject to try to save humanity, which is disingenuous—there's no evidence Ruth was trying to save anyone but himself—while the angelic choir that sings "Take Me Out to the Ballgame" over his deathbed scene reduces the entire scene to parody.

In *The Jackie Robinson Story*, religion was just background. In *The Babe Ruth Story*, it was subtext, although you'd have to be blind to miss it. 1951's *Angels in the Outfield*, however, put it front and center. The film about a group of baseball-loving angels who help turn a bottom-feeding franchise into a winner is better known today as the inspiration for its 1994 Disney remake about the California Angels. In 1951, the major-league Angels didn't exist yet, so the film's pitiable subject is the Pittsburgh Pirates, who at the time were the absolute laughingstock of baseball. It was widely reported that the film sold so many tickets in Pittsburgh because fans there would rather watch a fictional team than the one getting slaughtered at Forbes Field every night.

Just how bad were the Pirates of this era? It's fair to say they could have used supernatural assistance. Sure, they had Ralph Kiner, one of the league's most feared sluggers, but otherwise they were a team of scrubs. From 1946–57, the Pirates finished in the top half of the National League only once. In 1950, the year before *Angels* was released, they finished in last place, 33½ games out of first. Believe it or not, that was their high point for some time. They lost at least 100 games—a generally agreed-upon benchmark for total ineptitude—in '52, '53, and '54; in two of those years, they finished more than 50 games out of first place. That's hard to do if you're trying to be bad.

The setting of *Angels in the Outfield*, however, is owed more to savvy business strategy than the incompetence of its subject. Once again, Branch Rickey factors heavily into the narrative. The year after *The Jackie Robinson Story* came out, Rickey sold his stake in the Dodgers and took a position running the Pirates. Maybe he was selling high on a team that had just been immortalized on celluloid, or perhaps he just enjoyed a challenge, but his familiarity with the movie business paid off for Pittsburgh. At the time, MGM had not yet decided whether to make *Angels in the Outfield* about the Pirates or the Cubs, who were equally inept, and Rickey used his connections to lure them to the Steel City.

Although steeped in religious ideas, the film still has much in common with its secular counterparts. *The Pride of the Yankees, The Stratton Story, The Winning Team*, and *The Pride of St. Louis* tell stories of half-broken men who are put back together by the game and go on to be productive members of American society. In *Angels*, it's not a player who gets redeemed by the game but manager Guffy McGovern (Paul Douglas), known to all for his ornery attitude. On the field, he is prone to obscenity-laden outbursts at the umpires, although the film, still operating under the Production Code, scrambles his voice to make it sound like gibberish (or perhaps speaking in tongues?). Off the field, he has no purpose at all. Jennifer (Janet Leigh), an intrepid young journalist writing a profile of McGovern, follows him around to ascertain his habits; she finds a lonely, angry, and potentially violent man. He spends all his time either at the ballpark or a restaurant where he eats the same meal every night—steak, naturally, the most American food. Crusty old managers are nothing new to baseball cinema, even here in the genre's nascent stages, but there's nothing charming about McGovern's mood swings. He's cruel toward the players, insulting them in the clubhouse after a particularly tough loss. He comes across as a man in need of a spiritual revelation, and perhaps a good woman. By the end, he'll have both.

One night after a game, McGovern is visited on the field by an angel, who speaks to him from heaven and offers him a deal: He'll help the team win if McGovern will stop cursing so much and generally try to be a better man. It's all very Dickensian. "Look for a miracle tonight in the third inning," the angel tells him, in a line that surely reminded viewers of *A Christmas Carol*, which had already been adapted into six films by the time *Angels in the Outfield* graced screens. The angel, voiced by James Whitmore (known much later for his performance as Brooks in *The Shawshank Redemption*), acts more like a mortal than a celestial being. Sometimes he's funny. "Why can't I see you for one moment?" McGovern asks in exasperation. "Because I usually stay as far away from you as possible!" the angel replies. Sometimes he practices tough love.

"Stand still and listen, or I'll blast you with a bolt of lightning!" he shouts, as the thunder claps mightily above the field.

What he's not is particularly Biblical. The portrayal of heavenly beings in *Angels in the Outfield* is ultimately more opportunistic than genuinely spiritual, and a neat fit for those early postwar days when religion was a social good as much as a spiritual one. As the angels help turn the Pirates into a contender, everything seems to be going well until an orphan child (Donna Corcoran), whose prayer inspired the angels to act in the first place, catches sight of the team's heavenly helpers. Jennifer writes an article about it, turning McGovern, who woozily admits to seeing angels after being hit in the head with a line drive, into a national news sensation. A sportscaster harboring a grudge against McGovern reports him to the Commissioner of Baseball, who launches a trial to determine whether angels exist. It's all reminiscent of *Miracle on 34th Street*, which culminates in a similarly ludicrous trial to determine the existence of Santa Claus. Here, the "prosecution" calls a psychologist to testify that angels are a figment of America's collective imagination, while the defense calls a priest, a rabbi, and a minister to refute it. It sounds like a bad joke waiting to happen, especially when, after testifying to the existence of angels and by extension the sanity of McGovern, they ask to be excused early so they can catch the ballgame—together.

This trial business is an effective bit of manipulation by the filmmakers, somehow transforming those who believe in angels into a persecuted group. In 2016, a Gallup poll showed that 72 percent of Americans believe in celestial beings, and it stands to reason that number was even higher in 1951 (no polling was done at the time), when a higher percentage of Americans believed in God and religion was more of a galvanizing ideal. With the multi-denominational defense witnesses, the film acknowledges faith in the supernatural was ubiquitous across religions, but it pitches belief as diametrically opposed to rational thought, represented here by the psychiatrist. This wasn't just dangerous—the growth of private psychiatry in this era helped many U.S. veterans overcome their post-traumatic stress syndrome—but it also perpetuated a culture of victimhood among

American Christians that could be exploited for political gain. Consider the aforementioned words of McCarthy, whose Irish Catholic family first immigrated to the U.S. in the mid-1800s: "Ladies, and gentleman, the chips are down—they are truly down." He and the American Catholics who zealously supported him saw atheism as a major threat to their way of life. In *Angels in the Outfield*, that threat is represented by a psychiatrist, a journalist, and the Commissioner of Baseball, a stand-in for the U.S. government. I'll say it again: McCarthy must have loved this film.

That's not to say that *Angels in the Outfield* should be dismissed as propaganda. As pure entertainment, it's immensely satisfying, and it features some top-notch filmmaking to boot. The scene in which McGovern first converses with his angel is especially stirring. It's set in the cavernous Forbes Field after the game has been played, where the combination of shadows and moonlight seem to summon the supernatural events to come. It feels like a holy place, an actual cathedral. It's the kind of scene that can give you goosebumps. Whether you endorse its religious underpinnings or not, that's the feeling we go to the movies for.

We also go for the happy ending. In the end, McGovern and Jennifer get together, and they even adopt the young orphan girl whose prayer set off this entire wacky adventure. Yes, the lonely middle-aged man and the ambitious career woman both find happiness in the sturdy, traditional domestic unit. Baseball and God cure them of their woes—along with the Pirates, who received an angel named Roberto Clemente a few years later and saw their fortunes reverse—and it's easy to imagine where their life is headed from there: marriage, a house in the suburbs, a couple more kids, and, of course, church every Sunday.

Chapter 4

Fear Strikes Out (1957) and *Damn Yankees* (1958)

LET'S GET THIS OUT OF THE WAY: THE BASEBALL IN *FEAR STRIKES OUT* IS abysmal, maybe the worst you'll see in any baseball movie. It's painfully clear that to play Jim Piersall, a real-life major leaguer who suffered from bipolar disorder, had a mental breakdown on the field, and underwent extensive treatment before returning to the sport, actor Anthony Perkins had no interest in learning the game. Either that, or the filmmakers actively dissuaded him from it. If you told me they confiscated every ball, bat, and glove within a 100-mile radius until filmmaking began, I'd believe you.

In real life, defense was Piersall's calling card. He made it to the majors as an outfielder in 1950 based largely on his otherworldly range and cannon of an arm. The film mercifully only shows him defending a couple plays, but even those are awkward as hell. In one, we see Perkins tracking a fly ball into deep right-center field. It cuts away to the crowd cheering him on, and then cuts back to Perkins, who is now standing still as the ball flies toward him. Actually, "flies" isn't the right word. It is *slung* to him, clearly thrown by someone just off-camera. Perkins sticks his mitt out to his glove side, catches the ball, and hurls it back in. Filmmaker

45

Ron Shelton, the former minor leaguer who wrote and directed *Bull Durham*, called it "the low point in sports movies."

What's even worse is how the film tries to pass off Los Angeles' Wrigley Field, a minor league stadium where most baseball movies up to this point were filmed, as the legendary and inimitable Fenway Park, where Piersall played his home games as a member of the Red Sox. Director Robert Mulligan uses wide shots of Fenway to establish the setting, before cutting to inserts of the baseball action filmed at Wrigley. It's inelegantly done, creating whiplash for the modern viewer, but to be fair, the filmmakers were handicapped by the fact that Piersall played in such a distinctive stadium. There's virtually no slice of Fenway that could possibly pass for another park. Its dimensions and appearance are the stuff of baseball lore, so the transitions here are far more jarring than they were in *Pride of the Yankees*, which was also shot at Los Angeles' Wrigley, or in any other baseball film.

Strangely, none of this posed much of a problem when *Fear Strikes Out* was released in 1957. Bosley Crowther of the *New York Times* wrote: "Mr. Perkins plays the young fellow excellently, not only conveying the gathering torment but also actually looking like a ballplayer on the field." In the *Saturday Review*, Hollis Alpert argued, "The baseball stuff is adequately done, and there are some interesting scenes in Fenway Park." Obviously, Alpert had never been there, but it nevertheless shows how the standards for this sort of thing have changed over the years. Nowadays, if you make any mistake in a baseball film, fans will cry foul.

These particular flaws may be easier to forgive because *Fear Strikes Out* is not a traditional baseball movie, even for its time. Instead, it takes the baseball film and spins from its tropes a wrenching psychological drama about mental illness, the kind that afflicts not just shell-shocked veterans but regular people doing regular things. It arrived right on time. In the 1950s, psychotherapy was on the rise. Up until World War II, mental illness lived in the shadows and was largely treated in psychiatric hospitals. In the postwar era, however, it became more common as a form of outpatient treatment. The Diagnostic and Statistical Manual of Mental

Disorders, essentially the bible of psychotherapy, was first published in 1952, while Maslow's Hierarchy of Needs, which identifies parental love as crucial to an individual's emotional growth (a revolutionary thought at the time), also became popular within the decade. From housewives to Mad Men, therapy was becoming a fixture in American society.

Therapy was not yet common among professional ballplayers, however, and it still might not be, although every team in the major leagues now employs a "mental skills coach" or something similar to help players navigate the emotional stresses of the season. Regardless, the conditions that led to Piersall's breakdown are universal, especially for those children raised in the shadow of the postwar American fantasy. There was an overbearing father lacking ability to communicate with his child, an emotionally absent mother, and an overwhelming pressure to succeed in ways that his parents could not. *Fear Strikes Out* uses baseball not as a driver of its story but as a backdrop for its query into human psychology.

In one sense, the subject of *Fear Strikes Out* is baseball fever. Jimmy's father is a baseball obsessive who passes down his affliction onto his son. It wasn't the first film made about the subject. The 1949 comedy *It Happens Every Spring* revolved around a college professor who "should have had his PhD. years ago," except that half his year is completely and totally devoted to baseball. He eventually develops a chemical that repels wood, smears it on some baseballs, and becomes the best pitcher in the majors. The hitters literally cannot make contact. *It Happens Every Spring* is a comic tale, but its subject, baseball obsession among the American male, was ripe for more serious inquiry. The 1950s proved to be the appropriate time for it. In the early days of the Cold War, fear and obsession were invading the American soul. Children were rehearsing for nuclear attacks by hiding under their desks, while Sen. Joseph McCarthy was working hard to convince Americans that their best friend could be a Soviet operative. Everything and everyone were subject to suspicion. Why not baseball?

In *Fear Strikes Out*, the rebellion against the wholesomeness of baseball begins in the opening scenes with a game of catch between young Jimmy

Piersall (Peter J. Votrian) and his father John (Karl Malden). Instead of a friendly, leisurely game that strengthens the father-son bond, John hurls it harder and harder at Jimmy, who begins to wince with every catch. When the ball eludes him and Jimmy tracks it down behind their shed, he lingers there a moment to give himself a respite as tears run down his cheeks. It's a damning indictment of the father, showing how his determination to prepare his son for a career in baseball blinds him to his emotional realities. It's also a startling subversion of the reverence these films typically have for the national game. There is arguably no image more symbolic of America's postwar suburban bliss than a game of catch between father and son. In future years, it would be a key nostalgia point in *Field of Dreams* and *The Sandlot*. By subverting it in the opening scene, *Fear Strikes Out* puts the audience on notice that no mythology will be considered sacred here.

In the era of *Father Knows Best* and *Leave it to Beaver*, of Rockwellian portraits in the *Saturday Evening Post* depicting families relaxing in front of the fire, it would have been simple to flip the portrait and make John plainly evil, but instead *Fear Strikes Out* shows him as unknowingly abusive, making its psychological inquiry far richer. Malden's portrayal expertly captures the banality of his abuse. He doesn't yell, scream, or throw things (except baseballs). He never hits his child. Instead, he carelessly instills in him a destructive pressure to succeed on his father's behalf. When discussing Jimmy's career, he speaks as if they are doing it together. "We're on our way," he says. "Nothing can stop us." Later, when Jimmy is in a mental hospital, he tells him, "Stick around here, and they'll make you an invalid for life. We know that, don't we?" Malden wisely underplays it, infusing the character with superficial warmth and understanding, charming us as easily as he does Jimmy, so the abuse barely registers.

Everything about *Fear Strikes Out* is intended to startle the viewer and overthrow expectations. It offers you the expected elements of a traditional, inspirational baseball film, before revealing a world of trauma lurking just underneath. Up to a point, *Fear Strikes Out* is broadly indistinguishable from that of *Pride of the Yankees, The Stratton Story, The Winning Team,* or *The Pride of St. Louis.* It's about a kid who loves baseball and dreams of being a major leaguer, who works his way through the system and is eventually signed by his hometown team. It's only when he is on the precipice of stardom that expectations begin to shift. Piersall is called up to the major leagues, but they want him to learn a new position, and he melts down at the possibility. He finally agrees to the position change, but even as he displays the physical skills and mental toughness to succeed in the majors, his neuroses begin to infringe on his life. He internalizes his father's critical voice and starts needling his teammates incessantly, becoming thoroughly unpleasant to be around. Finally, it boils over. During one game, with his father in the stands, he hits a ball in the gap, sprints around all four bases for an inside-the-park home run, and keeps running right up to the netting that separates the players from the fans. He cries out for his father's approval, even climbing the net before he is subdued by his teammates. It's a haunting (albeit fabricated) moment that takes what has long been portrayed as the greatest achievement in America's game—the home run—and reframes it as a symptom of psychological dysfunction. It's a portrait of baseball in America as a shiny dream with a rotten core.

We see at this point that Jimmy's dream of succeeding in the major leagues isn't actually his own. He has fully sublimated himself into his father. That's why the film's penultimate line of dialogue—"I want to play"—is so meaningful. Piersall has finally figured out what he wants. It reminds me of the climactic scene in 1997's *Good Will Hunting,* in which Sean (Robin Williams) asks Will (Matt Damon) what he wants to do with his life, and he has no answer. *Good Will Hunting* owes something to *Fear Strikes Out,* and so do other therapy movies like *Ordinary People* and *The Prince of Tides* (not to mention *The Phenom,* a 2016 movie about a hot baseball prospect who loses control of his fastball and visits a therapist who delves into the pitcher's troubled relationship with his father). *Fear Strikes Out* was not the first film to broach the subject of mental illness—*Now, Voyager,* with Bette Davis as a woman who suffers from an overbearing mother but thrives when under the care of a handsome doctor at a mental hospital, came 15 years earlier—but it was the first to do so in a story about men, a major breakthrough at a time when masculinity was defined largely through strength and stoicism.

Despite its effectiveness as an advertisement for therapy and a thorough revision of the American Dream, *Fear Strikes Out* had its detractors, chief among them Piersall himself. In his 1984 autobiography *The Truth Hurts*, he said the film was "a lot of bullshit." He felt it put too much emphasis on his relationship with his father, which in his view was only one factor in his poor mental health. He also said Perkins "threw like a girl" and danced around the outfield "like a ballerina." Perkins' identity as a gay man was an open secret in Hollywood at the time, and it seems likely that Piersall's criticism of the film stemmed from homophobia. Audiences were less likely to know of Perkins' sexual identity, or how much of his unorthodox performance was the product of his experiences in the celluloid closet, but his nervous sensibility contributed mightily to the pull of the film, undermining the mythology of the unflappable star athlete and making the film more appealing to some female viewers. Again, Hollis Alpert: "About as tall and gangling as Gary Cooper; he looks a little bit shy and mixed-up; and he has enough charm and boyishness, when his face is magnified on the screen, to loose [sic] a cascade of motherly feelings throughout the nation." Alpert was onto something; three years later, Perkins would star in *Psycho* as Norman Bates, an icon of sexual repression and perhaps cinema's ultimate object of motherly feelings.

While Piersall's criticisms aren't particularly serious—putting his homophobia aside, all biopics take major liberties with the facts—he's right that the filmmakers left some of the most interesting material out of the final product. Piersall's breakdown actually came on slowly and wasn't marked just by his yelling at his teammates and eventually crawling into the stands. His behavior was more clownish. He liked to imitate his opponents and even, at times, his teammates. The crowd ate it up, hooting and hollering every time he acted up. He started playing to the crowd, bowing to the bleachers every time he took the field. Sometimes he would go over to the fence and talk to them during play, causing the umpires to call time and wait for him to return to his spot.

Eventually, his behavior worsened, but it was always more playful than the film made it look. Once, after managing a base hit against the great Satchel Paige, he took his lead off first while flapping his arms like a chicken and making pig noises just to annoy and distract the great pitcher. Another night, while arguing with the home plate umpire over a called third strike, he pulled a water pistol out of his pocket, squirted it in the umpire's face, and said, "Now maybe you can see it."

It's easy to understand why these scenes were left out. They could have easily been mishandled, come off as bad comedy, or distracted from the film's serious portrayal of mental health. It's a case of truth being stranger—and messier—than fiction, and *Fear Strikes Out*, for all its failings and omissions on the field, still stands out as a baseball film with something unique to say about the game and its place in the American landscape. The final scenes show Jim and John reconnecting on the grounds of the mental hospital. John is humbled now, aware of how his fathering contributed to his son's breakdown. The director frames the scene elegantly, with Perkins looming larger in the frame, as if Jim has finally gotten out from under the crushing weight of his father's expectations. What comes next? They play catch, of course, but this time with the ease, comfort, and genuine spirit of play that defines every man's dream relationship with his father. Jim has overcome his fears. America still had a long way to go.

Damn Yankees, the 1958 film adaptation of the award-winning Broadway musical, tells a similarly incisive tale of the national pastime. Like *Fear Strikes Out*, it points to the bruised core of the postwar American Dream, although its commentary is harder to notice amidst the catchy songs, the choreography, and one famously provocative (albeit tame by today's standards) striptease.

At the heart of this Faustian tale is Joe Boyd (Robert Shafer), a profoundly average, middle-aged man. Unlike Lou Gehrig, Jackie

Robinson, or even Jimmy Piersall, Boyd was unable to make it to the major leagues. His problem? Like the vast majority of those who love baseball, he lacks talent. To be clear, he's a fictional character, and we aren't given his full backstory. We just know that he spends every waking moment watching, rooting for, and obsessing over his favorite baseball team, the Washington Senators. The opening scenes show Joe watching a game on his TV, screaming at the umpires, and criticizing the players for swinging at pitches in the dirt. He's not just a fan. He has baseball fever.

A man can choose his own prison, but a wife doesn't necessarily choose hers. *Damn Yankees* shows how Joe's toxic fandom has left his wife, Meg, (Shannon Bolin) in a bind. In that opening scene, she tries to turn his attention away from the game, discussing the weather in between pitches and, when that fails, trying to entice him with some local gossip. He has no interest in her if a game is on, or according to the song his wife croons, for "Six Months out of Every Year."

> *"When we met in nineteen thirty-eight, it was November,*
> *When I said that I would be his mate, it was December.*
> *I reasoned he would be the greatest husband that a girl had ever found.*
> *That's what I reasoned,*
> *That's what I reasoned.*
> *Then April rolled around."*

It's a cheeky little number, but it harbors a dark undercurrent. Right from the start, *Damn Yankees* portrays baseball not as a building block of the American Dream, but as the thing that punctures it. Like most young women of her era, Meg Boyd dreamed of a happily-ever-after with her husband and their children in the suburbs. We're meant to believe that baseball ruined her marriage, and quite possibly, her chance at being a mother (while it's never stated whether Joe and Meg had children, their absence is conspicuous). It's hard to imagine a more radical thought: that baseball, the national game, has stolen a woman's maternal destiny. And lest you think Meg is an outlier, other women citing the same marital dysfunction pop up in bubbles around her head while she sings.

Making a musical about baseball, or any of the major male sports, might seem like an odd gambit, but *Damn Yankees* wasn't even the first one. In 1949, Gene Kelly and Frank Sinatra made *Take Me Out to the Ballgame*, a film about a pair of major leaguers who had a vaudeville act in the off-season and were torn between their two pursuits. Vaudeville was actually a common off-season profession for players in baseball's early days, back when they were treated like indentured servants—the famous "reserve clause," which prohibited players from signing with other teams and dramatically limited player salaries, wasn't eradicated until 1975. Babe Ruth used to go onstage and recite baseball terms while a band played behind him. Rube Marquand, the top pitcher of 1912, spent his off-season in an act with Blossom Seeley, one of the top vaudeville performers at the time—and then married her. Why did they do it? Money. Christy Mathewson of the New York Giants was one of the game's highest-paid players, earning $10,000 for the 1910 season, but he worked the vaudeville circuit that off-season and made $1,000 per week.

Another reason baseball lends itself to the musical form is what author Howard Good, in his 1997 book on baseball cinema, *Diamonds in the Dark*, called "the intrinsic choreography of the game." In 2024, baseball isn't the only aesthetically beautiful sport, but it may have been at the time of *Damn Yankees*. The dunk had not yet been invented in basketball, and football was still largely a game of attrition based on two- and three-yard runs. The long, spiraling 60-yard touchdown pass was not yet a thing. Meanwhile, baseball had the crisply turned double-play, the hook slide into home, the impeccable curvature of a runner properly rounding a base. It was geometry and movement on a grand stage. To watch baseball was to watch something uniquely beautiful.

It's also the silliest game. During the summer this book is being written, the New York Mets infielders have begun a routine of passing the ball between them every time they come off the field, hurling it behind their backs and over their heads as they come together toward the dugout steps like a well-trained juggling act. Sometimes they only use their feet and kick it like a hacky sack. They say it helps keep them sharp, but they surely also understand the entertainment factor. St. Louis Cardinals shortstop Ozzie Smith used to do backflips before games for the crowd's enjoyment. The barnstorming teams of the Negro Leagues, as we will discuss in a later chapter, made showmanship a key part of their job. This all came to mind while watching "Shoeless Joe from Hannibal, Mo.," the dazzling song-and-dance from the first act of *Damn Yankees* in which Rae Allen, playing the hard-edged reporter, comes up with her story idea to frame Joe Boyd as a mythical Midwestern hero, while the players dance around her, incorporating swinging bats, pounded mitts, and slides into their routine. The choreography by a young Bob Fosse is wonderfully inventive, and there is a strange delight in seeing real dirt kicked up by these dancers-cum-ballplayers.

The rest of the musical numbers represent a muddled mix of styles and quality. "You Gotta Have Heart" and "Lola" have stood the test of time; the former is a hummable ditty sung by the players and manager in the locker room that evokes a wholesome and romantic view of the game; the latter is a seductive, virtuosic dance number by Gwen Verdon, Fosse's wife, muse, and collaborator, that represents the carnal temptations inherent in the young ballplayer's lifestyle. In concert, the two numbers reveal the film's contradictions, its unwillingness to commit to a consistent morality, its desperate need to have it both ways. *Damn Yankees* is a story caught between the moralistic 1950s and the more liberated 1960s. Joe leaves behind his average suburban life—a wife, a job, and a house in the suburbs, those hallmarks of the American Dream—to live out the dreams of his youth. Once in the major leagues, he meets an array of sexually liberated women. Besides Lola, there's also the reporter, a working woman who jokes that she comes to the park "to see the naked men."

But Joe has no interest in the fruits of his fame. From the minute he gets to the majors, he can't wait to return to his old life, even renting a room in his old home from his unsuspecting wife, who doesn't recognize him in his younger form. Their co-habitation causes a stir, as Mr. Applegate, i.e., the Devil, spreads salacious rumors about this middle-aged woman sharing a home with a handsome, young ballplayer. In the end, the complications prove to be too much for poor Joe, who chooses to return to his old life and leave the dreams of youth behind, choosing, as Good put it in *Diamonds in the Dark*, "marriage over sex, work over play, middle age over eternal youth." For the baseball-obsessed viewer, *Damn Yankees* is a life lesson on how to watch the game without being overwhelmed by it, a reminder that the security of middle-age is preferable to the spoils of youth. A few years later, psychiatrist Arnold R. Beisser would write that fandom has an important social function in how it "tends to refurbish the individual for return to the monotony of his daily life." That's what happens to Joe. He lives out his childhood fantasy and sees that it's not all it's cracked up to be, which prepares him for being a better husband when he eventually returns.

Except for one thing: the film doesn't quite buy it. The plot may affirm the sanctity of a quiet life in the suburbs, but the filmmaking doesn't. "You Gotta Have Heart" and "My Old Girl," a pleasing ballad in which Joe writes a goodbye letter to his wife before departing for greener ballfields, are unimaginatively staged, with a static frame and virtually no choreography. They are nice songs expressing virtuous ideals, and the filmmakers seem utterly bored with them. Things change when Mr. Applegate and Lola arrive on the scene. Walston brings a slithery, kinetic energy to his portrayal of the Devil, while Verdon shimmies across the screen with a physical grace and exuberance not before seen in the American musical. She is overtly sexual ("Whatever Lola wants/Lola gets"), and it's not just hormones that make men in the audience perk up in their seats whenever she is on screen. She's utilizing the foundations of film as an art form—motion, light, and sound—to make the most of her appearance. It's as if cinema inherently favors the youthful, liberated lifestyle that Joe Boyd himself eventually rejects.

Next to Walton and Verdon, Tab Hunter blends into the wallpaper as Boyd, or as he becomes known in his younger form, Joe Hardy. Hunter was a singer, actor, and heartthrob, and was perhaps best known for his role in the 1955 WWII drama *Battle Cry*, in which he plays a soldier who has an affair with an older woman but ends up marrying the girl next door back home. His onscreen embrace of conservative American values intersected in fascinating ways with his personal life, where he was in a committed relationship for four years with, wait for it, Anthony Perkins. Their relationship dramatically affected their careers. Perkins in particular sought out more challenging roles—he desperately wanted to play Tony in *West Side Story*—but was rebuffed by studio executives who feared audiences would somehow sense his homosexuality. Instead, he and Hunter each ended up starring in a baseball film in successive years, which in prior years would have strongly reinforced their shared image as stereotypical heterosexual men. By the late '50s, however, the baseball film had cast off its simplistic masculinity. It played in the fields of secrets, lies, and repressed emotions.

Hunter surely drew on his own life to play Hardy, who carries a secret he can't reveal to his adoring fans. Writing in his 2005 memoir, Hunter explained, "[life] was difficult for me, because I was living two lives at that time. A private life of my own, which I never discussed, never talked about to anyone. And then my Hollywood life, which was just trying to learn my craft and succeed." Understanding the emotional realities of Hunter's personal life reveals another fascinating layer to his performance in *Damn Yankees*. It's there in Hunter's blank stare, which both captures the single-mindedness of the star athlete and implies an ocean of secrets hiding beneath his pleasant surface. It's in Hardy's reluctance to indulge in the pleasures that, for many young men, comprise a huge part of the appeal of being a ballplayer. When Verdon is dancing for him, Hunter looks like he'd rather be anywhere else, even at home with Hardy's loving but largely sexless, middle-aged wife (standing next to the young Hunter, she looks more like his mother). If he could play baseball without being surrounded by attractive, young women, he might have had a chance to be happy, but instead he chooses the lesser of two evils: domesticity and the suburban closet.

This subtext was largely lost on the viewers, as *Damn Yankees* and *Fear Strikes Out* came and went without a hint of controversy. A decade earlier, they would have been seen as provocative, the former for the overt sexuality of Gwen Verdon and the latter for its disturbing portrait of mental illness and its sharp revision of the icons of American exceptionalism. But by the late 1950s, America was ready for its postwar myths to be probed more deeply. Change was coming. The Civil Rights Era was in full bloom; by 1959, every Major League Baseball team was integrated. McCarthyism was waning, and America was a year away from electing John F. Kennedy to the White House. The social, political, and cultural dynamics that produced this first wave of baseball films had dissipated. It was bookended by a pair of films about the Yankees, the first one filled with *Pride* and the last one literally damned to Hell. What came next? It would take over a decade to find out.

Bathroom Break
The Most Popular Team
in Baseball Cinema

There's no simple, foolproof way to do this. You can do a keyword search on IMDb (the Internet Movie Database), but you'll end up sorting through a lot of baseball documentaries no one has ever heard of and never had a theatrical release. Those don't count. We're talking about real movies here. To determine which franchise is the champion of baseball cinema—the one most used by filmmakers—we'll have to talk this out.

Most teams have at least had one movie moment. The Twins (*Little Big League*), the A's (*Moneyball*), and the White Sox (*Eight Men Out*) have each gotten a film to call their own. The Cardinals had *The Pride of St. Louis*. The Red Sox had *Fever Pitch* and *Fear Strikes Out*. Heck, even the Brewers had *Mr. 3000*, an underrated comedy that got lost in the wilderness of baseball cinema in the early 2000s. The Giants had *The Fan*. The original *Angels in the Outfield* was about the Pittsburgh Pirates and was shot at Forbes Field. The Braves had *The Slugger's Wife*, unfortunately. The Guardians had the first two *Major League* movies. The Astros are featured in *Boyhood* and, more prominently, in *The Bad News Bears in Breaking Training*. The Tigers have *For Love of the Game*. The

Phillies have *Stealing Home*. By my count, the only major league teams not to have been featured prominently in a baseball film are the Marlins, Nationals, Reds, Rockies, Padres, Diamondbacks, Orioles, Blue Jays, Rays, Royals, and Mariners.

The Cubs have been in numerous films, but often as a joke. *Back to the Future Part II*, filmed in 1988 but set in 2015, earns a good laugh by predicting the Cubs would win the World Series that year. They came pretty close, as the Cubs finally won it in 2016. They also were the subject of two films—1933's *Elmer the Great* and 1935's *Alibi Ike*—starring Joe E. Brown, a film comedian in the 1930s who loved baseball so much that his contract included the creation of a studio-funded team to play games against semi-pro, college, and Negro League teams up and down the Pacific Coast. Of course, there's *Rookie of the Year*, which is perhaps the most popular Cubs film. Some Chicagoans will also argue that *A League of Their Own* qualifies as a Cubs movie, since the owner played by Garry Marshall is based on Philip K. Wrigley and the try-out sequence is set at Wrigley Field. *Ferris Bueller's Day Off* famously has a scene set at Wrigley (more on that in a later section), as does the sour 2006 romantic comedy *The Break-Up*, starring Vince Vaughn and Jennifer Aniston.

The Yankees are, of course, baseball's most famous team. Five thousand years from now, when some kid looks up baseball on Wikipedia, there'll be a photo of a Yankee, probably Babe Ruth. Frankly, the same photo might accompany the entry for America. As the nation's model franchise, the Yankees have been the basis for numerous films: *Pride of the Yankees, The Babe Ruth Story, Safe at Home* (an abominable film starring Mickey Mantle and Roger Maris as themselves), *Bang the Drum Slowly, The Babe*, and *The Scout*. Even when they're not the star, they loom large as the villain of our national nightmare. There are no Yankees in *Damn Yankees*, but they still made it into the title. In *The Bad News Bears*, the villainous Little League team is named after them. They even show up in *Moneyball*, when Billy Beane decrees, "If we try to play like the Yankees in here, we will lose to the Yankees out there."

A case could also be made for the Dodgers as cinema's team, although some of that is simply a question of proximity. They're obviously a huge part of *The Jackie Robinson Story* and *42*, which cover the team's time in Brooklyn. But several baseball films, including *The Naked Gun* and *Taking Care of Business*, were shot at Dodger Stadium, simply because it's near Hollywood. The nearby Angels might also have a case here, as they were the subject of both the 1994 remake of *Angels in the Outfield* and 1991's *Talent for the Game*. That's a lot of baseball cinema for a team who is considered a little brother in their own metropolitan area.

Speaking of little brothers, what about the New York Mets? Technically, there have been no traditional baseball films built around the Mets. No biopics of Tom Seaver or Dwight Gooden have ever gotten off the ground (and Gooden's would likely end on the no-hitter he pitched as a member of the Yankees). Still, they show up more than you would think. *City Slickers, Funny Farm,* and *The Odd Couple* all feature protagonists constantly adorned in Mets hats. Is there something funny about this franchise? Many would argue there is, although in the case of *City Slickers*, there is a practical reason. Billy Crystal is a lifelong Yankees fan, but the Yankees refused to donate to his *Comic Relief* charity drive, and the Mets did, so he rewarded them by wearing their cap throughout the movie.

There are countless scenes shot in the stands at Shea Stadium, where the Mets played from 1964 to 2009. In *Two Weeks Notice*, Mike Piazza nearly crashes into Sandra Bullock and Hugh Grant while chasing a pop-up. In *Three Men and a Little Lady*, Tom Selleck and Steve Guttenberg put a blindfold on their daughter before bringing her into the men's room in the Shea concourse. *Small Time Crooks, Old Dogs,* and *Keeping the Faith*—all middling comedies—each have a scene shot at Shea.

To be fair, the Mets have a distinct home-field advantage, as their city is a hugely popular location for films. Lately, Atlanta has become a second Hollywood due to its enticing tax laws, and of course, Los Angeles will always be atop the list, but the films shot in those cities are rarely set there, while New York–shot films are often about New York. Baseball is a big part of the city, and my hunch is that the Mets—who, over the course of several owners, were well-known for their thriftiness—were far more eager than the Yankees to build their brand and collect a few dollars by allowing virtually any production to be shot there, regardless of the quality of the film. No offense to *Two Weeks Notice*.

Being the underappreciated team in their own city has also made the Mets the subject of smaller, more interesting movies. 2012's *Gimme the Loot*, an indie film set in New York that premiered at the Cannes Film Festival, revolves around two teenage graffiti artists trying to "bomb" the home run apple at Citi Field. In the classic comedy *Coming to America*, Prince Akeem (Eddie Murphy) is seen wearing a Mets jacket; he and his manservant have chosen to live in Queens because they believe it's a royal land, and he wears the jacket to try to blend in. The joke is that Queens is anything but royal. The 2007 indie *Chop Shop* makes narrative hay out of the widely bemoaned environment around the Mets' stadium, which is littered with auto body shops and junkyards. The film by acclaimed director Ramin Bahrani follows a child who works at one such establishment, and it features a scene of him watching a Mets game from the roof.

Then there's *Bad Lieutenant*, Abel Ferrara's NC-17 masterpiece, in which Harvey Keitel, as a drug-addicted, sexually depraved police officer, becomes so enraged at a Mets' loss that he pulls out his gun in his car and shoot the radio while sitting in New York traffic. He had money on the game, but even without that, what Mets fan can't relate?

Numerous Spike Lee films feature the Mets, perhaps because he is from Brooklyn, which bequeathed much of the Dodgers' fan base to the team. Or maybe it's because he came of age as a filmmaker in the mid-1980s, when the Mets owned the city. They had two of the biggest Black baseball stars during that era, Dwight Gooden and Darryl Strawberry. In 1989's *Do the Right Thing*, Mookie, a character played by Spike Lee and whose name was perhaps inspired by Mets center fielder Mookie Wilson, argues that Gooden is "the best pitcher in the game." A few years later, things had changed. In 1990's *Mo' Better Blues*, a character played by Lee places a bet on the Pirates to beat the Mets because "the Mets need more Black ballplayers." The Pirates had Bobby Bonilla and Barry Bonds.

So there are practical and economic reasons the Mets have been featured in so many films. But there's also something in the team's innate character that lends itself to cinema: pure magic. The Mets have been known as a team that finds new ways to lose, but when they win, it's usually because of a miracle. The first magic came in 1969, when the Mets, who had never had a winning season in their history, rose from last place to first in the final two months of the season, and won the World Series against the Orioles in a relaxed five games. They were dubbed the Miracle Mets. Some people called them the Amazin' Mets, a moniker that has stuck.

The movies love miracles, and they love amazing things. The 2000 film *Frequency*, about a Queens cop (Jim Caviezel) who communicates with his deceased father (Dennis Quaid) in 1969 through a magic ham radio, revolves entirely around that amazing World Series. The son proves he's real to his father—and not some neighbor playing a prank—by predicting what will happen in the next game. Later on, the father proves his innocence to a detective who suspects him of murder (it's complicated, don't ask) with the same trick, by predicting the result of the series and convincing him that this time travel business is real. There is also era-specific Mets paraphernalia in the background of nearly every scene, but what's most striking is how the Mets are used as an inspiration for real-world magic. If that team can win the World Series, anything is possible.

This supernatural quality to the Mets also accounts for their role in the *Men in Black* series. In the first film, Mets left fielder Bernard Gilkey is seen being distracted by an alien spaceship, costing him a chance to catch a fly ball. Both the original and the film's sequel have scenes set in Flushing Meadows Corona Park, just around the corner from the stadium. Perhaps the best use of the Mets in any film, however, belongs in *Men in Black 3*, when the alien cops played by Will Smith and Tommy Lee Jones track a benevolent being to Shea Stadium. Played by character actor Michael Stuhlbarg, this creature has a gift (or curse) for being able to see every possibility at once. We find him standing on the upper deck concourse at night, chanting, "Let's go Mets!" The field is dark, but he's rewatching the 1969 World Series in his mind. "It's my favorite moment in human history," he says. "All the things that had to converge for the Mets to win the World Series. They were in last place every single season until they won it all." He watches the last out and says, "When that ball is pitched to Davey Johnson, who only became a baseball player because his father couldn't find a football to give him for his birthday, it hits his bat two micrometers too high, causing him to pop up to Cleon Jones, who would have been born Clara, a statistical typist, if his parents didn't have an extra glass of wine that night before going to bed." We see Cleon Jones catch the fly ball that ended the series. "A miracle is what seems impossible but happens anyway," he concludes. Mets fans already know this, and clearly so does baseball cinema.

· PART II ·

Watergate Baseball

Chapter 5

Bang the Drum Slowly [1973]

IT'S AN EASY MOMENT TO MISS, ESPECIALLY ON A FIRST VIEWING. IT COMES early in *Bang the Drum Slowly*, a drama about a backup catcher dying of cancer and the stud pitcher who befriends him over the course of one fateful season. The pitcher, Henry Wiggen (Michael Moriarty), is chatting in a hotel lobby with bullpen coach Joe Jaros (Phil Foster), who casually mentions a book Wiggen published in the off-season. Jaros apologizes for not having read the whole thing; instead, he says he's "only concerned with the parts that concern me." Wiggen's writing career is never mentioned again, although he is later seen with a notepad and pen. From this, we can reasonably assume that his voiceover narrating the film represents a book he is writing about his experiences that season—in essence, the film *is* that book—when he stuck his neck out for catcher Bruce Pearson (Robert De Niro), pushed back against a culture of bullying in his clubhouse, and led the fictional New York Mammoths to a pennant.

But what of this prior book mentioned by Jaros? His comment implies it's a nonfiction book about Wiggen's experiences in the majors, which sounds very much like *Ball Four*, the book published in 1970 by journeyman major league pitcher Jim Bouton. *Ball Four* sold millions of copies and dramatically changed the perception of the national pastime. It was a simple diary of a season, but it exposed dirty secrets that journalists

67

had for years ignored for the supposed good of the game. Within the first few dozen pages, Bouton reveals that Mickey Mantle is an asshole, general managers will nickel-and-dime even their biggest stars, and that players aren't the squeaky-clean role models they're made out to be. They curse and they womanize. Their favorite activity is "beaver-hunting," which is code for finding creative ways to spy on unsuspecting women on the road. Binoculars were their weapon of choice, but according to Bouton, one player even drilled a hole in his hotel-room wall to catch a glimpse of his neighbor in the nude. You know, a sex crime.

Bouton massacred every sacred cow in the game, and the world was ready for the slaughter. *Time* named it one of the 100 greatest non-fiction books written since 1923 (or since the beginning of *Time*), but that doesn't begin to describe the scope of its influence. Bouton himself reported in a later edition that he could hardly go a day without a mother approaching him and telling him that *Ball Four* was the only book they could get their son to read. The author's excavation of baseball's true nature permanently removed the sheen of heroism that rested above the game's grimy insides.

So why does *Bang the Drum Slowly* suggest that Henry Wiggen is a Bouton-like figure, a player-author who reported on the game from the inside? The idea first came from the novel on which the film is based. Written by Mark Harris and published in 1956, it describes Wiggen as a star pitcher who has just authored a baseball novel, presumably based on his own experiences. *Bang the Drum Slowly* was too dour to be made as a baseball film in 1956, but it's perfect for the *Ball Four* era, when illusions about baseball and America were being ripped apart. *Ball Four* was published the same year the National Guard killed four antiwar protesters at Kent State University, two years after the assassinations of Robert F. Kennedy, Jr. and Martin Luther King Jr., and two years before Watergate removed the final fig leaf from American politics. It was the total destruction of the wholesome, upright image America had built for itself in the postwar era, and baseball could not hide from the carnage.

"It's significant that you don't have a lot of big baseball movies in the '70s," argues Dave Zirin. Zirin is a writer for *The Nation* on the intersection of sports and politics, whose first book, *A People's History of Sports in the United States,* revealed the history of radicalism in professional sports that has been erased by the game's corporate interests. He's a fan of *Bang the Drum Slowly,* but he correctly notes that this era of baseball cinema is sparser than others, especially compared to the two decades that followed. "It's almost as if Hollywood was recognizing that the appetite for that kind of Americana just wasn't there." The baseball films of the 1970s were gloomier, more introspective, and designed around failure. Like *Ball Four,* they showed that the ballplayers once held up as role models for America's youth were not immune to human weakness. They could be just as greedy, pervy, and unpleasant as the rest of us.

Henry Wiggen is such a figure. He may look like a classic movie ballplayer—he's tall, blonde, and handsome. Some critics suggested he was modeled on Tom Seaver, the Cy Young Award winner who a few years earlier led the perpetually bottom-dwelling New York Mets to that miracle championship. Seaver was a mythic figure—all heart and muscle—but Wiggen is painfully human. As the film begins, he is holding out for a higher salary, sitting on the sidelines during spring training while his teammates prepare for the upcoming season. It wasn't until 1975 that the "reserve clause," which prohibited free agency in baseball, was dismantled and players became free to sell themselves like mercenaries to the highest bidder. At the time *Bang the Drum Slowly* was made, players could simply sit out if they didn't like their contract. Wiggen wanted his freedom. And his money.

When Wiggen finally receives an offer from ownership, the salary is well below his expectations, and he writes his response in magic marker on the offer's front page, "I was taught in school where slavery went out when Lincoln was shot." Even in 1973, when White men comparing themselves to slaves was seen as slightly more acceptable than it is now, his response would be considered petty and foolish. It's not until he learns that Pearson is ill that Wiggen starts to break good. Although the two players are not yet close friends, Wiggen accepts a lesser salary on the condition that Pearson's fate on the team be tied to his. If Pearson gets traded, so does Wiggen. If one man gets sent down (let's face it, it would only be Pearson), so does the other. The team's owner, general manager, and cranky old manager (Vincent Gardenia) reluctantly agree to his demands.

Securing Pearson's place on the team, however, isn't enough for Wiggen. His next move is to persuade his teammates to cease their endless ragging on him without revealing his illness. Their typical insults are both ordinary and merciless. A few players, including a lanky first baseman played by a young Danny Aiello, have a favorite joke to play on him. They ask him how tall he is, and when he responds in earnest, they reply, "I didn't know they piled shit that high." It seems a harmless bit of bullying, but when you're already an outsider trying to fit in, it stings. Pearson is an easy target. He's consistently described as dumb, and nothing in the script or in De Niro's performance will dissuade viewers otherwise. He's a Southern rube in the big city, and he's not much of a ballplayer either. Before Wiggen intervenes, Pearson is about to be sent down to the minors in favor of a hot young catching prospect who rides a motorcycle and carries a guitar wherever he goes. The new guy is a headache for the manager, but at least he can play. Pearson has talent but lacks the brains to make anything of it, or the personality to join in the players' reindeer games.

Wiggen is determined to make Pearson's final season be a happy one, so after persuading his teammates to stop ragging on him, he teaches him a few tricks to improve his game. It works. Pearson goes on a hot streak in the late summer that keeps him in the line-up as the Mammoths careen toward the pennant. More crucially, he finally teaches him to play TEGWAR (The Excellent Game Without Any Rules), a made-up card game used to sucker unsuspecting idiots out of their money. Early on, we see Wiggen and Jaros sitting in the lobby of their hotel, luring in baseball fans who are eager to sit at a card table with a major leaguer. At first, Pearson is a victim of TEGWAR—a symbol of his status as an outsider, as if he's not even a real teammate—but after his diagnosis, Wiggen lets him in on the game's secret, and by the end, he's having a ball making up rules alongside his buddy, taking cash from dumb fans who are all too eager to hand over their cash for a chance to hobnob with the pros.

It's a delight for Pearson and for us. Baseball is an insider's game—that's why Bouton's book caused such a scandal—but its popularity rests on the fantasy that any fan could stroll up to the plate and rip a single if they were given the chance. In reality, it's a world that is shut off to the vast majority of us. Most of us couldn't even make contact. If any of us ever made it to the show, it would be some terrible mistake and just a matter of minutes before we were sent down in favor of a real major-leaguer. That's how Pearson feels. So as Wiggen teaches Pearson the ropes, it feels like he's letting us in on the secrets of the game, too. He's doing in the movie what Bouton did in his book.

If it's so much fun, then why does *Bang the Drum Slowly* have the reputation of being a legendary downer? In part, it's because sad sports movies aren't a thing anymore, so its melancholia stands out. In the early '70s, however, they were a genuine phenomenon. *Bang the Drum Slowly* may be based on a 1956 novel, but its spiritual cinematic antecedent is 1971's *Brian's Song*, an ABC Movie of the Week that became a national phenomenon. It was the most-watched made-for-TV movie ever, earning an audience share of 48 percent, and is now often cited as one of the best TV movies ever made. Based on the friendship of NFL players Brian Piccolo and Gale Sayers, *Brian's Song* starts out as a sports flick and an interracial buddy movie, but as Piccolo is diagnosed with cancer, it morphs into a male weepie. Young people who were cut down in the prime of their lives was a mini-genre at the time—*Love Story*, starring Ryan O'Neal and Ali MacGraw as lovers with tragic timing, was the highest-grossing film of 1970, and it saved Paramount Pictures from bankruptcy. Imitators were sure to follow. Still, *Brian's Song* was more clearly the reason *Bang the Drum Slowly*, which had been optioned for a film several times before, was finally greenlit. Putting aside the racial themes, they're almost the same movie. They each follow a friendship among teammates, one of whom gets diagnosed with a fatal disease. There are laughs along the way and a glimpse behind the curtain of the modern athlete, but they ultimately confront viewers with the inevitability of death in a way that few sports films had, at least since *The Pride of the Yankees*.

These films reflected the national tragedy offscreen: a war that killed tens of thousands of young American men (and countless Vietnamese), was exceedingly unpopular at home, and would soon be widely understood as the first losing military effort in American history. It was also the first televised war, giving Americans actual glimpses into an environment that had up until this point been left unshown. Camera crews sent overseas showed the soldiers goofing off in non-combat situations, allowing Americans to connect with the soldiers personally, instead of seeing them simply as numbers. It helped turn the tide against the war and influenced how young Americans were portrayed in pop culture. Our illusions had been broken, necessitating a greater reality in our films.

Both *Pride of the Yankees* and *Bang the Drum Slowly* are about players on the Yankees—okay, the Mammoths aren't technically the Yankees, but their uniforms are clearly modeled on them—whose careers comes to a premature end due to deadly disease; one is based on a true story and the other is fictional, which makes *Bang the Drum Slowly* seem even more like a response, as if the filmmakers purposefully subverted the template of *Pride of the Yankees* to highlight the ways American attitudes toward war had changed. The broad outline is the same, but there is a drastic shift in tone. *Pride of the Yankees* is rousing—while Gehrig's death is certainly tragic, the film finds salvation in how his courage in the face of death inspired others. It ends with Gehrig calling himself "the luckiest man on the face of the Earth." Viewers walked out of the theater feeling encouraged. There is perhaps no more reassuring message in the midst of a World War than that you can be victorious even in death.

Bang the Drum Slowly sounds no notes of triumph. It finds redemption in how the players discover their better angels when they learn of Pearson's illness, but the film's structure doesn't allow for uplift. In *Pride of the Yankees,* Gehrig doesn't get his diagnosis until the film's third act, leaving plenty of time for love to flourish, laughs to be had, and skeptical immigrant mothers to be won over. Bruce Pearson receives his bad news before *Bang the Drum Slowly* even starts. The film opens on an establishing shot of the Mayo Clinic, where Pearson has just received his diagnosis. Instead of a traditional rise-and-fall arc, *Bang the Drum Slowly* sees life as a long, slow fade-out in which its players, mainly Wiggen, struggle to redeem a hopeless situation. Its climactic moment comes not during a game but in a long rain delay, when Piney Woods (Tom Ligon), the young, guitar-playing catcher who has arrived to replace Pearson, entertains the players by playing the song from which the book and the film gets its title, "Streets of Laredo," which is sung from the perspective of a slain cowboy: "Oh, beat the drum slowly and play the fife lowly / Sing the Death March as you carry me along." By then, almost everyone on the team knows Pearson is sick, and the song honors him through the simple, clear acknowledgment of his impending death. There is no victory to be wrung from it, just a graceful defeat.

The contrast with *Pride of the Yankees* is perhaps most stark in the tenor of its central performances. Robert De Niro was no Gary Cooper (or maybe Cooper was no De Niro). Cooper was a prototypical movie star, handsome and all-American with an inherent likeability. He played war heroes, cowboys, and ballplayers. He didn't transform into his characters; he was always Gary Cooper. He had a good face for the camera, and his subtle reactions played well on the big screen. De Niro didn't look like a movie star, although he and his peers quickly redefined what a movie star could look like. In the 1970s, ethnic types like Al Pacino and Dustin Hoffman became major stars and box-office draws. The success of Pacino and Hoffman in films like *The Graduate, Midnight Cowboy,* and *The Godfather* surely paved the way for De Niro to be cast as Pearson, a role for which he may not have seemed at first such an obvious fit. He didn't even look much like a catcher. A backup catcher only has to be big enough to block the plate and strong enough to frame a fastball that's a couple inches outside. De Niro looked like a stiff wind could blow him over.

Despite these physical incongruities, De Niro gives a remarkable performance that benefited greatly from the young actor's anonymity. De Niro was still a nobody in 1973, and it's even easier to transform when you're unknown to the audience. His résumé in the press notes for the film lists only company productions of *Cyrano de Bergerac*, *A Hatful of Rain*, and *A Long Day's Journey into Night*, as well as a few touring plays. He was still a few months away from making *Mean Streets*, which would transform his career. Much of the press around the film centered on De Niro's adoption of something called "method acting," which actors John Garfield and Marlon Brando brought to cinema decades prior but was still largely unknown to the American public. De Niro trained for the role of Pearson by spending time in Alabama and learning to chew tobacco. According to one report, for a scene in which he had to look very ill, he spun himself around just before the camera rolled until he got green in the face. Moriarty, who played Wiggen, was less enamored with De Niro's quirks and by method actors in general. "Unfortunately, they're fed by a lot of people who want to see those neuroses, they're fed by the acting teachers themselves. There are certain actors whose mannerisms were neurotic ones and those mannerisms were mistaken for talent." This tension, however, supports the film. There is no chemistry between Pearson and Wiggen. They come from different worlds, and even as they grow closer over the film, it never blossoms into a bromance. Their closeness is contrived and awkward. It's always an effort. Watching it unfold, you get the sense that doing the right thing brings no pleasure to Wiggen, and Pearson's illness has not magically made him more likable.

With its mournful tone and embrace of a bold, new acting style, *Bang the Drum Slowly* represented a welcome realism in the baseball film. Critics who were on board with Hollywood's turn toward more gritty material celebrated *Bang the Drum Slowly* as a triumph. *Cineaste Magazine* rightly called it "sentimental without being maudlin." The critics for the *New York Post* mused that while "it should be lugubrious, depressing and about as entertaining as a hangman, instead it is sweet, sexy, funny, satiric, and one of the few human movies to open all year." Richard Schickel of *Time* magazine called it "very possibly the best movie about sport ever made in this country." Even those hung up on the veracity of its baseball action found much to admire. In the *New York Times*, Peter Schjeldahl wrote: "I have yet to see a baseball film in which the game looked real. This may be because baseball is, in effect, a rival art form with spatial and temporal conventions all on its own; attempts to represent it on film invariably make it seem obscure and pointless. In any case, *Bang the Drum Slowly* falls down on the field and picks itself up in locker rooms, hotel rooms, and bars." Schjeldahl rightly observed how the real revelations of *Bang the Drum Slowly* come from what the players do off the field, just like in *Ball Four*.

In fact, the film had no greater champion that Jim Bouton himself, who did not write the source material but might as well have. In a guest review for the *New York Times*, he noted that "most people, especially baseball players, will not laugh at *Bang the Drum Slowly*. It seems too real. Too many details are perfect. The general manager negotiates a pitcher's contract by remarking how well the other pitchers are throwing…. The manager is named Dutch and says things like, 'Never mind the facts, give me details,' and he worries that the clap, an occupational hazard, will spread around his infield." Even a non-ballplayer can spot other wonderful details that could only be ripped from reality, like a coach comically scratching himself, or the manager smoking a cigarette in the clubhouse jacuzzi, asking Wiggen to lift up the lid of the toilet so he can deposit his ash. Taken together, these details fill out the world of the film and paint a portrait of baseball as it is, not how we have dreamed it up.

Nor was the connection between ballplayers and soldiers lost on the thoughtful Bouton. "The athlete's mocking humor has been compared to soldiers' humor, soldiers being another band of men who deal with boredom and tension and failure that in their case can mean death," he wrote. "Maybe that's why when baseball players get sent to the minors they call it 'dying.' A player just released from the team walks out of the manager's office and says, 'I died.' During the spring training cutdown, players walk around the locker room and say, 'Who died today?' Such 'deaths' take the pressure off a swollen spring roster. One man's death means another man's life."

That's the only redemption in *Bang the Drum Slowly*. Bruce Pearson dies—off-screen, after the film has ended—so that others can live. There's little hope that all the cruelty of baseball, war, and life will be redeemed by Pearson's tragedy, but maybe the people he touched will live slightly better lives. The Mammoths come together as a team in the wake of Pearson's diagnosis. The manager ceases to be such an irascible prick and learns the value of saying a kind word to his players once in a while. We never hear from the owners again; some people are beyond redemption. And Wiggen? He learns to stop being a bully. "From here on in, I rag nobody," goes the famous final line of the book and the film. Perhaps being a little kinder to his teammates seems like no major shift in thinking, but when you consider the alpha-male, frat-like culture revealed by *Ball Four* and *Bang the Drum Slowly*, in which brotherhood is forged only through competition, and death is just a curveball away, maybe it's not such a small change after all.

Chapter 6

Bingo Long and the Traveling All-Stars & Motor Kings (1976)

WHY DOESN'T ANYONE KNOW ABOUT *BINGO LONG AND THE TRAVELING All-Stars & Motor Kings*? Whenever the baseball movie canon is debated, *Bingo Long* rarely gets mentioned. Maybe it's the unwieldy title. It's a mouthful. Maybe it's the film's uncomfortable portrayal of America's racial contradictions. On the other hand, it stars Lando Calrissian and Darth Vader (Billy Dee Williams and James Earl Jones, to some) as Negro Leaguers who form a barnstorming team and travel throughout the land, crushing baseballs and entertaining the locals. Richard Pryor is in it, too, as Charlie Snow, whose whole deal is that he's learning Spanish so he can sneak into the pre–Jackie Robinson major leagues as a Cuban. It's a funny bit, and he calls himself Carlos Nevada, which is a cool name. Released in 1976, the film was a bonafide hit, grossing $33 million on a $9 million budget. Why don't more people know about it?

Okay, so it didn't win Oscars. It wasn't beloved by critics, but it wasn't reviled either. Vincent Canby at the *New York Times* called it "genial, slapdash, high-spited, and occasionally moving." In *Time* magazine, Jay Cocks wrote that while "it never fulfills the richest possibilities in the raffish misadventures of a barnstorming Black baseball team in the 1930s, it does come close from time to time." That's about right. *Bingo*

Long doesn't always work as a movie—its pacing is muddy, and outside of Pryor's riffing, none of the jokes really land—but it features entertaining performances from its central trio and a portrayal of the Negro Leagues that's both vivid and complex. It's the only studio film about the Negro Leagues in which its central characters don't get called up to the majors. Maybe it didn't make it into the canon because it told a story about baseball that baseball people didn't want to hear.

It's the only baseball film in which you'll hear the words "means of production," a Marxist term describing the advantages ownership has over its labor force, and certainly the only one that references W.E.B. Du Bois, the author and activist who co-founded the National Association for the Advancement of Colored People and saw capitalism as the primary underpinning of American racism. I wonder what he would have thought of *Bingo Long*, which weaves serious ideas about racial and economic justice into its underdog story but was also written and directed by White men who more than once take their eyes off the ball. Maybe *Bingo Long* has a small cultural footprint because it's too difficult to wrestle with. Its ideas are powerful, perhaps too powerful to be put into a light-hearted baseball movie, and are often undercut by middling execution. It's not perfect, but at least it tries.

The dual protagonists are Bingo (Williams) and Leon Carter (Jones), star players of the Ebony Aces, a Negro League team run by tyrannical owner Sallie Potter (Ted Ross). Things are good for Bingo and Leon. They're paid well enough, and their exploits on the field have made them celebrities in their Southern town. After the games, they get dressed up and go out to eat steak and mingle with girls. Leon even has the cachet to snap at a waiter and order him to bring his friend a plate. In a few simple strokes, the film paints a portrait of Black celebrity that had rarely been seen on film. These are Black Americans with influence and social power, even if it's just in their little corner of the world.

The fragility of their livelihood becomes startlingly clear when a beloved teammate, Rainbow (DeWayne Jessie), gets injured in a game and is unceremoniously released by Potter (it seems no coincidence that the owner shares a name with the evil banker from *It's a Wonderful Life*). Bingo feels for Rainbow and complains to Potter in front of the team; the owner fines him for trying to "foment rebellion." Bingo could surely catch on with another squad, but in Rainbow, Bingo gets a terrifying glimpse of his own future, so he convinces his teammates to quit the Aces and form a barnstorming team. It will be a true collective. He'll be in charge, but the profit shares will be equal. He brings Rainbow along to handle the money box, and also as a symbol of solidarity—on this team, no man will be left behind. Leon is initially opposed to the idea of trading his steady income with the Aces for the uncertainties of the road, but he's won over by Bingo's optimism and his desire to support Black entrepreneurship.

In theory, Bingo and Leon form a meaningful dialectic, representing two distinct approaches to Black advancement. Bingo is a salesman who is willing to use the tools of capitalism to create change. Not particularly concerned with politics, he only wants to get paid and to help his teammates do the same. He's willing to put on a show, and in his performance it's easy to see the wildly successful advertising pitchman Williams would become. Remembered as much for his commercials for Colt .45 malt liquor ("It works every time") as he is for his screen acting, Williams has the rare ability to make salesmanship feel earnest. Leon, on the other hand, is informed by a deep knowledge of the racial and economic struggle of his people. He quotes Du Bois' theories on the capitalist undergirding of American racism, and wisely steps in to correct Bingo every time he's about to take a wrong step. The game has already slowed down for Leon, and he sees all the moves ahead of time. Jones, whose physical stature and thundering baritone gave him an authoritative presence, was perfectly cast.

Amidst its conversation on divergent approaches to racial and economic progress, *Bingo Long* is rooted in the details of the Negro Leagues that both baseball and Hollywood had always been happy to overlook. Bingo and Leon, a flamboyant pitcher and power-hitting catcher, are clearly modeled on Satchel Paige and Josh Gibson, two of the greatest players of all time whose talent has been historically underrated, due to their lack of time in the big leagues. Bingo imitates Paige's famous wind-up, with the high leg-kick and windmill arms, as well as his gimmick of calling his defense off the field before he throws a pitch, as a demonstration of his confidence. Bingo calls it his "invite pitch," and he opens every game with it just to delight the crowd.

The fictional Bingo Long All-Stars are an idea patched together from real barnstorming teams like the Indianapolis Clowns, the Chappie Johnson Colored All-Stars, and the Harlem Globetrotters of Baseball. These squads rostered many skilled ballplayers but are mostly remembered for the few major leaguers who got their start there. One in particular deserves mention. In 1952, the Clowns signed a young slugger named Henry Aaron, who played with the team for a year before his contract was purchased by the Boston Braves; the rest is history. Much like the All-Stars, these barnstorming teams recognized that skill alone wasn't enough to bring in the crowds. They goofed around. They talked trash loudly enough for the crowd to hear. They brought out comically oversized gloves and engaged in "shadow ball," in which the players pantomimed a defensive play without an actual baseball. Each of these antics is faithfully reconstructed in *Bingo Long*, marking the first time many viewers had seen them, since little footage of the Negro Leagues exists.

Kudos to *Bingo Long* for getting these details right, but the emphasis on "clowning" remains the most challenging aspect of the film. As the All-Stars arrive in a small town for their first game, they prepare to go straight to the ballpark, but the local man who scheduled the game insists they put on a show first. He shows them exactly how to dance, and the players go along with it. They parade down main street in their uniforms, shucking and jiving, waving to the locals. At first, the camera shows us the White locals looking on disapprovingly, but as the parade goes on, Black residents show up in larger and larger numbers, smiling and dancing themselves, and eventually joining the parade as they make their way to the stadium. The film's theme song, "The Bingo Long Song (Steal On Home)," makes its first appearance on the soundtrack, rousing viewers with Thelma Houston's joyous gospel vocals. It's a party, and we're invited, and these scenes unsurprisingly comprise the most lasting image of the film. When the novel it was based on was reprinted in 1993, a still from this scene made the cover, even though the sequence is only glancingly referenced in the book.

What are we supposed to make of this dancing? It's complicated. Buck O'Neil, a Negro Leaguer with the Kansas City Monarchs who went on to coach for the Chicago Cubs, absolutely despised it. "It wasn't like that," he said in one interview. "We weren't no minstrel show." Elsewhere, he called the film a "farce." He also objected to the film's portrayal of the Negro Leagues as a ramshackle operation. "There were 16 Negro League ballclubs, each with at least 15 players," he said. "There were all those people putting on the games, booking agents, traveling secretaries, trainers. Baseball was Black entertainment and was important to Black communities." To O'Neil, the parade sequences were not a meaningful trade-off for representation. They were an insult to the real-life Negro Leaguers who played the game with as much pride and skill as their major league counterparts.

"There's just no way a Black team would have been shucking and jiving down main street," agrees Robert Daniels, a film critic specializing in Black cinema and an all-around smart baseball man. "No Black team would have been dumb enough to do that in the Deep South dressed in flashy uniforms in front of White people who are probably part of the Ku Klux Klan and ready to lynch somebody." As a representation of reality for Black Americans, especially those who lived in the era the film is set in, these scenes simply strain credulity, reflecting the film's conflicting goals. It wants to honor the Negro Leagues, while still entertaining White audiences at the movies on a Saturday night. Too much of the former would have surely gotten in the way of the latter. *Bingo Long* was supposed to be a hit. A $9 million budget wasn't nothing in 1976. They couldn't afford too much honesty.

For Daniels, however, the lack of reality isn't necessarily a flaw, as it demonstrates the way stories about the Negro Leagues spread. Exaggeration was part of their marketing. These games weren't covered by the mainstream press. They weren't televised, and box scores were near impossible to come by. They only lived on in the minds of those who were there, and so the cartoonish behavior we see in *Bingo Long* reflects a tradition of oral storytelling crucial to the Negro Leagues' success. "There's that scene where Esquire [Joe Calloway] is running for a home run and is speeding across fields and crashing through things," Daniels says. "It seems so outlandish, but it's the kind of Negro Leagues story you would have heard from someone like Buck O'Neil or something Satchel Paige or Rube Foster would have said about themselves. It feels like a glitch until you realize this is actually a feature. It captures how over-the-top all these stories were." Some of the Black press took a similarly measured stance upon the film's release. David Dugas of the *Atlanta Daily World* called the film "an exceptional picture that will get laughs from non-baseball fans as well as non-Blacks," but he also noted that "the comedy is mostly superficial, as though that era of racial prejudice weren't quite ready for the good-natured yet revealing backward glance it deserves."

Perhaps the best way to understand *Bingo Long*, both its victories and its complications, is as a piece of the so-called Blaxploitation film movement of the 1970s, a collection of low budget but artfully made films set in inner cities featuring Black protagonists. Everyone knows *Shaft*, the private eye played by Richard Roundtree with his own Oscar-winning theme song. Other key figures in the movement include Pam Grier, who played a sexy and powerful avenging angel of the inner city in *Coffy* and *Foxy Brown*, and director Melvin Van Peebles, who kicked off the entire genre with *Sweet Sweetback's Baadasssss Song*, an avant-garde masterpiece about a Black gigolo who becomes an urban folk hero for his defiance of the White police force. These films embraced their stereotypes; they often featured Black characters defined by their sexual prowess or racial anger (or both) and didn't shy away from portraying violent crime and drug addiction. They were also enormously successful, gave much-deserved work to talented Black actors, and opened conversations about subjects, like resistance to state violence, which were rarely voiced in the mainstream media.

As they were raising the profile of Black artists, these films were met with skepticism by some Black thought leaders. The term "Blaxploitation" was coined as criticism by Junius Griffin, president of the Beverly Hills–Hollywood branch of the NAACP, who felt that the films were "proliferating offenses" to Black communities for their perpetuation of harmful stereotypes. The concern was that the lesson White viewers would learn from these films was that all Black people were criminals, an example of the distinct challenge that fell on Black filmmakers at this time. As the first movies made by and about Black people to ever break through with White audiences, Blaxploitation films were held to an impossible standard of pleasing both Black audiences eager for an honest accounting of their experiences and the same White Hollywood executives who spent decades withholding access and opportunity. They were tasked with telling uncomfortable truths about America's racist past and present, while promoting a response to that oppression that only gently challenged the status quo. Few White filmmakers can understand that burden.

To be clear, *Bingo Long* isn't quite a Blaxploitation film. It is not set in the city. It doesn't portray its characters as criminals caught up in a broken system, or speak directly to the issues that affected Black Americans offscreen at its time. Instead, it confronts viewers with the humiliations and objectification of the entertainment industry. Wrote Roger Ebert, "As I sat through it, I almost began to feel like a member of one of the All-Stars' first White audiences, laughing at the cut-up antics of the players but never seeing the hurt underneath." If the humorous antics of Bingo's All-Stars provoked a complex reaction in viewers, maybe that's okay. Black minstrelsy, a popular art form in the last half of the 19th century, did the same thing. The performers traveled from town to town and performed separate shows, both including racial stereotypes, for Black and White audiences. Many minstrel performers became minor celebrities, especially to their Black fans. The fact that they relied on harmful stereotypes was not a deal-breaker. It was so uncommon to see a performer of color succeed on the stage in any capacity—particularly as the star—that their success empowered Black audiences. It seems likely that the Black barnstorming teams of the 20th century took their inspiration from these Black minstrels, or were at least unconsciously following in their traditions.

These complexities in *Bingo Long* are even more difficult to unpack when you consider it was made exclusively by White men who knew little of the lived experiences of Negro Leaguers. It was the directorial debut of John Badham, a filmmaker born in England and raised in Alabama in the 1940s; a year after *Bingo Long*, he directed the smash disco movie *Saturday Night Fever* and, despite a long and illustrious career, he never made another film with a Black protagonist. *Bingo Long*'s screenplay was written by Hal Barwood and Matthew Robbins, who met at film school at the University of Southern California and became successful figures in 1970s Hollywood. They based their script on the novel by William Brashler, who was studying at the Iowa Writers' Workshop when he was made aware by his professor of the barnstorming teams of the 1930s; Brashler loved baseball but initially had no idea such teams existed and knew little of the Negro Leagues. To complete his novel, he heavily researched the era and talked to many former Negro League players and their families.

Despite Brashler's limitations, the book feels more authentic than the film, and less susceptible to accusations of whitewashing. Consider its climax, in which one of the All-Stars, a former criminal, breaks into a White-owned auto dealer to steal a car; the All-Stars' car has gone kaput, and a criminal act is the only way they can continue their enterprise. He and his teammates know he'll be lynched if he's caught, and the scene is written with the expert tension of a taut thriller. Death hangs over the proceedings. When the scene is recreated for the movie, however, it's played for hijinks. The jazz on the soundtrack, reminiscent of "Sweet Georgia Brown" (the theme of the Harlem Globetrotters), discourages the viewer from taking any of it too seriously. It's similar to a scene in which a player is caught with a White prostitute and beaten to within an inch of his life. To escape his assaulters, he jumps out a window and lands in the backseat of a passing car as if he were Buster Keaton. The book, on the other hand, describes the wounds inflicted on the player by the brothel's muscle in gruesome detail. In both cases, the film smooths things over for White audiences, while the source material at least tries to tell a greater truth.

Perhaps the most racially astute sequence in the book takes place on a quiet creek, where the players are trying to catch their dinner in between games of a double-header. It's a relaxing afternoon until two White cops show up and ask if they have a permit. Once they recognize them as the All-Stars, the officers lighten up a bit. They begin asking them about baseball and their careers, and are excited to hear some of them played against Dizzy Dean, a favorite of White Southerners. They ask the All-Stars how they fared against Dean, and Bingo is about to brag about his success before Leon interrupts him: "No, sir. Dean is too tough for us. We can't touch him. Can't even see him." Leon understands the situation—that puncturing the myth of their heroes could inspire violence—far better than Bingo does, which means Brashler understands it, too, and he makes room in his novel to convey that understanding to the reader.

The film leaves this scene, and really any scene that conveys the lived experiences of Black Americans, out of the picture, which had the intended effect of making it easier to digest for White audiences. Black critics, like fans of Black minstrel shows, were mostly happy the film was made at all. They credited *Bingo Long* for raising awareness of the Negro Leagues, which had taken a backseat in America's collective consciousness at the time. "America probably will hear more about the old-time, Negro League baseball this summer than it has ever heard before," wrote A.S. Doc Young in *Call and Post*, a newspaper serving Cleveland's Black community, upon the release of *Bingo Long*. Angela E. Smith in the *New York Amsterdam News* credited the film for giving "historical insight on the Black Man's presence in baseball long before it made a millionaire out of Willie Mays."

The fading memory of the Negro Leagues may have made *Bingo Long* more urgent than ever, but it could also be responsible for the film's relatively dim legacy. *Bingo Long* was a story that needed telling, but did America know it needed it? Jackie Robinson died in 1972, while a new generation of Black stars—Joe Morgan, Lou Brock, and Reggie Jackson—who had never known the Leagues, were leaving their mark on the game. The percentage of Black players in MLB reached new heights in the mid-70s, up to 18 percent in 1976. Did a semi-fictionalized clowning Satchel Paige and Josh Gibson resonate at a time when Black players were thriving in the majors without resorting to such pandering? Did they need Bingo Long when they had Bob Gibson and Vida Blue? There is never a wrong time to learn the hard lessons of baseball history, and the film was a box-office hit, grossing $33 million on its $9 million budget. It's also possible that in a golden age for major league Black stars—when it seemed so many of them had "made it," to use Jackie Robinson's phrasing—a comedy about the Negro Leagues might have seemed inessential.

There is, of course, one more complication that arises while watching *Bingo Long*: the parallel between the fictional All-Stars and the very real cast of Black actors. "We ain't the circus," Leon says when he first objects to the parade. "You in show business," the promoter replies. Both onscreen and off, they're a group of Black men, overlooked by a cruel and abusive system, getting an opportunity to show their talents that their White counterparts got years prior. Just like the All-Stars, Billy Dee Williams and James Earl Jones are dancing for their lives, trying to make the most of their opportunity, while working to insert a little humanity into a profession that is more interested in myths and stereotypes.

The performance from Jones is worth lingering on. With a notable paunch and graying temples, Jones, like Leon, is an unimpeachable talent in an industry that has just started to open to Black stars. Jones had an illustrious stage career by the time *Bingo Long* was released and had already starred in a few films, earning an Oscar nomination for the 1970 boxing drama *The Great White Hope*. But neither that film nor *Bingo Long* catapulted him to real movie stardom; a year later, he'd voice Darth Vader, of course, but never actually be seen in a *Star Wars* movie. After that, his most memorable performances were supporting roles in *Matewan, Coming to America*, and—a film you might have heard of—*Field of Dreams*. Like Satchel Paige, he was too early. Or rather the industry was too late.

And yet the final scene of *Bingo Long* offers a poignant expression of his potential. The All-Stars have won the big game with the high stakes; they will replace Potter's Ebony Aces in the league. It should be a happy ending for Long's All-Stars, a night on the town with wine, women, and song. But then he hears the news that Esquire Joe (Stan Shaw) has been called up to the majors. Well, the minors first, but a plan is in place for him to break the color line. It turns out that we've been in a Jackie Robinson story—or an anti-*Jackie Robinson Story*—all along. Bingo is happy for his guy (in the book, he's overcome by jealousy, another harder truth) until Leon, one final step ahead of his friend, explains it to him. Once integration becomes official, the Negro Leagues are dead. Everything they worked for will be gone.

Once again, Leo was right. The Negro Leagues, according to historian Peter C. Bjarkman, "had once represented a thriving $2 million empire, one controlled by Blacks, employing Blacks, and providing crucial forms of cultural identification for millions of Negro fans. After Robinson, Black players were at long last playing in the big leagues, and none would have had it any other way. Yet fewer Blacks were making their living at baseball, and Black communities had suddenly lost an important life force that could never be replaced." *Bingo Long* deserves credit for addressing this discomfiting truth that films about Jackie Robinson, both those that came before and after, elegantly sidestep. In *The Jackie Robinson Story* and *42*, the Negro Leagues are portrayed as, at best, akin to a minor league that any Black player would be delighted to graduate from. These films shed no tears for their demise, which naturally followed Robinson's achievement. They don't even acknowledge it.

As *Bingo Long* nears its conclusion, we can feel the Negro Leagues on the precipice of extinction, but Bingo won't accept it, not right away. He slaps on a smile and starts pitching Leon on a new plan. They'll make it work. They have the talent and the showmanship. They have each other, the two biggest Negro League stars left. They might be too old for the majors, but they can still put on a show. After resisting for a minute, Jones' infectious smile creeps across his face. Leon decides to go along, not out of genuine belief but because there's no good reason not to try and hold out hope. Because Bingo deserves it, and so does Leon. For the players—both on the field and in front of the camera—all they have left is the hope that the future will be kinder than the past, and that the world will one day know the story of Bingo Long.

Chapter 7

The Bad News Bears (1976)

Somewhere in California, there's a Little League baseball field. Green grass, brown dirt. Sprinklers spray cool, clear water over the outfield. In the foreground, a team of young men are practicing. You can hear the infield chatter: "Okay, let's go for two now." "Not bad, not bad." "Okay, go for the bunt." It recalls in spirit the scenes from postwar baseball films in which youngsters play on sandlots and city alleys, not for money or fame, but just for the clean, wholesome fun of it. Maybe someone on the field will get discovered and go on to be a major league star. Have a movie made about him.

Oh, and who's this pulling into the parking lot? Could it be a scout ready to discover the next young stud? Nope, it's crusty old Walter Matthau as an ex-minor leaguer working off one hangover and building toward another. He shuts off the car, cracks a beer, pours out a drop, and then refills it with bourbon. That's breakfast for Morris Buttermaker, the closest thing *The Bad News Bears* has to a decent adult. Clean, wholesome fun is out the window.

A commercial smash that became a staple of Saturday afternoon cable programming, *The Bad News Bears* is the model for every future film about a ragtag group of lovable losers who eventually learn to put aside their differences, come together as a team, and win. This subgenre endured throughout the '80s (*Major League*), '90s (*Little Big League*), and

89

'00s (*Hardball*), but it was far more potent in the 1970s, when Americans had lost faith in the old power structures and were ready to throw their collective cultural weight behind the underdogs. *Rocky* came out the same year as *The Bad News Bears*. *Slap Shot* was released a year later. These are irreverent movies that reject the conventional sports narrative of a talented athlete who suffers a bad break, but overcomes it through grit and resilience, and becomes a champion. In these films, the heroes are regular people, and regular people lose.

To call anyone in *The Bad News Bears* a hero is admittedly a stretch. Buttermaker is an ex-pro who suffered a career-ending injury: a bruised ego. A talented pitcher in the minors, he quit before making it to the majors because he felt his talents weren't properly appreciated. One of the film's charms is its dexterity with exposition; we learn all we need to know about Buttermaker through a few simple lines of dialogue, first his oft-repeated story of the time he struck out Ted Williams in a spring training game and then his words of encouragement to his team when they propose disbanding after a devastating Opening Day loss: "This quitting thing is a hard habit to break once you start." It speaks volumes. Buttermaker is no role model. He's a pool cleaner who uses children— his ex-girlfriend's daughter, his Little League team—to perform unpaid labor, while he lays around and chugs beer. He only took the coaching job because a parent paid him under the table. He drinks constantly. He cusses at the kids. When things start going well, he gets obsessed with winning, eager to redress the regrets of his past, to the detriment of the kids' well-being. He's hilarious (and so is the film), but he's not a great guy.

If he seems at all heroic, it's only in comparison to the film's other adults. In *The Bad News Bears*, the kids are fine. It's the grown-ups who aren't alright, especially Roy Turner (Vic Morrow), the abusive manager of the rival Yankees, the best team in the league. Turner is a dictator on the field. He pushes his kids too hard, emphasizing winning above sportsmanship, and even slaps his own son in the championship game for throwing intentionally at a player, an aggression the boy clearly learned from his father. Turner, whose vileness is masterfully underplayed by Morrow, is the can-do American spirit turned sour in the Me Decade, eager to win at all costs and out only for his own aggrandizement.

He's a hypocrite, but at least he's transparent. Bob Whitewood (Ben Piazza), the other major parent figure in the film, is harder to figure out. At first, he seems like a model parent. The father of Toby (David Stambaugh), one of the less memorable Bears, Whitewood is a city councilman with a vested interest in fairness. Prior to the events of the film, he and other parents sued the league in order to get their kids onto a team. We learn this in an aside conversation offered by Cleveland (Joyce Van Patten), the league manager. "Class-action suits are gonna ruin this country," she says. "It wasn't so bad when they made us take in the girls. At least the ones that came could play. But now this." These kids are the true rejects, worse than girls, an insult that stands above all others on a ballfield or sandlot. But Whitewood stands for the little guy, supposedly.

Class-action lawsuits were all the rage in the 1970s, with an all-time high 3,061 such suits filed in 1975, the year *The Bad News Bears* was shot. Roe v. Wade was a class-action suit. So was the sex discrimination case of 1975 in which flight attendants won the right to continue working after marriage—yes, you read that right. As stated by lawyer David Berger, the class-action lawsuit is "the greatest, most effective legal engine to remedy mass wrongs." Hailed as a "class-action hero" by the *New York Times*, Mr. Berger won settlements for people living near the Three Mile Island nuclear reactor that melted down in 1979. This era also marked the peak of the fame and power of Ralph Nader, who became a celebrity for his legal crusades against nuclear power and corruption in government.

Contextualizing the Bears within the boom of legal activism offscreen makes its underdog ethos feel more substantial. The Bears aren't just a collection of kids who have been picked last. They represent all those American society has marginalized. It is lost on no one that the team is composed of, according to one player, "a buncha Jews, spics, niggers, pansies, and a booger-eatin' moron!" That's the kind of language that would surely get *The Bad News Bears* canceled today—indeed, it was sanded down considerably for the 2005 remake—but it bluntly expresses the crucial idea that these players aren't outcasts simply for their playing ability. They are ostracized because of their race, religion, sexual identity, and, with the addition of Amanda (Tatum O'Neal), gender. The player who utters these epithets is Tanner Boyle (Chris Barnes), a White kid, but the fact that no one objects to his rant demonstrates how they have internalized their own bullying. Watching them learn to overcome their low self-esteem and stand up for themselves is the film's greatest pleasure, as well as a powerful political statement. In the year of America's bicentennial, when displays of unexamined patriotism were ubiquitous, *The Bad News Bears* offers a revised view of what makes America great: the opportunity it offers for society's marginalized classes to band together and embarrass the rich kids on the field of play.

The parents, on the other hand, are less pure in their intentions. Whitewood claims he only wanted fairness, or a chance for his kid to play, but there are many leagues in the area, and this particular one is for the most talented athletes. Do these kids really need to play in the absolute best league? Or is this a political crusade for Whitewood, perhaps to bolster his public standing in advance of a run for higher office? Prominently displayed on the wall of Whitewood's office are framed photos of Martin Luther King, Jr., Bobby Kennedy, and John F. Kennedy. He pitches himself as a campaigner for a more level playing field, but when the chips are down, his selfishness is revealed. Over the course of the season, Buttermaker coaches the kids into being a respectable team. He successfully lures two ringers—Amanda, who sports a wicked curveball, and Kelly Leak (Jackie Earle Haley), a hoodlum with preternatural instincts for the game—onto the team. But winning corrupts him. With the championship in sight, he keeps the weaker players on the bench and encourages the team's stars to make plays all over the field, literally taking the ball out of the hands of the more average athletes. During the championship game, he realizes the error of his ways and reverts to a democratic approach, but this time, Whitewood objects. Buttermaker explains that everyone on the team deserves to play, causing Whitewood to snarl, "Don't give me that righteous bullshit! We've got a chance to win!"

In this exchange, Whitewood reveals himself to be just as selfish as Turner, the opposing coach, or maybe even worse. At least Turner is honest about his desire to win at all costs. Whitewood presents himself as a champion of the underdog, but it's just cover for his own self-aggrandizement. The film's portrayal of Turner and Whitewood, the two main parental figures in the film, forms a damning indictment of the grown-ups that doubles as an indictment of the entire American establishment. In any movie about children, parents are the only authority that matters. The kids know little of their government, and their understanding of the power of the corporate media is limited. The parents stand for all authority, and a film that depicts those parents as selfish, abusive, and capable of making only superficial gestures at justice and equality reflects a powerful disillusionment in American institutions.

Not only did *The Bad News Bears* fit into its era of underdog sports films, but its subversive spirit reflected profound changes in the film industry that were happening at the time. As Hollywood looked to capture the dollars of a generation of young Americans who had no interest in escapist spectacle, they gave big budgets and editorial control to youngsters like Martin Scorsese, Robert Altman, and Francis Ford Coppola, who delivered scathing critiques of the American political system in films such as *Taxi Driver, Nashville*, and *The Godfather*. Director Michael Ritchie, who helmed *Bears*, should be mentioned in the same breath. In 1972, he directed Robert Redford in *The Candidate*, which satirizes the American electoral system. That same year, he made the underseen *Prime Cut*, starring Lee Marvin and Gene Hackman, which, through its story of corruption and perversion in Kansas, tears through America's myth of the heartland like a combine through wheat. In 1975, he made the beauty pageant satire *Smile*, which lifts the veil on an American beauty pageant and finds only greed, sexism, and xenophobia.

The Bad News Bears fits neatly into his filmography. After fixing his lens on politics, agriculture, and small-town life, Ritchie chose for his next targets children and baseball, two virtues ripe for his wicked brand of satire. Having grown up in the 1950s, Ritchie was surely inundated with the same postwar imagery of good-natured children who got up to harmless trouble in television like *Father Knows Best, The Adventures of Ozzie and Harriet,* and *Leave it to Beaver.* Throughout the '60s, this didn't really change. In the media, adults were flawed, and teenagers could be hoodlums, but children remained unimpeachable. *The Bad News Bears* may have saved its harshest commentary for the adults, but portraying children who curse, fight, spit, and shove chocolate bars into their mouths was a sharp turn away from the Rockwellian images of kids sitting at their father's seat in submission. It's meant to shock those who still believed in the postwar fantasy of the angelic suburban child, and delight those who grew up in reality, where kids can be cruel, ruthless, and hilariously funny, all at once.

Ineptitude, for example, is very funny. If you've ever been to an average Little League game, you know it looks a lot like the baseball you see in *The Bad News Bears*, especially in the early scenes. Every ground ball is at least a triple, since neither the infielders nor the outfielders know how to knock a ball down, let alone catch it. Multiple errors on the same play are the norm, and baserunners routinely forget the rules of tagging up on fly outs. Finally, here was a baseball film to which children and adults could relate. Ritchie deserves a lot of credit. To supplement the physical humor, he built a sense of realism by using handheld cameras to survey the ballpark scenes, giving the film a documentary feel, and employing a desaturated color palette that may have been common in '70s cinema but is particularly effective here. It evokes the thick heat of a California summer, while draining the baseball of its pomp and circumstance. Even the American flag in the film's final shot looks limp and exhausted.

Today *The Bad News Bears* hardly feels controversial—except for those words that have since been barred from conversation—but at the time, it was considered by many to be a genuine threat to the social order. The producers didn't mind. They leaned into the controversy, presumably hoping that viewers who loved it would see it multiple times, and crusading moralists would pony up just to see the devil up close. The marketing of the film reflected this two-pronged plan. Consider the radio ad that played in New York featuring a well-known former Yankees sportscaster. "I'm Mel Allen, and I'm here to tell you about the latest candidates for Baseball's Hall of Fame. They are the Bad News Bears…." At this point Mel is interrupted by Tanner Boyle hollering, "Hey, you can take your trophy and shove it straight up your [BLEEP]." Undeterred, Mel proceeds to offer a few facts about the film before the Bears jump back in with some dialogue: "Shut up or I'll put this bat where the sun never shines." Next we hear Tatum O'Neal: "I'm almost 12 and I'll be getting a bra soon." Finally, a generic announcer voice reveals a controversial tagline: "The coach can't wait to pass out. The pitcher can't wait to fill out." The sexualization of a 12-year-old girl certainly wouldn't fly today, but the ad accomplished its goal of persuading the public that *The Bad News Bears* was a baseball film they'd never seen before.

The Catholics, however, still weren't having it. Although the Production Code was history by 1976—replaced in 1968 by the MPAA rating system that is still in place today—the religious right still had some influence to wield. The U.S. Catholic Conference released a statement asserting that the language used by children in the film has "no place in popular entertainment of this sort," and asked, "what right, in both the legal and the moral sense, does any movie producer have to put such dialog into the mouths of child actors?" The Little League of America also protested to Paramount about the foul language. Peter McGovern, president of the LLA, wrote to the studio before the film came out and asked them to excise the obscenities. Paramount rightly pointed out that the LLA had no right to object, since the name of the league is never actually mentioned in the film. In response, the LLA threatened public protests but ultimately decided against them, concerned that any public demonstration would only arouse more interest in the film.

It didn't matter, as interest was already robust. Inappropriate or not, America was ready to laugh their asses off at a bunch of cursing, fighting, spitting kids. *The Bad News Bears* grossed $42 million, making it the 10th biggest film of 1976. It was a bit too raucous for the critics, who only endorsed the film begrudgingly. The *New York Times* called it "surprisingly painless" and "occasionally funny." The *Independent Film Journal* took note of its "exuberantly spicy" language" but found it "thoroughly appropriate." Only *Sight and Sound*, the prestigious British film journal, really understood what the filmmakers were after. They noted Ritchie's "ruminations on the peculiarly American requirements for winning in sports, politics, and pageant" and praised the film for its "simple but consistent deployment of the silent movie dictum that there are few actions funnier than demonstrable incompetence." It's fascinating that a European magazine produced the most clear-eyed analysis, suggesting that *The Bad News Bears* so perfectly replicated the mood of the country that its politics were virtually invisible to American critics.

The incompetence referred to by *Sight and Sound*, of course, is the baseball itself, and that's the other notable thing about *The Bad News Bears*. Sure, it deals in broader themes, but those are just subtext. The real action is on the field. It's not much like *Pride of the Yankees*, which is a romance at heart, or even like *Bang the Drum Slowly*, a story about male camaraderie. *The Bad News Bears* is a story told largely through the action on the field. It featured more sheer baseball action than any film made to that point, and even though its cultural legacy is mostly limited to its shock value and broad comedy, its box-office success helped to overturn the stubborn Hollywood doctrine that baseball movies couldn't be profitable.

In the wake of *The Bad News Bears*, the first true baseball movie boom would commence, featuring a quality and quantity of baseball cinema that is unlikely to be matched. Hollywood also became obsessed with sequels and franchises in the '80s, but the baseball movie got there first. The producers of *The Bad News Bears* believed they had a replicable product and milked its success for two sequels of decreasing effectiveness over the next two years. Rushed into production and released in 1977, *The Bad News Bears in Breaking Training* is a perfectly fine children's sports film that rejects almost everything good about the original. First of all, Morris Buttermaker is gone. By the time the sequel was released, Matthau was deep into a contentious lawsuit with the producers over his cut of the first film. Instead, the kids are the stars of this one, mostly Kelly Leak (Jackie Earle Haley) the hoodlum who became the de facto team leader in the original film through his talent and utter coolness. In *Breaking Training*, the Bears have been offered a chance to play an exhibition game at the Houston Astrodome—in between games of a major league doubleheader—but they have no coach and no way of getting to Houston. Leak arranges everything. He borrows a van from a friend and drives the team there himself, pulling off a series of subterfuges to fool the adults who are rightly suspicious about a van full of adolescents with no parent in sight.

The film has only a few bits of inspired satire, most of which come at the beginning. There's a hilarious montage in which the kids all ask their parents for money for the trip. Lodging, they explain, has been arranged, but they need money for food and incidentals. Abdul Rahim, the Black kid, negotiates a decent amount. Engelberg, who eats his weight, needs $80. The two Latino boys need only $4. It's a neat insight about the distinct racial strata in American society, but the most cutting critique of the parents—a *Bad News Bears* tradition—comes when Leak convinces the local groundskeeper to pose as the team's coach. He's presented, in a moment as cancelable as anything in the original, as an imbecile too stupid to even form complete sentences. Leak teaches him to say, "Hello, how are you?" And when the parents arrive to drop their kids off and meet the new coach, nobody notices that he is incapable of saying anything else. All they need to see is a middle-aged White man in a suit, and they're comfortable sending their kids off on the highways of America. The kids have gotten smarter, but the grown-ups are still as dumb as rocks.

The only other adult of note in *Breaking Training* is the top-billed William Devane, who plays Mike Leak, Kelly's dad. He's the real reason Kelly wants to go to Houston. The father and son are estranged, and their first meeting, in which Mike, leaving the factory after a shift, looks right at his son but doesn't recognize him, is genuinely heartbreaking. Why

Leak's parents split up is never revealed, but we can gather the details: Mike, sporting an Army jacket, is a Vietnam veteran who returned from the war and could not conform to family life. He moved to Houston, got a union job, and now spends his time drinking and dating young girls. In a sense, *Breaking Training* is his movie, as he's the only one with a character arc.

Kelly asks him to pose as the team's coach so the Bears don't get kicked out of their hotel, but soon Mike starts coaching them for real. We see the source of Kelly's athletic instincts. Mike knows baseball. And his time with the team changes him. By the time the big game rolls around, Mike has ditched the Army jacket, a symbol of post-traumatic stress disorder made iconic one year earlier by Robert De Niro in *Taxi Driver*. Instead, he's wearing a cornflower blue Lacoste shirt, a uniform for conspicuous consumers in the next decade. In his transformation from rattled loser to competitive yuppie, you can see the '70s become the '80s in real time.

The shift was even more pronounced in *The Bad News Bears Go to Japan*, which was released in 1978 and is, quite simply, one of the worst baseball movies ever made. It features almost no actual baseball, instead centering its story on Marvin Lazar, a Hollywood hustler played by a mugging Tony Curtis, who's trying to score a fortune by organizing a game in Tokyo between the Bears and a Japanese team. There is a bland love story between Kelly, still played by Haley, and a teenage geisha who speaks no English, but the film is still more interested in Lazar than it should be. His exploitation of the children is less appealing than Buttermaker's, in part because Matthau is a more charismatic actor but also because his exploitation was only half-hearted, anyway. He just sat there, drinking beer. Lazar drags them halfway across the world and lets them rot in a hotel while he goes off and tries to close deals.

This shift from the layabout Buttermaker to the criminally desperate Lazar signals the new decade that was coming. Apathy would no longer be tolerated. The idealism of the '60s morphed into the nihilism of the '70s and was reborn as shameless materialism. In the '80s, everyone was hustling to make their fortune. It was the decade of *Lifestyles of the Rich and Famous,* in which British entertainment reporter Robin Leach toured mansions for the pleasures of the proletariat. It was the decade of *Wall Street,* which taught us that "greed is good," of *Family Ties* and Alex P. Keaton, played by a young Michael J. Fox as an enthusiastic Reaganite who rejected his parents' countercultural values. His character resonated so deeply with the audience that the producers retooled the show after the pilot episode to make him—and not the aging hippie parents—the focus.

The Bad News Bears Go to Japan did not resonate with audiences, and neither did *Breaking Training,* although it earned a modest haul of $19 million at the box office (*Japan* made only $7.3 million). Besides being, um, less good than the original, they lacked the courage and conviction of the first film, especially in their endings. In neither sequel do the Bears lose the big game. *Breaking Training* ends with a rousing Bears victory. *Japan* concludes with the game being called off for fighting; instead, the kids go play in a sandlot, far away from the greedy adults who sought to profit from their love of the game. It's a neat ending that upholds the purity of the game, but it hardly measures up to the subversive power of the original. Scan the baseball films that came prior to *The Bad News Bears,* and you won't find one that ends with a loss. Everything in that original film pointed to a win in the final scenes, where Buttermaker would be rewarded for his transformation to being a responsible adult, and the kids could get their first taste of the sweet nectar of victory. That's how movies, especially comedies, worked in those days. But instead, Kelly Leak gets thrown out at the plate, and they lose. The Yankees compliment the Bears on their play—which the film tricks us into thinking is one of those moral victories that baseball cinema thrives on—but the real victory comes moments later when the Bears throw their second-place trophy back at the Yankees, Tanner Boyle tells them to shove it, and little Timmy Lupus musters the courage to shout, raising his voice for the first time in the film, "And wait till next year!"

Rousing as it may be, the film still ends on a loss, and in its efforts to wrest some moral victory from it, we can sense a comment on America's view of itself in 1976, one year after the Vietnam War had ended badly, and with the country still reeling from the disillusionment of Watergate. In the same year *The Bad News Bears* was released, *Rocky* conquered the box office and won three Oscars, including Best Picture. *Rocky* doesn't end with a win either, instead simply celebrating Rocky's survival, his refusal to give up, as a high achievement. This was a country dealing, for the first time in a long time, with loss, and just like *Rocky*—and *Bang the Drum Slowly* and, in its own way, *Bingo Long*—*The Bad News Bears* has no illusions about the fate that awaits us. Its characters endeavor to squeeze some dignity out of life before the world cuts them down for good. The closest they could get to a victory was to embrace their defeat. By the time the next batch of baseball films rolled around, losing was no longer cool.

Beer Run

The Top 10 Baseball Scenes
in Non-Baseball Movies

Because baseball is such a potent symbol in cinema, it's often used outside of dedicated baseball films as a shorthand for widely accepted American virtues: masculinity, freedom, ambition, and patriotism. It's a way for characters to bond. It's how a father and son communicate. It's the best thing to do on a summer day. For some, it's a way out of their circumstances, or a brief moment of liberation from an otherwise joyless existence. Baseball is a language all on its own in American cinema, a common tongue that brings audiences together, and an important tool for filmmakers seeking to speak to a diverse, mainstream audience. Here's a ranked list of where it has been most effectively used outside of those films devoted to the game.

10. *Hook*

Steven Spielberg's divisive Peter Pan movie uses baseball to tap into the most persistent theme in the director's filmography: parental abandonment. It opens with Peter Banning (Robin Williams) missing his son Jack's Little League game because he's stuck at work, another in a long series of broken promises. Later, after Jack (Charlie Korsmo) has been kidnapped by Captain Hook (Dustin Hoffman) and manipulated into accepting him as his new father, the villain sets up a game of "pirate baseball" for Jack, complete with the death penalty for base-stealing. Hook plans to win the young man's heart by giving him the attention his father withheld and the self-esteem every adolescent craves. The game, in other words, is rigged. The pirate Smee (Bob Hoskins) offers up a meatball, and Jack hits one out, giving him the glory that few baseball-loving kids experience in real life. No matter, Neverland provides.

9. *City Slickers*

Billy Crystal is a famous baseball fan. He made a baseball movie for HBO, *61**, which chronicled the 1961 pursuit by Roger Maris and Mickey Mantle of Babe Ruth's major league home run record. Crystal is all over Ken Burns' *Baseball*, perhaps most famously talking about the excitement of going to his first game at Yankee Stadium. He liked that speech so much that he re-used it in *City Slickers*, his 1991 comedy-western, when Mitch (Crystal) and his friends Phil (Daniel Stern) and Ed (Bruno Kirby) each take turns describing the best day of their lives. Mitch's life peaked the day he set foot in Yankee Stadium and saw the green grass and brown dirt, after having previously only watched the game on his black-and-white television.

Baseball comes up again in *City Slickers* when Bonnie (Helen Slater), the lone woman on their excursion, complains that all men talk about baseball too much. Ed offers a snide remark, but the recently divorced Phil, perhaps seeing an opening, says, "I guess it is childish, but when I was about 18 and my dad and I couldn't communicate about anything at all, we could still talk about baseball. That was real." The speech offers a window into the way men use baseball as a substitute for emotional intimacy. And it works. Phil and Bonnie end up together, showing that baseball need not be a hindrance to all male-female relationships. In the movies at least, it can actually bring them together.

8. *The Warriors*

"Warriors, come out and plaaaaaay." In Walter Hill's 1979 cult classic, a Coney Island gang must make its way from the Bronx back to their home turf, while a litany of rival gangs tries their violent best to stop them. One such gang is the Baseball Furies, who the Warriors encounter outside the 96th Street station on the Upper West Side. They look a bit like if the rock band KISS formed a baseball team: clad in generic uniforms, wielding wooden bats as their weapon of choice, their faces painted with clownlike makeup. The Furies are given no backstory, but according to *Warriors* canon—created after the fact by superfans of the film—they're real major leaguers who prowl the neighborhood surrounding Riverside Park at night. Their run-in with the Warriors doesn't go well; the Baseball Furies have their bats turned against them and get beaten into submission.

But does this film even qualify as a non-baseball movie? The sport is subtly woven into *The Warriors* throughout the story. Each gang has nine members, just like a baseball team. They are identified only by their uniforms. As the Warriors make their way home, an anonymous disc jockey sends reports of their progress out to the other gangs, much like a play-by-play announcer. After they beat the Furies, she states: "The Warriors have rounded second base and are headed for home." Although the film is clearly more inspired by the real gangs that dominated New York City at the time—reportedly, the Baseball Furies are based on the Second Base Gang, who didn't paint their faces but wore letterman jackets with "Second Base" printed on the back—someone involved was clearly a fan of the national pastime.

7. Brewster's Millions

In this 1985 comedy, Richard Pryor plays an aging minor league pitcher who finds himself in the unique position of having to spend $30 million in thirty days without accruing any assets. If he can do it, he'll win $300 million. If not, he gets nothing. It's such a clever idea for a comedy that the film has been remade thirteen times, including four times in India.

Accompanied by his catcher, played by John Candy—and boy, there was an actor born to play a catcher—Brewster comes up with a series of inventive ideas to spend the money. One of his best is hiring the New York Yankees to play an exhibition game against Brewster's Hackensack Bulls. The sequence is decently shot, but it's mostly worthwhile for Candy's trash talk to the opposing hitters. It may not seem an original strategy—see *Major League* and *The Sandlot* for very similar examples—but this was the first time it happened on screen, and there's something admirable about Candy's direct and dirty approach. "I saw your wife on TV last night," he says as the pitcher deals. "Sure is an ugly bitch." Only an actor as inherently likable as Candy could make it work.

6. One Flew Over the Cuckoo's Nest

So here's the set-up. McMurphy (Jack Nicholson) has gotten himself transferred from a prison to a mental hospital, where he is warring with the tyrannical Nurse Ratched (Louise Fletcher) for control of the group. His latest battle is over whether the patients will be permitted to watch a World Series game. She thinks it will rile everyone up. He thinks it will help them feel normal. They take a vote, and he loses. His fellow inmates are too scared to vote against their warden.

McMurphy, however, starts a rally. He sits in front of the unlit television and, in an act of defiance, starts calling the game as if it were on. "Koufax kicks and delivers...it's up the middle for a base hit." He really sells it, and one by one, his fellow patients shuffle toward him. By the end, they're cheering along with him, fully persuaded by his passionate delivery that the action he's describing is real. It's an iconic moment in the Oscar-winning film, one of the most indelible scenes of Nicholson's career, and a testament to the power of a good play-by-play announcer.

5. *Twilight*

Once the superhero era began, the baseball movie's decline was sealed. How heroic can a ballplayer seem when viewers have Iron Man and Batman to look up to? *Twilight*, the first in a box-office-smashing franchise of films based on Stephenie Meyer's young adult series about vampires in love, gives us an idea of how it could work. There's a scene, much derided by cynical cinephiles, in which the vampires play baseball in a thunderstorm. The film never bothers to explain who's on which team, or how they're keeping score. It's more like a Home Run Derby, in other words largely unnecessary and pretty darn fun. The vampires essentially have superpowers. Nearly every swing produces a bullet line drive. The outfielders scurry up trees to snag fly balls. Edward Cullen (Robert Pattinson) has an arm that would make Roberto Clemente shake his head in amazement. Yes, it's profoundly silly, but I wish the makers of other fantasy franchises would take note: Baseball doesn't have to be boring.

4. *Life*

1999 was an exceedingly strong year for film, with seemingly an entire generation of American masters releasing early-period masterpieces. *The Sixth Sense, Magnolia, Fight Club, The Talented Mr. Ripley,* and *Being John Malkovich* all came out that year. So did *For Love of the Game,* half a great baseball movie (and half a trite romance). Perhaps this abundance explains why *Life*, a funny and poignant comedy starring Eddie Murphy and Martin Lawrence, has been so overlooked. The comic stars play as bootleggers convicted of a murder they didn't commit in 1920s Alabama, and the film tracks their life sentence—and the sentences of several other Black men who have perhaps been wrongly convicted—with laugh-out-loud humor and a keen understanding of the lived experiences of racism.

The film concludes—spoilers, sorry—with the two friends finally out of prison and taking in a Yankees game in the Bronx, but more substantial is the middle section when they start a prison baseball team. For the film's incarcerated, baseball is a source of joy and liberation, and it even earns one character his freedom. Can't Get Right (Bokeem Woodbine) is a mute, perhaps simple-minded inmate who can absolutely destroy a baseball. He draws the attention of a Negro League scout (Noah Emmerich), who convinces the judge to commute his sentence so he and his bosses can profit from the young man's talent. This development produces a conflicted response; happiness for the young player, sadness for our protagonists, who nurtured the talent of Can't Get Right but aren't permitted to leave with him, and a sad resignation that all a young Black man in the South could do at this time to earn his freedom was prove himself useful to powerful White men.

3. *Good Will Hunting*

There's an early scene in this Oscar-winning film in which Will Hunting (Matt Damon) and his buddies watch a Little League game in their neighborhood and banter about the players as if they are major leaguers. But that's not the scene I'm talking about. The one I'm talking about has no actual baseball in it. It's the story told by Will's psychiatrist, Sean (Robin Williams), about meeting his wife in a bar before the biggest game in Red Sox history, the sixth game of the 1975 World Series, when Carlton Fisk's game-winning home run kept the Sox's championship hopes alive and turned Boston into bedlam.

Actually, Sean doesn't just tell the story. He acts it out like a little kid, running around the imaginary bases in his little office, pushing Will aside just as Fisk barreled through the fans who had jumped onto the field to celebrate. Will gets into the act, too, imitating Fisk's famous attempts to will the ball fair with his outstretched arms. Director Gus Van Sant gives us a few snippets of the telecast for context, so technically, there's some baseball in it, but really that's unnecessary. Williams and Damon capture the euphoria of being a fan in a big moment as well as any telecast ever could.

2. College/The Cameraman

Silent film star Buster Keaton adored baseball. "As far back as I can remember," he wrote in his autobiography, "baseball has been my favorite sport. I started playing the game as soon as I was old enough to handle a glove." He was also an athlete by trade; his physical comedy required incredible agility and precise timing, and the sport proved an integral part of his creative process. At the Keaton Production Company, he would order his employees to play a game of baseball every time they were faced with a difficult problem on set. If a solution struck in the middle of the game, they'd throw down their mitts and resume shooting. One of his biographers summarized, "Baseball was his religion."

It was only natural that he incorporated baseball into his films. In 1927's *College*, Keaton plays a brainiac who, upon arriving at university, decides he has a better chance of wooing his lady love if he becomes a star athlete. He tries out first for the baseball team and makes a fool of himself. Few of Keaton's trademark pratfalls are present here, just general baseball incompetence; he makes some routine errors, overruns his teammates on the basepaths, and gets his foot stuck on first base. It's a little dull by today's standards but must have been a blast in 1927, long before the "sports blooper" became a popular comic trope.

In the next year's *The Cameraman*, Keaton plays an aspiring news cameraman assigned to photograph Babe Ruth. He arrives at Yankee Stadium, only to find out the game is in St. Louis, so instead of working, Keaton takes the field in an empty stadium and lives out a childhood fantasy. He pantomimes a pair of at-bats, one as the pitcher and another as a batter hitting an inside-the-park home run. Keaton's athleticism and understanding of the game is on full display. What makes it funny is its realism, the way he emphatically shakes off the catcher, drops down a tag on the runner, and, finally, chugs around the bases with wild abandon. It was easily the best baseball action ever put on film at this point in history—all done without a baseball.

1. *Ferris Bueller's Day Off*

Ferris Bueller, as played by Matthew Broderick in John Hughes' classic 1986 comedy, is not a real person. I don't just mean he's fictional, like most movie characters. Rather, there is no person who behaves quite like Ferris Bueller. He fits somewhere between a precocious child's idea of a cool teenager and a middle-aged dude's fantasy of his high school self. The way he schedules his day playing hooky with his friend Cameron (Alan Ruck) and his girlfriend, Sloane (Mia Sara), does not align with the priorities of any actual teenager in 1986 or at any other time. In real life, they'd probably spend more time smoking pot in the woods and less time having an existential moment at an art museum. The fact that he can hop on a float at a parade and have John Lennon's voice come out of his mouth is hard evidence we're not dealing with reality.

If you are a child imagining a day off from school, going to a baseball game would almost certainly be atop your wish list, and if you're going to any stadium on a sunny afternoon when you're supposed to be in school, it's definitely going to be Wrigley Field. That's what it was designed for. The Cubs' stadium was built in 1914, but it was in the mid-1930s when Bill Veeck, whose father was club president at the time, figured out that a team could make more money even in losing seasons if they made the stadium itself an attraction. His goal, according to his biography, was to make Wrigley "thought of as a place to take the whole family for a delightful day." He introduced fan appreciation nights, player names on uniforms, fireworks displays, and a more varied food selection than peanuts and Cracker Jack. Most importantly, in 1937, he came up with the idea of lining the outfield walls with ivy. It worked. The ivy is now perhaps the most memorable element of any baseball field in the world (give or take a Green Monster), and win or lose, people show up to bask in great Wrigley's glory.

Ferris doesn't seem like a particularly devoted Cubs fan (no Ryne Sandberg reference, really?), but that's irrelevant. Unless you're a South Sider, no perfect Chicago day is complete without a trip to Wrigley. In the middle of their inordinately busy afternoon, Ferris and his friends spend probably an hour or so in the left-field stands at Wrigley Field. It's a pitcher's duel—the score is "nothing, nothing" according to a local pizza man—but the lack of offense doesn't break their spirits. Ferris catches a foul ball and gets on TV. Cameron teaches him how to razz the opposing hitter ("Suh-wing, batta"). Sloane tolerates it all like a champ. Ferris might have broken his thumb catching that foul ball, but the pain seems to wear off quickly. It's a land of fantasy, but it's one born of reality. Anyone who has ever played hooky and gone to Wrigley on a weekday afternoon knows there is nothing else worth doing. It's the essence of baseball as lived by a child and conceived by an adult. Just as Ferris escapes his dreary life by spending an afternoon at Wrigley, we escape ours in *Ferris Bueller's Day Off*.

· PART III ·

The Nostalgia Boom

Chapter 8

The Natural (1984) and Field of Dreams (1989)

WHEN AUTHOR BERNARD MALAMUD EXITED THE CINEMA AFTER HAVING watched the film adaptation of his book *The Natural*, he said to his wife, "Now I am an American writer." What took so long? Malamud published *The Natural*, his debut novel, in 1952. He went on to publish seven more novels, win the National Book Award twice, and garner the 1967 Pulitzer Prize for Fiction for *The Fixer*, an imagined account of a Jew imprisoned in Tsarist Russia. He even has an award named after him, the PEN/Malamud Award for short fiction. A child of Eastern European immigrants, Malamud always saw himself as a Jewish writer. It's a testament to the awesome power of cinema that a single film can reshape the way we perceive the author of its source material. Even more incredible is that it can change the way that author feels about himself.

Somewhere between the page and the screen, *The Natural* changed from a Jewish book to an American film, from a fable of failure to a hero's journey, and from a story about America's dark underbelly to one that redeems an entire nation with the single swing of a bat. Malamud's book grapples honestly and heroically with the postwar despair that at the time existed largely in the American subconscious. It's about the fallacy of second chances, with a cast of characters that includes cynical baseball men, heartless journalists, greedy owners, murderous femme fatales, and cold-blooded gamblers. It ends with our hero coming up to bat in a big spot—and striking out. If Malamud's novel had been faithfully adapted, it might have been the first baseball movie to cross over into film noir, the only genre that dared reflect the burgeoning darkness of America in the years after World War II.

Instead, director Barry Levinson wrestles the text of *The Natural* into an uplifting work of American nostalgia that, like many films of its era, hints at national anxieties but instead chooses the politics of triumph. It came to theaters at just the right time, when Americans were desperate for a cultural reset. The 1970s were an era of demythology, in which long-held illusions, such as the purity of baseball and American righteousness, were painfully exposed. In 1979, president Jimmy Carter spoke candidly about these disillusionments in his notorious Crisis of Confidence speech, accusing Americans of "worship[ping] self-indulgence and consumption," of defining oneself "by what one owns." Less than a year later, Ronald Reagan accepted the Republican presidential nomination by nudging those anxieties aside and embracing a glowing portrait of our past: "Not so long ago, we emerged from a world war. Turning homeward at last, we built a grand prosperity and hopes, from our own success and plenty, to help others less fortunate. Our peace was a tense and bitter one, but in those days, the center seemed to hold." *Time* magazine wrote that Reagan believed "the past is our future." The *Washington Post* called him "the candidate of nostalgia, a political performer whose be-bop instruments dates from an antediluvian choir." Americans wanted a return to carefree days. Reagan won in a landslide.

Hollywood, which is ever eager to reflect the changing moods of its customers, jumped right on the bandwagon. Writing in his book *Back to Our Future: How the 1980s Explains the World We Live in Now—Our Culture, Our Politics, Our Everything*, political activist and Oscar-nominated screenwriter David Sirota argued that Hollywood ushered in "an entire industry organized around idealized nostalgia, and particularly midcentury, pre-1965 schmaltz." Instead of reckoning with social problems, Americans found comfort in reminiscence. Films like *Diner, Stand by Me, Peggy Sue Got Married, Back to the Future, The Right Stuff, La Bamba,* and *Hoosiers* looked back longingly at a simpler time—i.e. when its filmmakers were children—while smoothing over the uncomfortable realities of the past. Was life better in the 1950s? Probably not, but it seemed that way if you were young, middle-class, and White. Even 1978's *Superman* fits the pattern as a folk tale about an immigrant (albeit from another planet) raised in the Kansas countryside as a real American.

So does *The Natural*, although its perspective blurs the line between old-fashioned and reactionary. Its main action is set in 1939, when, if you go by the film, men were noble warriors, and women were either supportive-wife types (Glenn Close) or promiscuous single women (Barbara Hershey, Kim Basinger) who will destroy your life. *The Natural* thinks the worst thing that ever happened to baseball was the influence of gamblers; like other films of its era, it is inspired by the Chicago Black Sox scandal, viewing it as a symbol of American corruption. Its focus on one social ill, however, reveals an embarrassing blind spot for baseball's actual original sin: segregation. There are no Black players on the film's fictional New York Knights. In fact, there are no Black actors in the film at all. There is, to be fair, a narrative justification for this. If you follow the timeline, the film is set just moments before baseball's color line is broken. It begins with Hobbs as a teenager during the 1920s and then picks up 15 years later, when he is in his mid-thirties and just young enough to still be able to play the game. So while it can't be directly criticized for omitting Black players, the choice to set a nostalgia narrative in the last gasp of segregated baseball is, at the very least, troubling. The reactionary politics of *The Natural* didn't stand out to the mainstream media at the time, in part because there were fewer critics or journalists from marginalized communities to ask the right questions. Data from this era doesn't exist, but in 2019 only 6.5 percent of journalists identified as Black, and that's after 35 years of progress.

Miraculously, the film still feels largely apolitical today, in part because it is so thoroughly grounded in myth, lending the story an air of timelessness. *The Natural* is constructed from bits of Homer, Arthurian legend, the Bible, superstition, and even magic. Its closest corollary is to the tale of the Fisher King, which first appeared in Chrétien de Troyes' *Perceval, the Story of the Grail*, an unfinished 12th century French text, but has been told and retold in Arthurian literature in various forms. The consistent elements are a young Knight (the kind with a sword, not a bat) named Perceval who encounters a wounded King and, in most versions, saves his life. The version of the story I remember is from the 1991 film *The Fisher King*, in which Robin Williams plays a homeless man on a quest to steal the Grail from a Manhattan apartment. As he explains things, the knight unwittingly saves the king, who is dying of thirst, by serving him a cup of water out of the Holy Grail. "How did you find this cup?" asks the recovering King, who had sent all his wisest and bravest men to look for it. "I only knew you were thirsty," the knight replies.

Roy Hobbs (Robert Redford) is our Perceval, an aging farm boy and wanderer who joins the New York Knights, a last-place team led by the cursed Pop Fisher (Wilford Brimley). Through sheer talent, Hobbs has the ability to heal Fisher, who is suffering from various maladies including player incompetence and a cruel contract with the team's evil owner that will force him to sell his share of the team if the Knights fail to win the pennant. Fisher's mood is understandably sour, his field fallow and dusty, but Hobbs' first home run unleashes a torrential downpour, bringing the Knights and maybe Fisher himself back to life. Like Perceval, Hobbs doesn't set out to heal Fisher. He's only thirsty for baseball.

From there, the film incorporates the icons and underlying rules of a wide range of mythologies. There's the motif of the lightning bolt. "Again and again, it is the hurling of the thunderbolt, the blinding flash of lightning, the raging storm that awakens the hero in man," wrote mythologist Dorothy Norman, and she might as well have been talking about the quick-cut opening montage of *The Natural*, in which Roy's father plays catch with him in a field—an image that had lived in the

American imagination for over a century—and tells him to be mindful of his gifts. Shortly thereafter, his father dies, and as Roy grieves, a storm rages outside his window. A lightning bolt splits a tree in half. From the tree, he forges Wonder Boy, his bat, his sword, his Excalibur. Once Roy finds success in the majors, with a lightning bolt carved into the barrel of his bat, the other Knights adopt the same image, wearing patches adorned with a bolt in the hopes that Hobbs' light will shine on them.

Lightning and thunder recall the Greek god Zeus—his thunderbolt was the most powerful weapon in the universe—but there are other icons of Greek mythology in *The Natural*, like the gambler with the glass eye, a clear stand-in for the Cyclops from Homer's *The Odyssey*. Memo (Kim Basinger) and Harriet (Barbara Hershey) are the sirens who lure young sailors to crash against their rocks and die. More crucially, Roy has a tragic flaw common to the subjects of Greek myths: hubris. At 19 years old, he is invited to try out from the Cubs. On his way to Chicago with a drunken scout (a type that dates back to *The Stratton Story*), he meets the greatest ballplayer who ever lived, The Whammer (Joe Don Baker), a clear facsimile for Babe Ruth, on the train. While killing time during a water stop, Hobbs and the Whammer have a little competition. Hobbs strikes him out on three pitches, and Harriet, the mysterious, beautiful stranger clad in black, turns her eyes from The Whammer to Roy.

As the two would-be lovers spend the evening chatting in the dining car, she asks him what he wants out of the game. He tells her, "When I walk down the street, people will look at me and say, 'There goes Roy Hobbs, the best there ever was in the game.'" It's a line cribbed from Ted Williams, the last man to hit .400 in a major league season and probably the best hitter who ever lived. Harriet repeats the question the next day in the hotel room before she unexpectedly shoots him in the gut and jumps out a window, killing herself and setting Hobbs' career back a couple decades.

Malamud was clearly inspired by the story of two-time All-Star Eddie Waitkus, who in 1949 was lured into the hotel room of Ruth Ann Steinhagen, a stenographer who had developed an unexplained obsession with the ballplayer, and shot him in the chest. Waitkus wasn't quite as great as Hobbs, although he was called "the natural" by a few sportswriters, and Ted Williams reportedly said Waitkus had one of the best swings he'd ever seen (notably, he did not say he was the greatest hitter who ever lived). Waitkus was no country rube—he spoke four languages and loved ballroom dancing—although his son described him as an "easy-going, trusting guy at the time, and kind of flippant with women," before noting that the "shooting changed [him] a great deal. He became almost paranoid about meeting new people, and pretty much even stopped going out drinking with his teammates." That sounds a lot like Roy Hobbs when he gets to New York, before another woman, Memo, lures him into the same immoral lifestyle that interrupted his career the first time. According to *The Natural*, drinking and hanging around with loose women will get you killed, while country living and fidelity to the mother of your child will save your life.

The other mythology that *The Natural* draws on is the folklore of baseball itself. "Wonder Boy" is a baseball term that goes back a century; it was used to describe country bumpkins with no education but who had pure, raw, and natural talent. It sounds a lot like Mickey Mantle, who grew up in the Oklahoma wilderness and debuted in the majors at 19 years old, just a year before Malamud published *The Natural*. Hobbs' dedication to his bat recalls the lore of Black Betsy, the beloved stick of Shoeless Joe Jackson, another country bumpkin whose baseball instincts seemed to have sprung from the land itself. When Bump Bailey (Michael Madsen) crashes through the outfield wall and dies, baseball historians will think of Pete Reiser, outfielder for the Brooklyn Dodgers, Boston Braves, and Pittsburgh Pirates, who patrolled the grass with such abandon that he often injured himself playing the outfield. In 1946, Bama Rowell hit a shot off a clock on top of the Ebbets Field scoreboard, and glass rained down on a Dodgers outfielder. Hobbs does the same thing in *The Natural*.

Finally, *The Natural* draws on America's national mythology—which is distinct but not wholly disconnected from the lore of baseball or cinema—including the sanctity of the land and the blessedness of those who till it. In film, the farm isn't for raising animals or growing crops; it's a metaphor for the pioneer spirit and those sturdy, old-fashioned values that are constantly threatened by progress. "I shoulda been a farmer," is the first line uttered by Pop Fisher, and he looks like one, weary and weathered by the elements. Hobbs grew up in the heartland, and when he reunites with Iris (Glenn Close), who is now living and working in Chicago, he asks her, "Did you sell the farm?" "No, I'll always have that," she answers. "Good," he says. "It's home." The same year *The Natural* was released, there were three other films about family farms—*Places in the Heart, Country,* and *The River*—each featuring women protagonists fighting to protect their land from banks or other corporate interests. This focus on the family farm was a clear response to the rural crisis offscreen. In his 1980 campaign, Reagan heavily focused his energies on rural America, traveling throughout the heartland and reiterating a Republican platform position that pledged "to make life in rural America prosperous again." But a combination of overproduction, high prices for farmland, and an end to exports to the Soviet Union devastated the Midwest. Small-town banks failed. Main streets were filled with boarded-up windows. Many family farmers simply gave up; suicide and rural murder rates skyrocketed. By 1984, the *Washington Post* editorialized that "farm policy has proven to be a disaster area for the Reagan administration."

Reagan did little to help farmers, but he did adopt their lifestyle to endear himself to the American electorate. Whenever possible, he was photographed at his California ranch, clearing brush, riding horses, and often wearing a cowboy hat, echoing a career as an A-list star in westerns that never quite existed. John Wayne, he was not; most of Reagan's leading roles came in B-movies. Cowboy iconography, however, has an inexorable pull on the American citizenry, especially when the chips are down. The real people of rural America needed hope, and the easiest place to find it was in an imagined past. This was something movies like *The Natural* could help with.

Despite playing Grover Cleveland Alexander in 1952's *The Winning Team*, Reagan wasn't a baseball fanatic, but he pulled from the same rural mythology on which baseball was founded. For years, it was widely understood that baseball was invented in the farming town of Cooperstown, New York, by former Army officer Abner Doubleday. The Baseball Hall of Fame's subsequent construction and continued presence in Cooperstown upholds the legend. According to the *New York Times*, the story had "taken a position in the pantheon of great American myths, alongside George Washington's cherry tree, Paul Bunyan, and Johnny Appleseed." The only problem is that it almost certainly isn't true. Yes, Doubleday's role in the invention of baseball was confirmed by the Mills Commission, created in 1905 by sporting goods entrepreneur Albert Spalding to settle the debate on the game's origins. But the Commission was composed of baseball figures not historians, and it was later revealed that their only evidence was a letter from the elderly Abner Graves, a five-year-old resident of Cooperstown in 1839 who spent the last years of his life in a mental hospital.

No one knows with certainty when baseball was invented. In all likelihood, it was a rolling series of innovations and adjustments to previously known games like cricket; this is much like cinema itself, which has had its invention attributed to various figures over the years. One of the most respectable guesses is that baseball as we know it was coined sometime in the 1840s by Alexander Cartwright, a founding member of the New York Knickerbockers Base Ball Club, and that the first game was played in Hoboken, New Jersey, just across the river from Manhattan and a few miles south of where Aaron Burr fatally wounded Alexander Hamilton in their 1804 duel. Hoboken wasn't much of a city in the 1840s, but it was hardly rural. We do know that the game first became popular among members of the social elite. Only "gentlemen" were allowed to play, a fact hidden by baseball mythmakers who position the sport as inherently democratic, played by kids on sandlots and country bumpkins in open fields. There's a contradiction, even a deception, at play here that serves as a synecdoche of the American experience, in which the common man is elevated and flattered by clever politicians to provide cover for their enrichment of the upper class. Baseball's lie about its origins might be its most American quality.

As a cinematic interpretation of the Cooperstown myth, *The Natural* embraces a gauzy vision of the American baseball hero and inherently rejects the more new, modern athlete, who, in the years after the demolition of the "reserve clause," was viewed as more interested in endorsement deals and free agency than the purity of the game. Salaries were skyrocketing in baseball at this time. In 1970, the average major league salary was $29,000. By 1984, it was $329,000. "Hobbs embodies a kind of approach to being a sports hero that was beginning to fade," explained legendary sportscaster Bob Costas in a documentary on the making of the film. "He was the opposite of the arrogant person with a sense of entitlement figuring that everyone else was just a foil for him and lucky to bask in the glow of his greatness." It's true; Hobbs doesn't care about money. He's a country kid, unfamiliar with the ways of the big city. A Wonder Boy, whose gifts seem to spring forth from the land itself. He encounters all manners of temptation in the major leagues: money, sex, drink, fame, and his own arrogance. But he conquers his demons and emerges a hero, returning to the farm to raise his son on family land. The final scenes of him playing catch with his son are hopelessly hokey and impossible to resist.

Of course, that's not how the book ends. "It ends on a strikeout," points out Dave Zirin. "It ends with him crying and with the ambiguous question of if he struck out on purpose [to placate the gamblers]. It reflects to me the torturous nature of the sport. You get that feeling at the end of *The Natural* that even though he took the payout, he was actually going to try at this point, and he still fails. It's devastating. Then the movie ends with the ball hitting the goddamn lights." As a wounded Hobbs crushes a pennant-clinching home run into the stadium lights, Randy Newman's triumphant score kicks in, and by that point only the most hardened heart will refuse to swell. It's one of the most arresting images of baseball cinema, expertly lensed by cinematographer Caleb Deschanel, who uses dramatic, high-contrast lighting to make the field look like a stage fit for Shakespeare, and was Oscar-nominated for his efforts. Despite its troubling underlying politics, and for all the reassuring changes that make the film more commercially appealing than the book, *The Natural* gets how baseball *feels*: timeless and mythic, like the only thing that lasts in a world teeming with ephemera. It captures the moment of transformation from men into gods that's possible every time you turn on a baseball game.

As Hobbs rounds third base, the sparks rain down on him like seeds being scattered to the earth. We cut at once to him and his son playing catch in the wheat fields. In truth, *The Natural* scattered its own seeds. It opened as the number one film in America and came in 14th that year in domestic box office. Not a World Series contender, but certainly a playoff team, and popular enough to finally shatter the stubborn myth that baseball movies were box-office poison (already disproved by *The Pride of the Yankees* and *The Bad News Bears*, but studio executives are slow learners). It was nominated for four Oscars in total, including one for Glenn Close, who humbly credits her nomination entirely to Deschanel's backlighting of her in the famous crowd scene. More importantly, its success launched the baseball-movie boom that would last a decade and produce some of the most beloved baseball films of all time. It marked the creation of a new legend: for baseball cinema, for the heartland, and for America itself. Finally, decades after Lou Gehrig and Gary Cooper made history, the baseball movie star was back.

Field of Dreams, released five years after *The Natural*, concludes with a similar but far more famous scene of a father and son playing catch on a farm. This time, the son is a grown man: Ray Kinsella (Kevin Costner), a Berkeley grad who majored in "the sixties," moved to Iowa, became a farmer, and had a daughter with his flower-child wife, Annie (Amy Madigan). One evening, while wandering through the cornfields—this guy was already a dreamer—he's commanded by a voice: "If you build it, he will come." In the book on which the film is based, it's a booming stadium announcer. The filmmakers wisely changed it to a god-like whisper. Later that night, Ray is looking out onto his dark field when a bolt of lightning splits the sky. That's when he realizes he's supposed to build a baseball field so that Shoeless Joe Jackson, his late father's hero, can come back and play the game he loved.

Is Ray Kinsella much different from Roy Hobbs, whose father died suddenly and who watched a bolt of lightning form his destiny? *Field of Dreams* is grown from the same soil as *The Natural*, and it tangles with the same thorny politics. It's a Boomer movie that appeals to rural conservatives, aging hippies, and conflicted yuppies all at once. Its politics are profoundly White and definitively male. Its blind spots on racial and gender issues are glaring. But just like *The Natural*, it puts its finger on something fundamentally true about baseball, and not just its recreation of those beautifully old uniforms or its references to players, like "Smoky" Joe Wood or John McGraw, whose names are known only to baseball lifers. It understands the simple, immutable power of the game. It sees the magic contained between those white lines. It knows what happens in a baseball field at dusk. It knows that this game, as Ray says in the film, is "perfect."

If you also understand this, you'll be on board with *Field of Dreams* from the very first frames. If you don't, the film won't make a lick of sense. Imagine trying to explain the plot to someone: "It's about a farmer in Iowa who hears a voice telling him to build a baseball field even though the loss of crop yield could cost him his land, his house, and even his family," you'd say. "He does it, anyway, and the ghost of his father's favorite ballplayer comes back. Then the voice tells him to go to Boston and take a reclusive civil rights writer to a baseball game, where the voice shows up again and tells them to go to a small town in Minnesota to find an elderly ex-ballplayer who only got into one major league game before retiring from the game. When they get there, they discover he's dead, but they meet his ghost. He won't come with them, but they pick up a younger version of him on the road and bring him back to the farm to play baseball with a bunch of other ghosts. Meanwhile, the farmer's brother-in-law is trying to get the farmer to sell the field and all his land to him and his business partners, but he won't, and then their problems are solved when thousands of strangers magically arrive to buy tickets to watch the dead ballplayers."

None of this should work, neither on the page—the film is based on the 1982 W.P. Kinsella novel *Shoeless Joe*—nor on the screen. So why do we believe it? "If there's one subject to get earnest and sentimental about, it's baseball, especially baseball as it relates to your family," according to Michael Schur, an acclaimed television producer, author, and podcast host who is such a big fan of *Field of Dreams* he once tried to adapt it into a TV series. "Regardless of gender, you inherit your team from your parents, and they inherited it from their parents. That movie is a bit of a magic trick because it manages to very delicately capture this feeling that you get when you are watching a sporting event, and you have a familial link to the team involved, and then they win, and you're not just thinking about how they won, but you're also thinking about the time you played catch in the backyard when you're 11, and *Field of Dreams* is like, 'What if we made a whole movie about that feeling?'"

That's a poetic explanation of how *Field of Dreams* holds together, but there's also a practical reason. There's a trick in it. "I have this theory that audiences willingly suspend disbelief if you help them," said Phil Alden Robinson, the film's writer and director. "If the characters acknowledge the craziness of their actions, it's okay." One of the film's running bits is that its characters often call Ray out on his lunacy. When he first tells Annie of the voice, she asks if he's having an acid flashback. When Ray tells Terence Mann (James Earl Jones), the '60s writer he kidnaps, that they share a destiny because Mann once named a character after Ray's father, Mann quips, "Oh, you must have a whole team of psychiatrists working on you." Annie's brother Mark (Timothy Busfield) seemingly exists in the script only to call Ray crazy for choosing the baseball field over financial stability. Even Ray himself acknowledges the irrationality of his quest. "I never did a crazy thing in my life until I heard the voice." It's a script that defies logic at every turn, but you'll never once find yourself shouting at your screen because the film anticipates your shout and gets there first.

Unlike *The Natural*, *Field of Dreams* isn't really girded in myth, except for the bit about the lightning. Instead, it's molded out of reliable emotional truths. You may have never had a falling out with your father as a teenager—although you probably did—but I bet you have a yearning to return to the innocence and idealism of your youth. Maybe you were a little bit afraid of losing your vitality as you stumbled toward middle age, and I reckon you've had more than one moment in your adult life where you thought about doing something completely and totally irrational just to feel alive. Odds are you didn't do it—maybe you didn't have an improbably supportive spouse to give you permission. Ray does, though, and his indulgence in a whim often dreamt of but rarely acted upon turns *Field of Dreams* into a fairy tale of wish fulfillment. We all get to be Ray, quitting our job to build a baseball field with our daughter, to whom we pass on stories about old ballplayers. We get to drive through the country in a van—that symbol of countercultural liberation also fetishized in *The Bad News Bears in Breaking Training*—and go to baseball games in old cathedrals. We get to hang out with Pulitzer Prize–winning writers who ask us gently probing questions about our childhoods. Maybe he'll write a book about us one day.

Field of Dreams locates our inner dreamer so precisely and powerfully that its flaws, of which there are many, are easily brushed away. I remain unconvinced Ray Liotta was the best choice for Shoeless Joe Jackson, and not just because he erroneously bats right-handed. There's something hollow in Liotta's eyes that, when set against his pockmarked face and aggressive laugh, hints at a void of feeling. As a dangerous ex-boyfriend (which he had just played in *Something Wild*) or a ruthless gangster (which he would play the following year in *Goodfellas*), it works marvelously, but in *Field of Dreams*, it often feel as if Liotta has wandered in from a different movie, maybe an old James Cagney flick or even *The Untouchables*, the Prohibition-era drama Costner starred in two years prior. Then again, all the dead players do. Their broad performances seem cribbed from fiction rather than human experience.

It's nearly impossible, on the other hand, to imagine anyone but Costner as Kinsella. The actor's baseball movie bonafides and athletic ability were established a year earlier in *Bull Durham*, but that's got nothing to do with the greatness of this performance. He doesn't need to be any kind of an athlete in *Field of Dreams*. In fact, when he throws a few pitches to Shoeless Joe—the one scene in which Costner actually plays baseball—the joke is that Ray is in no way qualified to share a field with him. Instead, Costner's portrayal resonates because of how he embodies the film's conflicting ideas in his stoic disposition. His Ray Kinsella is perfectly pitched between rural and suburban, between farmhand and country club. That's the contradiction that *Field of Dreams* holds in its gentle hands, and Costner spent his entire career earning it. Technically, Costner appears in the hippie elegy *The Big Chill*; he plays the friend whose suicide brings the group of conflicted yuppies together. He shot a flashback scene that was cut out, so all we see are a few scant body parts as they dress his corpse for the funeral in the opening montage. By 1989, Costner had already made one western, 1985's *Silverado*, and was in production on another, the Oscar-winning *Dances with Wolves*. Over the course of his career, he'd make all kinds of films (including another baseball movie, 1999's *For Love of the Game*), but he always returned to the western, which shares with *Field of Dreams* a profound appreciation for the land. Costner is like that land. He has an easy stillness, and a calmness in his expression that grips you. "As the taciturn, ruggedly handsome Ray," wrote Stephen Holden in his *New York Times* review of *Field of Dreams*, "Mr. Costner bears an eerie resemblance to the 1930's Gary Cooper, a Hollywood icon of America's pioneer spirit if ever there was one."

Mr. Holden went on to cite another movie cowboy: "The movie's exhortation of a purer, more innocent America, symbolized by a ghostly baseball team that is visible only to those who have been converted to Ray's vision, is very close to the mythic American past invoked by that quintessential conservative Ronald Reagan." Thematically, *Field of Dreams* fits neatly into the conservative culture that Reagan fostered and Hollywood embraced, even if the characters themselves are as far from Reaganites as you could imagine. Like *The Natural*, it's a film about second chances—all it wants is for Moonlight Graham to take a major league at-bat, for Shoeless Joe to touch grass, and for Ray to play catch with his father—but its nostalgia runs even deeper. If the film has a prevailing ethos, it's that the past exists to be re-lived. Ray tells Annie that he doesn't want to grow old in the same way that his father did, but his real motivation is to recapture the ideals of his youth in 1960s Berkeley. It's there in the wild, pie-eyed look Ray gets when he gazes out onto his baseball field. It's certainly there during the lively PTA meeting in which Annie invokes the spirit of the counterculture to win over a crowd of hostile reactionaries trying to ban books. Finally, it's there in the journey of Terence Mann, a cross between James Baldwin and J.D. Salinger (in fact, it *was* Salinger in the book), who fought on the front lines of the Civil Rights Movement before growing disillusioned and dropping out of public life. Ray lugs Terence along on his journey of rediscovery, and by the end, Terence has promised to begin writing again. The spirit of the '60s has come back to life.

In its unabashed embrace of both rural and countercultural values, *Field of Dreams* attempts to be all things to all people and exemplifies the limits of that approach. It's profoundly muddled, for example, on gender issues, depicting Ray's wife, Annie, as a tough, spunky housewife who has broken away from her stuffy family, while also reducing her to clichéd role of Supportive Wife (it's still superior to her characterization in the book, where the author Kinsella comments on her "perky nipples" and portrays her as constantly groping her husband). Her great moment in the film comes when she defeats the fascist book burner in that PTA meeting. In the hallway afterward, she crows about "halting the spread of neofascism in America," but Ray can barely be bothered to notice, as he is too wrapped up in his own obsession. The film never accounts for his failures as a husband, and in doing so, does a disservice to the women it claims to respect.

Things get even cringier when you start parsing the politics of Terence Mann. Turning J.D. Salinger into a radical Black author and activist opens up a discussion about race, baseball, and politics that the film is in no way equipped to handle. The screenplay tells us that Mann grew up with a simple reverence for Jackie Robinson, which makes sense, but a public intellectual would surely have come to a more nuanced understanding of baseball's shameful racial history. You'd never know it from his climactic speech, inspired by a sea of dead, White ballplayers on Ray's field, in which he opines, "Baseball reminds us of all that was once good and can be good again." He's right, of course: We do idealize baseball, just like we idealize our past. But by having Mann utter those particular words, the film suggests that his activism was merely a pose of sullen adulthood and that reviving that little boy whose pure love of Jackie Robinson blinded him to more complex racial realities is somehow preferable. When Mann says he's going to write again, we gather it's not about politics but about this post-political, post-racial place where baseball dreams can come true.

These concerns were voiced at the time by conservative commentator Charles Krauthammer, who wrote in the *Washington Post* upon the film's release, "Baseball does not remind us of all that was good—it was, to take only one example, most cruelly segregated for over half a century—but it does remind us of all that is youth. At the heart of all baseball sentimentalism is this confusion of the young and the good." Krauthammer liked the film, but he aptly identified the film's weak spot. In viewing the past under a glaze of nostalgia, it asks us to undo the years of serious thought about race that have made us more responsible baseball fans and better citizens.

Phil Alden Robinson, who wrote the script and was responsible for changing the character from Salinger to Mann, defended the choice in strange terms. "J.D. Salinger has moved me to tears with his writing, and I feel great pain for him not being allowed his privacy," he wrote. "Why hurt him? He's somebody I respect and admire. So, I decided to create a character as far away from Salinger as I could but still keep the story intact." It's reasonable to change a real-life character to a purely fictional one—for liability reasons, if nothing else—but Robinson's explanation reveals a major error. He was quite aware of his own feelings, and the feelings of Salinger, but the impact of his portrayal on Black audiences was not in his sphere of concern. In an uncritical story about nostalgia and baseball, there may have been no other way to do it. Nostalgia is a much more complicated subject for Black Americans than it is for White ones, and bringing actual racial politics into the film would have surely killed the buzz. Still, the film's racial problems only seem more glaring three decades later.

No matter how you slice it, *Field of Dreams* is a complicated movie. It's a film made in the 1980s about a character who grew up in the 1960s but mourns the loss of his relationship with his father, whose values were born in the 1940s and 1950s. Trying to pinpoint its politics would be an exercise in futility, but in my conversation with Dave Zirin, he came close: "Ray is quite clearly seen as someone who lost something by becoming a radical. He lost his connection with his father. That loss, as Phil Alden Robinson is saying, needs to be accounted for. You can't just say the '60s were good because we believed in free thought and we bought farms and we moved the country forward through activism. That might be true, but at the same time, a generational price was paid."

One reason *Field of Dreams* continues to resonate is that America is still in the midst of this conversation, stuck somewhere between the postwar American Dream and the countercultural rebellion. It's still negotiating the generational price. Half the country wants to go back to the days of TV dinners and *Father Knows Best*, and the other half is willing to transgress every social boundary in the hopes of making a more just society. "Make America Great Again" may have been the rallying cry of Donald Trump, but Ronald Reagan was the first president to say it, and Bill Clinton said it, too. In baseball, movies, and America as a whole, an uncritical remembrance of things past is just business as usual.

And so it hardly came as a surprise when Major League Baseball partnered with the official *Field of Dreams* farm in Dyersville, Iowa, to host a regular season game there in the summer of 2021. They left the original field intact and built a new one on the same property, with the revenue from the game surely compensating for, if the film is to be believed, a devastating loss of crop yield. The new field had more seating and plenty of spots for high-definition cameras, but it featured the same cornrows for fences. In the pregame ceremony, Kevin Costner walked out of that corn and wandered around the outfield in what was meant to be a stirring image but looked more like an old, confused man searching for his car in a parking lot.

But then: He turned toward the corn, and the players—the real-life Yankees and White Sox—emerged like ghosts in old-timey uniforms and began striding toward the infield. That's when we all got chills. There was something elemental in watching these young athletes materialize from the corn, like living embodiments of the baseball heartland myth. It seemed for a moment as if baseball was being conjured into existence before our very eyes. As the players drifted toward the infield, Costner stood at the microphone and spoke these words. "Thirty years ago, on the other side of that corn, we filmed a movie that stood the test of time." It did indeed, but it was also a self-fulfilling prophecy. Major League Baseball came back for another game the following year, and it won't be the last. The league will ensure people never forget *Field of Dreams* because it holds in its powerful, dirt-strewn hands the image of baseball the way they want us to see it: childlike, beautiful, and "perfect."

Chapter 9

Eight Men Out (1988) and *Major League* (1989)

AS SHOOTING WRAPPED ON *EIGHT MEN OUT* IN THE FALL OF 1987, SEVERAL of its key actors came to the producers with a request. They wanted to keep their costumes, specifically those authentic 1919 Chicago White Sox uniforms in which they had lived out their dreams of being professional baseball players, if only for a few weeks. It's not uncommon for actors to keep their wardrobe, but in this case, the request was swiftly denied. The reason given? The uniforms were promised to another production. The actors scoffed, certain that they were being lied to. There was just no chance there was another Black Sox movie being made at that exact moment. They must have felt a bit foolish when *Field of Dreams* came out two years later.

What is it about Shoeless Joe, anyway? He appears three times in the baseball movies of the 1980s, and never before or since. Why were the filmmakers of this era so fascinated with the 1919 Chicago White Sox, eight of whom were permanently banned from professional baseball for throwing the World Series? Specifically, why were they obsessed with Jackson? *The Natural* drew from his legend to tell the story of Roy Hobbs, who gets mixed up with gamblers but ultimately redeems all of baseball by doing the right thing in the end. *Field of Dreams* literally brings Shoeless

Joe back to life. Then there's John Sayles' *Eight Men Out*, the most direct telling of the story of the Chicago "Black Sox." It's a true ensemble piece, with no single figure dominating the narrative. It probes the World Series from all sides: the players, journalists, gamblers, wives, owners, and fans, each with a different perspective on the historic scandal. But it ends on Jackson. He's disgraced by then, playing on a semi-pro team in Hoboken, New Jersey, under an assumed name. The final, sepia-toned shot is a freeze-frame of him looking almost directly into the camera, as if he had been the main character all along. Along with Jackie Robinson, he's one of the most central characters in all of baseball cinema.

Broadly speaking, his story was not unique. By the time the Black Sox scandal disrupted the baseball world, myriad players had already been involved in gambling scandals. In 1865, three players on the New York Mutuals, a club that would later become a charter member of the National League but at this time was mostly made up of New York firefighters, were the first to be banned from baseball for throwing a game. In 1905, star Philadelphia Athletics pitcher Rube Waddell suffered a suspicious late-season injury that kept him out of the World Series against the New York Giants. The team claimed that he injured his pitching shoulder in a wrestling match with teammates, but rumors persisted he was paid off by gamblers to sit out the series. Tris Speaker, Smoky Joe Wood, and Ty Cobb, three of the best to ever play the game, were all at various points involved in alleged gambling scandals. Gambling and payoffs were so fundamental to baseball that in 1878, a mere two years after the National League was founded, a St. Louis newspaper wrote that the sport had already been ruined by corruption. "The amount of crooked work is indeed startling," read an editorial in *The Spirit of the Times*, "and the game will undoubtedly meet the same fate elsewhere unless some extra strong means are taken to prevent it."

Every other baseball controversy, however, was eclipsed by the Black Sox, who swiftly became an emblem of America's adolescent loss of innocence. In *The Godfather Part II*, Hyman Roth suggests a statue should be erected to Arnold Rothstein, the gambler typically credited with organizing the fix. F. Scott Fitzgerald's Jay Gatsby brings Nick Carraway to lunch with Meyer Wolfsheim, a clear stand-in for Rothstein, and later brags that "he's the man who fixed the World Series in 1919." Not every misdeed gets appropriated by the greatest artists who ever lived. Only when it upends or confirms the cultural mores of its time does a scandal morph into legend. This one came at the end of World War I and the Spanish Flu, and at the start of the Roaring Twenties, when a national case of existential despair gave way to a decade of hedonism and greed (or just a good time, depending on your perspective). The Black Sox were a product of their environment, and their environment became a product of them. The fallout from the scandal led to major changes throughout baseball. It inspired the owners to create the Office of the Commissioner to signal to the public that they were serious about keeping baseball clean. This was immediately followed by a surge in power throughout the league; Babe Ruth went from hitting 29 home runs in 1919 to 54 in 1920, and other hitters followed suit. Claims that the owners juiced the ball to boost ticket sales remain unproved, but they clearly did nothing to correct the power surge—like pushing the fences back or bringing the mound closer to the plate—instead allowing the popularity of the home run to coax fans who had lost interest after the scandal back to the ballpark. In essence, the power game we know today was formed in the wake of the Black Sox.

As for Shoeless Joe, there are a cavalcade of reasons he became the fulcrum of this legend. He was a legend before he even got to the big leagues—the story about him playing a textile-league game without his shoes was passed around until it somehow became national news. When he made it to the White Sox, he quickly became one of the best hitters in the league and eventually accrued a Hall of Fame résumé. By the time he was kicked out of baseball, he had amassed 1772 hits over a 13-year career, and a lifetime slash line of .356/.423/.517 (that's a .940 OPS). He stole 202 bases, notched 168 triples, and had earned a lifetime bWAR of 62.2, which was not a measured statistic in his day but would now place him among the elite. He was also showing no signs of slowing down. In

1920, his final year as a pro, he had an OPS of 1.033, the third highest of his career. He was the best hitter on the team, and the only player who took a bribe but clearly and definitively didn't try to throw even a single game (as devotees of any of these films will know, he hit .375 and played error-free baseball during the 1919 series). Finally, he was the object of one of the most memorable sentences in American history: "Say it ain't so, Joe," a line so perfect it could have been written by Fitzgerald himself.

The version of Shoeless Joe we see in *Eight Men Out* is not a golden god like Robert Redford, or a Chicago-style gangster with haunted eyes like Ray Liotta, but rather a Southern hayseed with a knack for baseball and no other discernible skills. Played by up-and-comer D.B. Sweeney, he's something of a beautiful idiot, half Roy Hobbs and half Bruce Pearson, and it makes him a mark for his teammates' playful scorn. He can't read or write, which comes in handy for the team's ruthless owners when they want to sign him to a crappy contract, and especially for the team's lawyers, when they coerce him into signing a criminal confession he doesn't understand. In truth, functional illiteracy wasn't that uncommon among early ballplayers, but historians and filmmakers saw his ignorance as an opportunity to bolster their case that Jackson was an innocent soul.

Although it lands definitively on Shoeless Joe in the end, *Eight Men Out* fully separates itself from other iterations of the Black Sox scandal through its interest in the whole roster. It's a film with a single question at its core: Why did these men, lionized daily by the press and the public for their play on the field, tarnish the game they loved and risk their reputations? The simplest answer is economics. Shoeless Joe earned a salary of only $6,000 a year; the gamblers promised him $20,000. Rather than view their willingness to accept this bribe as a sign of weakness or corruption, the film shows how weakness and corruption were endemic to their era. Vice is central to *Eight Men Out*, but Sayles isn't interested in condemning any one party. Instead, he investigates with a sympathetic eye the wide array of motivations and perspectives of the players, finding a series of flawed, human responses to acute economic and cultural conditions, and ultimately offering the richest portrayal of baseball's human element since *Bang the Drum Slowly*.

It's so rich and so detailed, in fact, that it could have been easy for the viewer to get lost. Sayles realized this, so he made sure to introduce every player multiple times. "I've got a bunch of White guys in old-timey uniforms with no names on their backs," he said in a documentary chronicling the film's 20ᵗʰ anniversary. And so we meet them first on the field, and then in the bars, the owner's office, and their homes. First baseman Chick Gandil (Michael Rooker) is the ringleader, initiating the entire scheme out of pure greed, working to persuade his teammates to join the conspiracy, and struggling to keep the group unified after the gamblers take back a portion of their upfront payments. Shortstop Swede Risberg (Don Harvey), his second-in-command, and pitcher Dickey Kerr (Jace Alexander) sign on immediately, gleeful in their pursuit of the almighty dollar. Good-time center fielder Hap Felsch (a well-cast Charlie Sheen) also turns out to be an easy get. Starting pitchers Eddie Cicotte (David Strathairn) and Lefty Williams (James Read), crucial to the scheme's success due to the outsized influence a pitcher has over the game, need a little convincing but ultimately go along to ensure their families' financial stability. Shoeless Joe (D.B. Sweeney) agrees mostly to fit in with the other guys.

Not everyone bends to the pressure. Third baseman Buck Weaver (John Cusack) rejects the proposal outright. He views himself as a role model for the city's youth and values his standing in the community. Infielder Eddie Collins (Bill Irwin) and catcher Roy Schalk (Gordon Clapp) weren't asked, but it's clear from their upright attitudes that they weren't likely candidates to join, anyway. Collins is an outsider in the group, frequently mocked as "College Boy" for his education and moral character. It's no matter: The conspirators don't need the whole team for the scheme to work. A few key players, especially the starting pitchers, would get it done.

In these opening scenes, Sayles captures a roster of husbands, fathers, bachelors, rubes, snobs, and criminals, but he also deftly establishes the world in which they live, where everyone is a hustler, even the local kids who sell newspapers on the street and steal the signal for the local game broadcast off a homemade radio. Heck, even Ciccotte, one of the most morally upright characters on the team, throws a "shineball" by surreptitiously rubbing the ball on a grease spot on his uniform in between pitches. In a few quick strokes, Sayles locates his characters in an environment where heroism is obsolete, and the upstanding character of the game, a given in so many baseball movies, is a load of hooey.

That *Eight Men Out* immerses the viewer in a corrupt world without losing its own sense of morality is one of its great achievements, but it's hard not to take sides when one character holds such considerable power over the rest. I'm talking about team owner Charles Comiskey (Clifton James), one of the cheapest men in baseball, if not in the running for cheapest worldwide. A fact that goes curiously unmentioned in the film: They were called the "Black Sox" not because of the black mark they left on the game, but because Comiskey often skimped on laundry detergent, which slowly turned their home white uniforms a dark shade of gray. Such a story would have fit well within Sayles' portrayal of Comiskey, who, after his White Sox win the pennant in the opening scenes, stiffs his players on their promised bonuses, and instead deliverrs to their locker room a few bottles of flat champagne.

A further indignity is inflicted upon Cicotte, who, as the film starts, is nearing the end of a long career as one of the game's best pitchers. He's counting on ownership to do right by him and his family, but an early scene reveals the depths of Comiskey's penny-pinching. Cicotte requests a bonus that, according to his contract, must be paid when he wins 30 games. In the 1919 season, Cicotte only won 29 games, but he argues to Comiskey he would have won more had he not been held out of game action for two weeks that summer. Comiskey claims he did it to save the pitcher's arm for the World Series, but the way Sayles stages the action, with Cicotte coming hat-in-hand to request his fee and Comiskey lounging relaxedly in the seat of power, it's clear that Comiskey has held him out in order to depress his statistics and keep the cash for himself. "Thirty," the owner says coolly, "is not twenty-nine."

It's a key moment that creates enormous sympathy early on for Cicotte and, by extension, all his teammates. "This man took the money in the hopes of giving his daughters a college education, and he was loath to do it because he was ethically and morally a good man," said Strathairn in a DVD extra. "When he was deceived by Comiskey, and then by the guys who placed the bets, I think he was destroyed by that." The film shares Cicotte's disillusionment and extends it to even the most minor characters in its world. The pitcher's bitter disappointment is no less poignant than that of the child who begs Jackson, in the film's famous penultimate scene, to tell him it ain't so. If the game is crooked at the core, what's the point in playing it straight? Cicotte may have had the biggest ax to grind, but all the players were underpaid compared to the value they brought to the team, and they knew it. When you are feted in the street, and insulted by your bosses behind closed doors, something's going to give.

With its radical, working-class politics, *Eight Men Out* is an expected take on the material by Sayles, who by this point had burnished a reputation as a consistently progressive, pro-labor filmmaker. His debut film, 1979's *Return of the Secaucus Seven*, chronicled a reunion between friends and peace activists from the late '60s (Lawrence Kasdan has long claimed he hadn't seen it when he wrote *The Big Chill*, which has a similar premise). In 1983, Sayles used his winnings from the MacArthur Fellowship to make *The Brother from Another Planet*, about an alien who escapes slavery on another planet and crash-lands on Earth, where he takes the form of an African American. Then in 1987, just a year before *Eight Men Out*, he released *Matewan*, a stirring dramatization of a coal miners' strike in West Virginia in 1920 that culminated in a shootout between labor organizers and union busters.

The critical success of *Matewan* paved the way for *Eight Men Out*, another period piece with pro-labor themes. Looking back, it's an odd fit in its decade, when baseball cinema was more interested in remythologizing itself rather than breaking down with painful precision one of the sport's most traumatic memories. It turns out Sayles wrote the screenplay eleven years earlier—in the heart of American disillusionment—but wasn't able to get it made until the '80s. "To me, it was like *All the President's Men*," he told me. "I was interested in conspiracies because they very often fall apart because some of the people are ashamed of what they're doing. And they don't have enough meetings." Although conceived in the '70s, *Eight Men Out* surely felt more urgent under the decidedly anti-labor presidency of Ronald Reagan. A former union leader with the Screen Actors Guild, Reagan became a hero to the anti-union crowd when he stood up to the striking air traffic controllers in 1981, enacting a lifetime ban of those workers who did not return to their jobs within 48 hours (the ban was lifted by President Clinton a decade later). Reagan's handling of the air traffic controllers had a huge influence over American labor culture. Chair of the Federal Reserve Alan Greenspan later cited Reagan's firing of the air traffic controllers as "perhaps the most important contribution" to America's labor economy. "Reagan's action gave weight to the legal right of private employers, previously not fully exercised," he said, "to use their own discretion to both hire and discharge workers."

The same thing happened to the eight players on the 1919 Chicago White Sox. Like the air traffic controllers, they were banned for life. To properly convey their story—both the seriousness of their crime and the injustice of their punishment—Sayles needed to get his baseball right. We have to see them play well so that when they start to play badly on purpose we can tell the difference. Sayles understood this and, in the first act, insisted on making Sweeney hit "an honest triple," according to the actor. In a single, unbroken shot, we watch him hit a line drive into right field and run the bases—the camera dollies left up the third-base line—before sliding into third. Sweeney claims it took 35 takes to get right.

Robert Redford may have raised the bar for baseball movie realism with his sweet stroke in *The Natural*, but Sayles doubled down on it, hiring former major leaguer Ken Berry, a Gold Glove–winning centerfielder for the Angels and White Sox, to run a two-week baseball camp for the players. This is now de rigueur for baseball movies, war films, and other genres in which realism is expected, but it was a major innovation at the time. "I gave him a week with the guys and a shopping list of the skills they had to show on camera," said Sayles. He didn't need them to look like All-Stars. "I wanted them not to get hurt, so I asked for lots of baseball stretching. And I wanted them to be able to turn a double-play, or whatever simple thing they'd need to do. And he got them up to snuff in most places." Some of the actors took their training more seriously than others. D.B. Sweeney went hard in his preparation to play Shoeless Joe, spending two months with the minor league Kenosha Twins, learning to hit left-handed, and generally perfecting his baseball acumen.

All of that effort paid off with the critics, who recognized in Sayles a filmmaker who cared deeply about the details of the game. In his praise of the film, Lewis Archibald of *Downtown* magazine mirrored Sayles' literary tone: "He loves the easy I-can-do-anything lope of a man who's just hit a homer and is gliding around the bases like a carefree gazelle, and the 15 different choices an outfielder has to make in deciding if a hit is going to go foul or not, and even all those mysterious, virtually incomprehensible signs a catcher makes to a pitcher with his free hand between his legs. Sayles loves that stuff and does his best to catch it in the sort of baseball stadiums where the game can emerge best, short of neon surroundings, concessionaires tramping through the stands like scavengers, and all the modern-day distracting glitz." Archibald hits on a key point. There's a beautiful contradiction in *Eight Men Out*, which faithfully recreates an era that we often think of as a "simpler time" and then proceeds to diligently dissect its moral complexities. It's not a nostalgic film, but it benefits from our need for nostalgia. It's a wish for baseball as it once was—and for America as we still pretend it is—while acknowledging that it never actually was that way in the first place.

Confronting your nostalgia is a key part of growing up, for people, for baseball, and, most especially, for baseball movies. When Buck Weaver (John Cusack) tries to explain to one of those street kids why his teammates threw the Series, he uses vague language about the complications of an adult world the kids couldn't possibly understand. So why didn't he take money, too, the kid asks? "I guess I never grew up," he replies. Buck Weaver was 29 years old when this all went down, but Cusack, in his first adult role after starring in teen comedies *Better off Dead* and *One Crazy Summer*, was only 21, barely more than a kid himself. He was the right actor to deliver this important sentiment that explains why these filmmakers, raised in the '60s and maturing into adults in the '80s, continued poking at the legend of Shoeless Joe and the 1919 White Sox. With these films, they are revisiting the game of their youth and working to uncover the complicated adult realities behind them. In their way, they're all just trying to grow up.

Released in April of 1989, *Major League* didn't impress critics like *Eight Men Out*, and it certainly wasn't nominated for any Oscars like *Field of Dreams*. It's a straight sports comedy whose basic narrative is stolen outright from the superior *The Bad News Bears*; it centers on a group of outcasts and misfits that come together, defy the odds, and transform into a championship-caliber team. Made specifically with adults (or at least man-children) in mind, it lifts most of its macho, politically incorrect ethos from 1977's *Slap Shot*, a hockey comedy starring Paul Newman as the aging player-coach of a second-rate hockey team.

And yet it shares some DNA with *Eight Men Out* in its portrayal of a cruel, spendthrift owner whose underpaid players band together to defy. It would be too generous to cast *Major League* as a pro-labor movie about the plight of the working man. It's not committed enough to its ideas. Instead, it is mostly remembered for its jokes and its cast, for its perfect execution of well-worn sports comedy tropes and for its invention of a few others. No film had ever sought to replicate the rhythms of a full major league season before, from spring training to the postseason. *Major League* does that, and its successes spawned imitators, both in baseball cinema and in the actual major leagues.

In the opening scenes, the Indians' new owner Rachel Phelps (Margaret Whitton) instructs her general manager (Charles Cyphers) to put together a team of losers that will torpedo the team's attendance, releasing them from their lease with the city and allowing Phelps to move the team to Miami (if this plot sounds familiar to younger readers, it was stolen wholesale for the first season of *Ted Lasso*). Four years before the expansion Florida Marlins debuted, *Major League* understood the appeal of an MLB franchise in South Beach.

The roster she puts together, with the exception of millionaire Roger Dorn (Corbin Bernsen), is composed of players representing a wide array of America's overlooked and marginalized classes. There's Jake Taylor (Tom Berenger), a past-his-prime catcher with bad knees and no prospects for middle age; Rick Vaughn (Charlie Sheen), a convicted car thief whose prison sentence gets commuted so that he can make the tryout; and Pedro Cerrano (Dennis Haysbert), a Cuban defector who is mocked in the locker room for his religious beliefs. The film's admirable attempt at a rainbow coalition falls apart a bit with its portrayal of Willie "Mays" Hayes (Wesley Snipes), an unfortunate iteration of the flashy, me-first Black athlete stereotype created in part by this era's media. He's Rickey Henderson without the skill; in the first game of the season, he brags to the first baseman about how many bases he will steal that year—then promptly gets picked off.

In a sport of five-tool players, the roster of *Major League* is filled with one-tool players, guys with some natural talent but little baseball know-how. Vaughn could throw 96 mph (fearsome for its time, more like average today), but he lacked command, to put it mildly. Hayes could run like Mays, but, in the words of skipper Lou Brown (James Gammon), he "hit like shit." Cerrano can only hit fastballs; the curveball is the devil's work to him. Under the tutelage of Brown and Taylor, who essentially acts as a player-coach, the players gain confidence and hone their skills, becoming well-rounded professionals by the final reel. Of course, it's an exigency of the genre that they grow as ballplayers and as human beings, but writer-director David S. Ward creates for them a motivation that contributes to the film's populism. They don't come together as a team until they learn of their owner's secret plan to move the franchise and replace them with better players. It gives them something to rally against, and they ride their resentment all the way to postseason. As framed by Ward, it almost qualifies as a revolution.

And to be quite honest, Cleveland needed one. In 1989, the city was America's underdog. Known for decades as "the mistake by the lake" for its many economic foibles, Cleveland was once supported by a thriving steel industry, but the Great Depression, rampant inflation, and foreign competition took its toll. A city's descent is incremental, but every now and then, a symbol tells the whole story. To wit: Cleveland factories routinely dumped their waste into the local waterways, and in 1969, the Cuyahoga River caught fire, creating flames that were five stories high. The fire was extinguished with no casualties, but you couldn't find a better metaphor for a fading metropolis. The incident was immortalized by singer-songwriter Randy Newman, whose song, "Burn On," plays during the opening credits of *Major League* beneath images of urban youths playing stickball in the shadow of towering smokestacks.

In the 1970s, Cleveland went bankrupt. By the 1980s, city residents were fleeing en masse to the suburbs. Inflation, globalization, and the war against the unions had taken its toll on the factory workers. None of its professional sports teams had won a title since 1964, when the Cleveland Browns won the NFL Championship; the Indians had not won the World Series since 1948. At the time of the film's release, the Indians' attendance was low, and their stadium was falling apart. There was real talk of moving the franchise to Miami. In the film, few of the players are actually from Cleveland, so to demonstrate the city's hard-earned pessimism, the film shifts focus to the fans. In periodic cutaways, a wide swath of Cleveland residents gets their say: guys in the diner, a waitress, longshoremen, even the stadium grounds crew who possess a rooting interest in the team ("They're still shitty."). Battered and beaten from years of losing, and not just on the diamond, they refuse to believe the hype about the team until it puts together a legitimate winning streak, and then the fans turn out in full force for the climactic game. The crowd shot was a staple of baseball cinema before this, but there are more of them in *Major League* than in any earlier film. Fans had never been centered to this degree, nor had an attempt been made to link a team's character to a city's culture.

Ward, who grew up in the Cleveland suburbs, knew what he was doing. "I remember the 1954 World Series and how upset my father was that the Indians, after such a spectacular season, were swept by the Giants," said Ward. "That's when I realized how important a baseball game could be. After that, things went into a decline in Cleveland. Just grim, awful, hopeless years. I thought, the only way the Indians will ever win anything in my lifetime is if I make a movie where they do. And obviously it has to be a comedy because nobody would believe it as a drama." There were times Ward doubted himself, particularly during the difficult shoot. *Major League* was independently financed, so the filmmakers worked with little time and even less money. (The budget was a mere $11 million.) "What kept me going was I just didn't want to be another Cleveland failure."

Major League was no failure. It grossed $49.8 million, finishing 23rd in that year's box office (right between *Working Girl* and *Beaches*), and inspired two sequels, 1994's *Major League II* and 1998's *Major League: Back to the Minors*. You don't become a hit of that nature by appealing only to Clevelanders, or even residents of other Rust Belt states similarly harmed by mismanagement and poor economic policy. The political context of *Major League* is there if you want it, but, unlike *Eight Men Out*, it's easy to enjoy it as a pure baseball movie, the kind that journalists have been clamoring for since they lamented that *Pride of the Yankees* was too much of a love story. It's the story of a team, not an individual. It follows the Indians from spring training to the playoffs, and depicts the drudgery of the season, the shifts in momentum, and the thrill of big-game baseball. Over the course of the film, you get to know these players just as you would the stars of your favorite real-life team. Even as a broad comedy, *Major League* is the way baseball looked and felt in 1989.

Before its virtues can be more loudly sung, however, there are some errors and hypocrisies to get out of the way. For starters, baseball aficionados (and anyone from Cleveland) will notice that *Major League* was not shot at Municipal Stadium, the home of the Indians from 1932 to 1993. Instead, the production used Milwaukee's County Stadium. The reason? Cleveland was a strict union town, and hiring non-union workers was an easy way to save money. It's ironic that a film about the downtrodden working-class would abandon its underlying principles and cut corners so demonstrably, but the hard realities of making an independently financed film may have required it.

It's also a shame that a film gesturing so emphatically toward the empowerment of marginalized groups would be so cruel to its female characters. "It's the gold standard of baseball film misogyny," according to Ellen Adair, actress, regular guest on MLB Network's talk show *Off Base*, and host of the baseball movie podcast *Take Me In to the Ballgame*. Says Adair, "*Major League* is such a good movie, and it's so incredibly misogynist in how terrible the character of Rachel Phelps is. She's not just the bad guy because she's bad. She's also the bad guy because she's a woman." Phelps, as conceived by Ward and portrayed by Margaret Whitton (who had just played another domineering woman in a male-dominated industry in 1987's *The Secret of My Success*), represents the threat supposedly posed by feminism to the working-class male. Her very presence atop the Indians organization shows how things had improved for women, but the film tips the scales against her. She hasn't paid her dues. She simply married the aging owner and took over when he died. Before that, she was a showgirl in Las Vegas. The film frames her as a contemptuous gold digger and asks us to applaud when the players reduce her to what they see as her primal form. You know the scene I'm talking about. It was in the trailer, and if you were an 11-year kid attracted to women the first time you saw *Major League* (like I was), it was your favorite part of the movie. The players create a cardboard cutout with a piece of clothing to represent every game they need to win to make the playoffs, and they remove each one with every victory. When the Indians win their final game, they reveal Phelps as she once was: naked, but with stars covering her nipples. Their victory on the field is a reassertion of their dominance over the working woman, reducing her to the disempowered sexual object she once was.

Major League doesn't do much better with its unfortunate romantic subplot involving Jake Taylor and Lynn (Rene Russo), his ex-fiancée whom he once cheated on routinely but, now that she's engaged to another man (a prototypical yuppie who owns fancy artwork and hangs out with old people), is desperate to win back. To do so, he ignores her every social cue and basically becomes her stalker. He corners her at a restaurant, follows her to work at the local library, and tracks her down at her fiancé's apartment, even entering without permission. Later, he does the same at her apartment, showing up in her living room completely unannounced. It's okay, though. She sleeps with him there, then immediately exits the picture before showing up in the final scene without her engagement ring, demonstrating that (according to the film) a good boinking by a working-class stiff is all a librarian really needs.

So here is a film that celebrates misogyny, reduces women to sexual objects, stereotypes Black athletes and Latino players, and displays racist headdresses worn by fans referring to a team name that was changed in 2021 because of its offense to Indigenous people. It begs the question: Why is *Major League* still so darn good? Because it deeply understands what fans love about the game, and it found a way to express that love through cinema. *Major League* improved upon the baseball film's trusted conventions in multiple ways, and it resonated so deeply with the public that many of its innovations are still a part of baseball culture today.

The first invention sits in the broadcast booth. When he was cast as Harry Doyle, the hilarious, drunken broadcaster of the Indians, Bob Uecker was already in the midst of an illustrious career as the play-by-play announcer for the Milwaukee Brewers and host of the sports-comedy show *Bob Uecker's Wacky World of Sports*, where he showcased baseball bloopers and oddities, and even acted in the occasional comedy sketch. Known as "Mr. Baseball" (almost certainly a moniker he gave himself), Uecker made over 100 appearances on *The Tonight Show*, where he regaled Johnny Carson with humorous anecdotes and witty one-liners. He was a more polished Yogi Berra. A list of his best jokes would comprise dozens of pages, but he was best at self-deprecation. "In 1962, I was named Minor League Player of the Year," he said once. "It was my second season in the bigs."

Uecker's irreverence enlivened a character—the play-by-play announcer—that had long been taken for granted in baseball films. Typically, their role was to set the scene for the film's climactic game with flowery prose, or as in *Angels in the Outfield*, act as foil to the players or manager. Ward and Uecker collaborated on a true innovation of the genre by turning this archetype into a comic Greek chorus, punctuating the clownish action on the field with perfectly delivered zingers. It was a breath of fresh air for the baseball film, which had perhaps become overly solemn in the '80s with *The Natural, Field of Dreams*, and *Eight Men Out*.

The part was designed as comedic, but Ward has since acknowledged that Uecker improvised much of his dialogue and brought inspired timing even to the scripted lines. Uecker was a baseball lifer who had probably forgotten more about the game than Ward ever knew, but setting him free to make the character his own was a directorial masterstroke. "Juuuust a bit outside" was on the page, but Uecker made it funnier by stretching it to its breaking point. If *Major League* had no other legacy, at least it would have this. There isn't a play-by-play announcer in the game who hasn't once paid homage to the film by impersonating Uecker's delivery of that line, and it's easy to draw a line from Uecker to some of the goofier announcers in today's game, like the Mets' Keith Hernandez, whose on-air role is largely defined by his comical asides, inadvertent sighs into the microphone, and frequent references to his pet cat.

Even more influential than Uecker's comic posturing was the film's embrace of the closer entrance song. Rick Vaughn is a starting pitcher for much of *Major League*, but in the final game, he gets benched in favor of Eddie Harris (Chelcie Ross), the crafty veteran with a grease spot on his shoulder. But Vaughn comes out of the bullpen to get a key out in the top of the ninth inning, and when he does, "Wild Thing" by The Troggs blares through the loudspeaker. It had already become his theme song—inspired by his punk hairstyle and lack of control—but this is the first time we get to hear it in its full glory, with 50,000 Cleveland fans standing, cheering, and singing along.

It wasn't technically the first time a closer had used walk-up music. In 1972, new Yankees closer Sparky Lyle walked to the mound to the tune of "Pomp and Circumstance," but it was played by the stadium organist. Al Hrabosky, closer for the St. Louis Cardinals in the 1970s, used Franz Liszt's "Hungarian Rhapsody No. 2" to accompany his warm-up pitches, a gimmick inspired by his nickname, "The Mad Hungarian." Also played by the organist, it hardly matched the jubilant, get-the-crowd-going vibe of "Wild Thing."

Real-life closers were paying attention. After joining the Cubs in 1989, pitcher Mitch Williams, known for his long hair and dramatic pitching motion, adopted the moniker "Wild Thing," and the Wrigley Field organist played it every time he came out of the bullpen. When Williams was traded to the Phillies a few years later, they switched to a recording of the pop song, a la *Major League*. It didn't end as well for Williams as it did for Vaughn——he gave up one of the most famous home runs in World Series history to Joe Carter in 1993—but the trend caught on. In 1998, San Diego Padres closer Trevor Hoffman began using AC/DC's "Hells Bells" as his entrance music. After playing the Padres in that year's World Series, Yankees closer Mariano Rivera chose Metallica's "Enter Sandman" as his. Another closer, Billy Wagner, independently began using "Enter Sandman" the same year. As recently as 2022, Mets closer Edwin Diaz's entrance song—"Narco" by Timmy Trumpet—became so popular that Mr. Trumpet was invited to Citi Field to perform the song live as Diaz jogged in from the bullpen, while fans waved toy trumpets given out at the gates.

The closer entrance song is a marketing opportunity born of two ascendant cultural institutions: MTV and professional wrestling. At that time, hair metal was dominating the airwaves, and wrestling icons like Hulk Hogan, Ric Flair, and Randy "Macho Man" Savage were virtually indistinguishable from rock stars, with their long hair, brightly colored spandex, and throngs of adoring fans. Vaughn's gimmick took wrestling's showmanship and added an MTV soundtrack, enlivening a pastoral sport that had begun to feel antiquated in the flashy, neon-tinted '80s. With his leather jacket and punk hairdo, Vaughn was the perfect spokesmodel for a game seeking younger and hipper fans.

In the film, Vaughn's entrance music comes in the climactic game, a one-game playoff against the hateful New York Yankees to decide the division title. Complaints about the film's first half—its sexism and racial stereotyping—are valid, but the final game is unimpeachable. It has everything you want in a baseball movie climax. There are contributions from all its stars, including a key stolen base from Hayes and a radar-gun-busting strikeout from Vaughn. It features a player overcoming his season-long weakness, when Cerrano finally learns to hit a curveball in the biggest spot possible. There's a brilliantly conceived trick play, when Taylor ends the game by calling his shot like Babe Ruth but then laying down a bunt and, despite his aging knees, legging out a single that scores the hard-charging Hayes from second base.

Ward films the baseball action with such skill and precision that you forget you're watching a movie at all. Uecker drops the funny stuff and calls the game straight, even shutting up at key moments to let the images of a team celebrating its big hits and clutch strikeouts speak for themselves, just like iconic Dodgers broadcaster Vin Scully used to do. If *Major League* hadn't been a success, Ward could have seamlessly transitioned to directing actual baseball broadcasts. His generation of baseball filmmakers, which included Barry Levinson, John Sayles, and Phil Alden Robinson, were the first to have grown up watching the game on television, but while those directors looked to baseball's distant past for inspiration, Ward drew on the visual language of contemporary telecasts to make a modern masterpiece. The result is a final act that feels like you're watching a real major league game, barely heightened for drama. The shot of Jake Taylor, for example, calling his shot in the final at-bat comes from an angle—from the dirt below, looking up—that would not have been possible in a TV broadcast at the time. It's a hero shot that accentuates the moment without drawing too much attention to itself, conjuring the way baseball feels at its most thrilling.

Getting the baseball action right was just as important in *Major League* as it was in *Eight Men Out*, albeit for different reasons. *Eight Men Out* needed to set up a baseline of athletic excellence so that viewers could feel it when they start to purposefully falter. *Major League*'s attempt at replicating the look and feel of modern baseball was essentially an open invitation for nitpicking fans to complain. They had to nail it. "One of the things I did with all the actors before I cast them was play catch to see how well they could play," Ward said. "I had actors coming in and saying that they had played Triple A with the Cardinals. Then I'd take them outside, and they couldn't throw it 15 feet. They just lied." As had quickly become customary, Ward put his players through a boot camp to improve their skills, but it only got them so far. Former major leaguer Steve Yeager (who ran the boot-camp) stood in for Berenger during certain shots—basically, whenever his face could be hidden with a catcher's mask—and Ward filmed Snipes in slow motion whenever he was running to hide the fact that the guy playing the team speedster was, well, slow.

One actor took his quest to look like a big leaguer further than the others, even putting his health and reputation at risk. Can you possibly guess who it was? Charlie Sheen was probably the most naturally talented of the cast. "I had a great arm," he told *Sports Illustrated*. "I was just born with it." As a man known for hyperbole, it's hard to take Sheen at his word when he claims he was the standout on his high school baseball team or that he was on the verge of being scouted by pro teams when he quit and decided to become an actor, but Ward acknowledged Sheen could throw a fastball in the 80s. At least, with help. "It was the only time I ever did steroids," Sheen said years after the shoot. "I did them for like six or eight weeks. You can print this, I don't give a f—. My fastball went from 79 to like 85." *Major League* came almost a decade before the Steroid Era blossomed in baseball, but even at the time, performance-enhancing drugs were present in the sport and Hollywood. Mark McGwire acknowledged trying steroids in 1989, the same year

Major League was released, while muscle-bound '80s movie stars Arnold Schwarzenegger and Sylvester Stallone later admitted to using steroids to maintain their surreal, action-star physiques.

It's a case of art imitating life, and life imitating it back. With the fictional Indians transforming—much like Sheen's fastball—from forgettable to formidable, the offscreen Indians would soon do the same. Just a few years after *Major League* became a hit, the Cleveland Indians were suddenly a winner. They put together a team of Hall-of-Fame-caliber players like the sluggers Albert Belle, Manny Ramirez, and Jim Thome, speedy centerfielder Kenny Lofton, and veteran pitchers Dennis Martinez and Orel Hershiser. Squint and you can see Cerrano, Hayes, and Vaughn. They had a winning record each year from 1994 to 2001, sporting the best regular season record in baseball two years in a row ('95–96).. They survived the looming threat of relocation and built a beautiful new stadium, then known as Jacobs Field. In 1997, it became one of the few ballparks in history to host an All-Star Game and a World Series in the same year.

Between the success of the film, the excitement and stability of the new stadium, and the winning product on the field, it was a high point for Cleveland baseball. And yet. The Indians didn't win that World Series. They didn't win any World Series. They still haven't won a World Series, not since 1948. The fact that this franchise could put together such a dominant team and not come away with a championship only feeds its deep-seated culture of disappointment. Perhaps that's why the film continues to resonate with the city's players and fans. In 2021, Guardians All-Star Jose Ramirez was seen wearing a necklace with the film's logo on it—a baseball with a mohawk and sunglasses. In 2022, as the team embarked on a playoff run, a popular shirt among fans read: "Win the Whole F—ing Thing," echoing Jake Taylor's locker room rallying cry.

Toward the end of that season, I had a conversation with Jeremy Feador, the Guardians' official historian and a lifelong Cleveland fan. It was the morning of a contest that could have been right out of the movie: an elimination game against the New York Yankees. The Guardians had been up 2–1 in this American League Division Series, but they lost a potential clinching game the evening before. If they failed that evening, it would be the third playoff series loss to the hated Yankees in six years, and although Jeremy was hopeful his team could advance, he and the rest of the Cleveland faithful were prepared for a loss. They had a ritual. "You always have *Major League* to fall back on," he told me. "If the worst happens this year, and we don't win the World Series, I'll just go back and pop on the DVD."

America needs the movies for its happy ending—a glossy photo of a past that never existed—and so does baseball. Only one team gets to win the World Series every year. The rest have to find hope where they can. The Guardians lost that game to the Yankees, ending their season. Jeremy surely felt better after his annual viewing of *Major League,* and he wasn't alone. After my New York Mets lost in the Wild Card round against the San Diego Padres, I also popped in a DVD of *Major League* and found myself getting choked up when the team tied the game in the eighth on Cerrano's homer, got out of a jam in the ninth with Vaughn's strikeout, and then scored the winning run on Taylor's trick play. It didn't matter that I wasn't a Cleveland fan. The filmmaker told a story about one downtrodden city and its frustrated fanbase, and in aiming for something specific, they created a major work.

Chapter 10

Bull Durham (1988)

IT WAS NEAR THE END OF SPRING TRAINING IN 2015, AND OUTFIELDER Mark Canha felt good about his chances to make the Oakland Athletics. He'd had a good spring and performed especially well in the final few games, with a walk-off homer in one contest and another home run in the final exhibition game. He was 26 years old and had spent four full seasons in the minor leagues. If not now, when?

Then came the throng of reporters. "They're asking me questions after I hit the walk-off," he told me, "and I had never had to deal with the media before. I didn't understand the dynamics. So somebody asked me one of those questions that's hard to answer, something like, 'What kind of statement do you think you made with your performance today?' I didn't know how to answer it, so I answered honestly and said, 'I'm a little bit tired, and it's been a long spring. I think I showed that I can perform in a marathon-type season when you're fatigued or you're not 100 percent.' The reporter then went right over to the manager and said, 'Mark Canha says he's tired. Are you overworking him?'"

Canha was promptly called into the manager's office and chewed out for his transgression. If he were a more established player, it would have been no big deal, but at this precarious stage of his career, it felt like a consequential error. "I really felt like I had put my career in jeopardy," he said. "I was so mad and upset, and I decided there and then that the next time this happens I needed to take a page from Crash Davis."

In *Bull Durham*, Crash (Kevin Costner), a career minor leaguer, offers sage advice to Ebby Calvin "Nuke" LaLoosh (Tim Robbins), a young flamethrower with great stuff and no command. Even at this low-level of the minor leagues, LaLoosh acts like he's on the verge of stardom, and Crash has been tasked with mentoring him, not just on his pitching but also on surviving the bigs. "You're gonna have to learn your clichés," he tells him on the team bus. "You're gonna have to study them, you're gonna have to know them. They're your friends." Canha, who had watched *Bull Durham* dozens of times already by that fateful spring day, knew the clichés by heart, but he hadn't understood their utility until a few days later. He made the club and had a huge day in his major league debut, driving in four runs. Suddenly, he was standing in front of serious reporters asking him the same kind of vague, open-ended questions that had gotten him into trouble the first time.

"I'm just here to help the ballclub, and give it my best shot," he said with a glint in his eye. "And the good lord willing, things will work out." These are the very clichés Crash instructs Nuke to memorize. At the end of the film, we see Nuke repeating them in his first major league interview. Canha was the next ballplayer to use them.

For Canha and all else who love it, *Bull Durham* is an immersion into the language, the rhythms, and the realities of a career in baseball. Like a Rosetta Stone course for the national pastime, it will teach you what "the show" is (it's what they call the major leagues in the minors). You'll learn the difference between a "dying quail" (a bloop single) and a "ground ball with eyes" (a poorly hit grounder that squeaks through the infield for a hit). You'll find out about "bonus babies" (rookies who receive a large signing bonus from the organization). You'll learn that a "deuce" is a curveball, and that a rookie pitcher should never, ever, ever shake off his veteran catcher in a big spot. Baseball is built on unwritten rules, and *Bull Durham* will teach you them all.

Baseball, the film tells us, is not like the other movies say it is. It's harder, colder, realer, and funnier. Consider the early plate appearance of Crash, newly demoted to A-ball, a lower level of the minor leagues, for the sole purpose of mentoring bonus baby LaLoosh. He calls the batboy over to clean his bat. "Get a hit, Crash," says the batboy. "Shut up," Crash responds. Historically, the heroes of baseball movies are kind to children. We see it in *Pride of the Yankees* and *The Babe Ruth Story*, whose central figures literally save children's lives through their baseball heroics. Even *Eight Men Out* makes room for Buck Weaver, its most honorable figure, to be a friend and role model to the children of Chicago. In *The Bad News Bears*, Buttermaker's storyline is defined by it. In these films, the innocent child reflects back to the more grizzled hero an earnest love for baseball. The game rejuvenates the child, and the child rejuvenates the adult. This is how baseball has always worked.

But not for the flawed hero at the center of *Bull Durham*. At the film's start, Crash has yet to graduate to the majors, either in baseball or in life. He's a career minor leaguer and lifelong bachelor with no use for rookies or kids. When the sweet, young, batboy encourages him to get a hit, Crash doesn't smile, pat him on his head, and say, "You got it, kid. I'll hit one out for you." He can't even muster a wink. Instead, he tells him to shut up, and that kid is never seen again. More importantly, we understand why Crash responds as he does; the film has put us inside his head during the at-bat, where an inner monologue expressing a delicate balance of fragile confidence and raging self-doubt is constantly running. Crash puts enough pressure on himself. The kid was just gonna mess him up.

It's the demolition of the sacred idea that ballplayers are role models. *The Bad News Bears* showed us a former major leaguer who was morally questionable, but he wasn't a player anymore. Grizzled managers are allowed to be beaten down by life. So there's something special about watching '80s hunk Kevin Costner wear the uniform of a professional ballplayer while cussing, fighting, talking frankly about sex, and being mean to children. It's a glorious demythologizing of baseball—in that way, this is more of a '70s movie than an '80s movie—that is so good and so profoundly rooted in truth that it ended up creating a new standard for the baseball film.

It took someone with inside knowledge of the sport to so brazenly break the rules. A first-time filmmaker, writer-director Ron Shelton would go on to direct two other classic sports movies, *White Men Can't Jump* and *Tin Cup* (and the not-so-classic *Cobb*), but *Bull Durham* is his best because it's the most personal. From 1967 to 1971, Shelton played in the Baltimore Orioles minor league system. As a player, he wasn't great, nor was he terrible. His best year was with the A-ball team in Stockton, California, where he batted .277 with a .360 on-base percentage and stole 32 bases. Two years later, he was out of baseball, but before he left, he made the acquaintance of some unusual players. One was Steve Dalkowski, a pitcher who threw at least 100 mph (some say he touched 110) but had terrible control. He once struck out 20 and walked 20 in a single game. When Dalkowski got to Triple A, he was ordered to room with a 36-year-old veteran of the minor leagues who had been instructed to "mature the kid" and get him ready for the majors. Things didn't work out for Dalkowski—he was injured during his only major league spring training—so he'll have to settle for being the inspiration for a famous movie character with "a million-dollar arm and a five-cent head."

For Crash, Shelton drew from Mike Ferraro, who had a few cups of coffee in the majors in his early twenties, but spent a career in Triple A, despite having all the tools of a major leaguer. What took so long? He was a third baseman in the Orioles system, and the guy who manned the hot corner in the majors—a fellow by the name of Brooks Robinson—never took a day off. The organization wanted Ferraro to stay sharp and play every day in the minors, so he could be ready in case Robinson got injured. This is all according to Shelton, who claimed that Ferarro was the inspiration for Crash Davis; "not his personality but his dilemma." They were players who deserved their shot in the big leagues, but for whom the organization had other plans.

With his inspiration in mind, Shelton set out to craft a baseball film that audiences had not seen before. There are no tense moments, when the game is on the line. He films a meaningless pop-up, just because. There are no big games at all in *Bull Durham*, which starts after the season has already begun, and it ends before it concludes. This is true to the rhythms of life in the minor leagues, where players routinely skip levels in the middle of the year and a team's roster wildly fluctuates. The end result doesn't matter. Player development does. That's why the organization is willing to send its Triple A catcher down to the lowest level just to help their stud pitching prospect grow up a little.

This rarely authentic portrayal of minor league life is supported by a novel approach to filming the game. "You cannot compete with television," Shelton has said. "The television can put 17 cameras everywhere. Therefore, what the film can do is put this one camera where the television's 17 cameras cannot go, and that includes inside the head of the athlete." He's referring to Crash's inner monologue during that first at-bat, and he also shows us Nuke talking to himself on the mound. Maybe Nuke isn't intelligent enough to have any *inner* monologue at all, but the result is still the same. We see the neurotic anxiety behind the sturdy image of the stoic star athlete. This approach could be seen as a response to the larger-than-life melodrama of *The Natural,* still the gold standard for baseball cinema at this time. These guys weren't heroes or gods. They were just guys.

Shelton also takes us to actual physical places that the TV cameras can't go, like inside the locker room to capture a pregame tryst between Nuke and Millie (Jenny Robertson), the team's resident groupie, as well as a full-squad, postgame ass-chewing by the team's weary manager (Trey Wilson), in which the players are chastised for "lollygagging." We also see what happens on the team bus, where players who are stuck together all day and all night will eventually come to blows, and where the rare minor leaguer who has had his cup of coffee in the majors—in this case, Crash—will regale his young teammates with stories of life in "the show."

I'll single out two moments that showed me, a lifelong baseball fan who has never gotten near the field of professional play, a glimpse of baseball away from the TV cameras. The first is an argument between

Crash and the umpire after what Crash perceives is an incorrect call at home plate. In recent years, internet sleuths have learned how to slow down, zoom in, and read the lips of managers and players arguing with umpires, but in 1988 these conversations represented an unknowable mystery. We would see them standing face-to-face while screaming at each other, with no idea of what was being said. Shelton shows us. Costner starts shouting about the call, and he and the umpire come face-to-face. Costner bumps his chest, and the umpire starts yelling back. Costner cries out: "You just spit on me!" He starts stomping all over the field, lamenting the umpire's "cocksucking call." The umpire dares him to call him that word again. "You want me to call you a cocksucker?" Costner asks, his face inches from the ump. He whispers: "You're a cocksucker!" That's when the umpire tosses him from the game, followed by a cutaway to Millie, listening on the radio while she tries on her wedding dress, who offers the perfect punchline: "He must have called him a cocksucker." We had always heard there were certain words that, when said to an umpire, merited an automatic ejection. Now we know at least one of them.

Then there's the mound visit. For over a century, fans had wondered what is said when players and coaches congregate around a struggling pitcher. *Bull Durham* gives us an idea. The pitcher complains that his father sitting in the front row is making him nervous. The first baseman requests a live chicken sacrifice to get a hex off his glove, and the pitching coach makes some wedding gift suggestions for the unexpected nuptials of Millie to the roster's resident evanglical. If Shelton's gestures toward verisimilitude would have made *Bull Durham* feel at home in the previous decade, his gift for comedy made him a good fit in the '80s, which produced a major film comedy boom. In this decade, stars like Steve Martin, John Candy, Bill Murray, Chevy Chase, and Eddie Murphy—all of whom honed their chops on *Saturday Night Live* or *SCTV*—collaborated with writers, directors, and craftspeople of the 1970s to make some of the funniest and most technically-sound comedies ever made: *Beverly Hills*

Cop, Fletch, Ghostbusters, Stripes, and *Planes, Trains, and Automobiles. Bull Durham* is as funny, smart, and well-made as any of them.

The secret of *Bull Durham's* success is the blend of Shelton's fresh comic voice with his real-world experience. In some cases, Shelton simply put the stories he remembered from his time in the minor leagues right up on the silver screen without alteration. The portrayal of a Latino player who is devoted to voodoo might seem politically incorrect today, but it was a real phenomenon. "I knew a lot of ballplayers from the Caribbean who were involved in voodoo and various forms of witchcraft," he has said. "On Puerto Rican baseball teams, the 25th roster spot was for a witch." This explains why there was a similar character—Pedro Cerrano—in *Major League.* It's not racism. It's reality. He also claimed to have known a religious player who married a "Baseball Annie," which is ballplayer lingo for the women who hang out around the team to sleep with the players. (The character named Annie Savoy is a nod to it.) And that brainstorm of Crash's in which he floods a field in order to secure a rainout the next day? Shelton actually pulled it off, although he picked the wrong location. "A night off in Amarillo is worse than playing a doubleheader," he joked, "because there's nothing to do in Amarillo."

Not all of the reality was played for laughs. Another moment we'd never seen in a baseball film before comes early in the film when the Bulls manager calls a player into his office and informs him of his release. It's excruciating. The player tries to talk his way out of it ("I hit the ball hard today!") like a teenage boy getting dumped by his dream girl. It's the moment every ballplayer fears, not just for the shame of being fired but for the sudden end of an entire way of life. Most ballplayers wake up every morning thinking about the game. Being prepared to perform on the field is the driving force that shapes their diets, their exercise routines, their sleep patterns, where they live, who their friends are. They refer to being cut as "dying." Life, as they know it, is over. You can see why this player reacts the way he does, moving from desperate pleas to throwing a chair around the room in anger, and it makes Crash's reaction when he eventually gets cut—resigned acceptance—even more poignant.

Michael "Kip" Coons, a sportswriter for the *Durham Herald-Sun* in the late 1980s, had a clear view of how this moment resonated with the players. He had a non-speaking role as a journalist in the film, but his strongest memory of the entire experience was from the premiere. "We're in the Carolina Theater in Durham, and the team the Bulls were playing that weekend were invited along with the Bulls. They're all having a good time and joking around. We get to the scene in which the player is released, and you could have heard a pin drop. Every player in the theater recognized at the same time, 'That could be me tomorrow.'" It's like a slasher movie for ballplayers. A gruesome murder that comes out of nowhere. Other baseball filmmakers must have been struck by the incomparable drama of this scenario, as similar scenes were used in *Major League II* and *Little Big League*, where reluctant managers are forced to cut beloved veterans, and the players are devastated.

It's a testament to the charms of *Bull Durham* that the film's melancholia over the painful losses of middle-age doesn't derail what is ultimately a very good time. For that, much credit must go to the actors, even Tim Robbins, who looks and moves nothing like a major league pitcher but creates a compelling human being out of what was surely a cartoonish character on the page. His failures in portraying an athlete are well-established. According to Bill Miller, the assistant general manager and groundskeeper of the real-life Bulls, "The guy was almost hopeless on the mound. The first time I saw him try to pitch, he sort of stood behind the mound, took a couple of steps up, and launched himself off the rubber as if he were throwing a shotput." Miller says special foam baseballs were created for him because he "hit some people he wasn't supposed to." Even after working on it for a while, Robbins' pitching motion looks unorthodox at best. It seems like Shelton and Robbins were going for some blend of Fernando Valenzuela and Luis Tiant, but it's just as likely they would settle for anything to distract the audience from Robbins' lack of coordination. It's a clever bit of misdirection, as a wild delivery is harder to criticize for a lack of realism.

Costner, on the other hand, needed no such tricks. He wasn't Gary Cooper, who trained for weeks just to barely pass the eye test. When

Shelton was first shopping the script around, Costner took him out to the batting cages in Van Nuys, California to convince the former minor leaguer that he had the chops to play Crash. Consider us convinced. Costner is perhaps the most realistic ballplayer ever put on screen. He has the athletic physique and the grizzled good looks. He has a good sense of humor, but he doesn't go cracking jokes all the time. Costner has an inherent flatness that can pass for stoicism or maybe even wisdom. These are the same qualities that he would employ in *Dances With Wolves* a few years later, and in the many, many westerns he would later make. Shelton saw all this in Costner, who had just played a gunslinger in 1985's *Silverado*. "I thought of [Crash] as a man without a past, without a home, without a town," said Shelton in a commentary track for the film, "and a man who goes from town to town looking for a fight wherever they'll pay him to ply his trade. That cynicism, romanticism, and mean streak his character has, and that Kevin so wonderfully portrays, is really that of the archetypal American hero." This characterization pays off in the film's funniest scene, when Crash and Nuke face off in a duel behind the bar, and Crash challenges the youngster to hit him in the chest with a baseball. It might as well be set on a dusty street next to an old saloon. "If this was the 1880s," Shelton said, "they'd have guns."

Westerns and baseball movies are both traditionally male-driven genres, so maybe the most subversive thing about *Bull Durham* is the agency it offers its women. Shelton claims his initial goal for the film was to write about sexual liberation from a female perspective. There was no better choice to play Annie Savoy than Susan Sarandon, who forged a new kind of acting career for women in the '70s and '80s by centering her sexuality without sacrificing her strength or intelligence. She started with the *Rocky Horror Picture Show*, then moved on to the erotic lesbian vampire movie *The Hunger* and, in the year before *Bull Durham*, starred in the Biblically tinged sex comedy *The Witches of Eastwick*. In each one, Sarandon plays a variation of the same role: a timid, pre-feminist bookworm who is sexually awakened through an encounter with an otherworldly being, and eventually learns the advantages and the limits of her new lifestyle.

That's not Annie Savoy, who is grown up, fully formed, and preternaturally confident in her sexuality. She sees her job as not only satisfying each player's carnal desire but also enriching him with poetry, music, and even spirituality. She makes them better people. She's also the film's voice, narrating its opening and closing moments with her thoughts on the sanctity of the game. Because this is in many ways Annie's story, her values permeate the film. Karina Longworth, who spent a season of her film podcast *You Must Remember This* on the erotic films of the 1980s, is fascinated by *Bull Durham*'s sexual politics, particularly its appreciation for male bodies. "You see Tim Robbins' butt before you see his face," she points out. She also draws attention to the scene in which Costner's character is cut from the team while wearing the skimpiest of towels. "There may not be much baseball left in his body," she jokes, "but the body is something else." It's also worth lingering on the brief moment when, after Annie invites both Crash and Nuke to her house, the guys assume it's for a threesome. No homophobia invades their thinking, as you might expect from two jocks playing in perhaps the most culturally conservative sport. Instead, Crash winks at Nuke, and the trio heads back to Annie's place. The misogyny and homophobia that creeps into many baseball films—and most other films—of the 1980s is hard to find in *Bull Durham*.

Then there's the language. Never before have a film's baseball players talked so openly about sex. "I believe in the soul, the cock, the pussy," says Crash in his famous speech. Sex is constantly referred to as "fucking," rarely with a euphemism. In *Bull Durham*, sex is many things: an act of pure lust, a training tool, a warmup routine, a way to protect yourself, a way to make yourself vulnerable. Longworth points out that the sex scenes are actually rather tame, but the film was still marketed as an adult movie and given an R rating by the MPAA's Ratings Board. "The rating comes almost entirely from the dialogue." Shelton's words are lurid—and often florid—but they serve his thoughtful approach to gender equality.

Sexual oppression lives in the shadows, and when the realities of sexual dynamics are exposed to the light of day, women have a far better chance to create a level playing field.

Of course, *Bull Durham* might also have received its R rating simply because it showed two women—Annie and Millie—who have multiple sexual partners at the same time. The MPAA is famously conservative when it comes to sex. Kirby Dick's landmark 2006 documentary *This Film is Not Yet Rated* detailed how easily the board tolerates blood, guts, and gore, while even the slightest bit of explicit sex typically earns an R rating. The board seems particularly concerned about portrayals of female pleasure. The surest way to an R is to portray a female orgasm onscreen.

I'm not sure we ever see one in *Bull Durham*, but it's certainly implied. Crash, unlike Nuke, knows how to please a lady. What we do see is a single, working woman choosing her own sexual partners, talking frankly about her sexual desires ("I want you," she tells Crash plainly), and never once apologizing for either of them. "There's a gender-swapped way they look at sex," said Ellen Adair. "For Crash, it's a matter of the heart, and for her, it's just something humans do for fun. It's another thing the film does really well, not making things cut and dry in its gender lines." The film never once condemns Annie as a groupie or a slut—the words are never uttered, not even about Millie—and even when the script requires her to settle down with Crash and support him on his next adventure as a manager (and for Millie to surprisingly and suddenly marry the team's resident Christian), it doesn't paint this decision as a correction to her days of carousing. She just fell in love, that's all. *Bull Durham* is too kind to punish its character for their politics. It respects Annie because she respects the game. Whether she's sleeping with the stud pitcher or married to a minor-league manager, her love of baseball never falters. That's the real secret of *Bull Durham*'s success. It loves the game, and offers its secrets, its beauty, and its inherent silliness as a gift to anyone else who does.

Chapter 11

A League of Their Own (1992)

Just like *Bull Durham*, *A League of Their Own* makes a point of showing us a meaningless pop-up, but the context changes its meaning. Let me set the scene: The Rockford Peaches have just been informed by Ira Lowenstein (David Strathairn), publicist for the All-American Professional Girls Baseball League, that the league will be shut down before season's end if their sagging attendance does not increase. The players are devastated, but it's not over for them yet. Lowenstein has lured a photographer from *Life* magazine to the game. He pleads with the girls to do something special that day.

Catcher Dottie Hinson (Geena Davis) hears him loud and clear. Tracking a foul pop-up behind the plate, she does the splits at the last moment and catches the ball while splayed out on the ground, her already-short skirt riding further up her legs. The photographer snaps a photo and puts it on the cover. Attendance begins to skyrocket. Although the result of the play is the same as it was in *Bull Durham*—an out—the comparison tells you much about what *A League of Their Own* has in mind. Women aren't allowed to just be ballplayers. They have to work twice as hard as their male counterparts. To satisfy the public, they have to turn even a routine play into something sensational.

Taken together, *A League of Their Own* and *Bull Durham* represent the apex of the baseball movie genre for how they tell stories about people who had long been relegated to the sidelines in baseball cinema—women and minor leaguers—with incredible craft, great humor, and strong baseball acumen. Due to their outsider status, the women and minor leaguers of baseball cinema have a shared experience that is deeply divergent from life for the men in the majors. They get paid next to nothing. They take long bus rides to the opponent's stadiums instead of private planes. Their facilities are subpar at best. The showers are disgusting, and the dugout is basically just a hole in the ground. These gritty details enliven a genre that often relies on convention, but they also make the characters more relatable. For most of us, it takes a major leap of imagination to stand in the shoes of Lou Gehrig or Roy Hobbs. They're gods who walk among us, or at least near us. But Crash Davis is an old, broken-down veteran on the verge of baseball death, which makes him human, and the women of *A League of Their Own* are even more sympathetic. They never dreamed they'd even have a shot to play professional baseball, under the lights and before a cheering crowd, which makes them ideal surrogates for 99 percent of viewers.

Making a baseball film about women might have felt revolutionary at the time, but looking back, it was kind of inevitable. The line from erasure to representation for women in baseball cinema was relatively straight. In the 1930s, there were several attempts to put female stars on the big-screen baseball diamond, but, with good reason, few are remembered. 1937's *Girls Can Play* is about a women's team that serves as a front for the owner's bootleg liquor business. The players are chosen solely for their looks, and in the end, the owner's girlfriend (a young Rita Hayworth) is fatally poisoned because she has witnessed his illicit activity. There are also short films from the same era, like *Gracie at the Bat* and *Fancy Curves*, that feature sexist and unfunny tropes, like players who powder their noses in the dugout. Ain't women silly? In the postwar era and beyond, women were typically framed as supportive wives, like Eleanor Gehrig or Ethel Stratton, whose roles were largely defined in relation to their husbands; the more emotional support they offered, the better wives they were. Elsewhere, the women of baseball cinema are laughed at or diminished for their relative ignorance of the game; see Katharine Hepburn in *Woman of the Year* or Janet Leigh in *Angels in the Outfield*. Susan Slusser, longtime beat writer for the A's and Giants, and first female president of the Baseball Writers' Association of America, explains, "The trope is that the girls are just the moms and the girlfriends. They're the love interests. They're the thing the two players are fighting over. They're the reporter slipping a player her number. Support the player or seduce the player, that's pretty much all they were allowed to do."

The first crack in the baseball movie's glass ceiling came when Tatum O'Neal showed up in *The Bad News Bears* and almost stole the movie out from under Walter Matthau. Says Slusser, "That was the first time I thought women could play baseball and excel at it. She's the second-best player on the team after Kelly Leak, and she also manages to be super cool." Still, when the male Boomer directors of the 1980s dabbled in second-wave feminism within the genre, the progress came with caveats. As mentioned, *Field of Dreams* featured Amy Madigan as a feisty wife who stands up to small town fascists, but the film eventually disempowers her, slotting her into the role of a supportive wife who encourages her husband to chase his crazy dreams. Annie in *Bull Durham* gets a similar treatment. A product of the sexual revolution, she's a single, sexually liberated 40ish woman with a career of her own and an impressive knowledge of the game. Yet the film ultimately relegates her to the same submissive position as most of her predecessors. Her last words in the film are spoken while sitting on a small-town porch swing, encouraging Crash Davis to chase yet another dream, this one of being a minor league manager. "You'll be great," she says, looking up at him with wide, eager eyes. It's like the '60s never happened.

There's also the curious case of 1983's *Blue Skies Again*, which starred Robyn Barto, an unknown actor, as a die-hard fan of the fictional Denver Devils who travels to spring training in Florida to seek a try-out with the big-league team. Don't be surprised that you haven't heard of it. *Blue Skies Again* is out of print on all physical media and isn't available to stream. It looks more like a TV movie than anything you'd see on a big screen, and its story is thoroughly predictable, which, to be fair, isn't usually a deal-breaker for fans of baseball movies. But it's also more honest about the trials of a woman in baseball than you might expect for its time. As soon as the main character sets foot on the field, her potential teammates let rip with the misogyny. One jokes that he'd "like to take a shower with her." When she's at the plate, another yells, "The bitch can't hit!" *Blue Skies Again* eventually arrives at its preordained, feel-good ending, but there are gems of insight buried within. Unfortunately, they stayed buried; the film made less than $1 million at the box office and was never heard from again.

The most important women's movie of this era wasn't a baseball movie at all, even though it brought together the lead actresses from *Bull Durham* and *A League of Their Own*. 1991's *Thelma and Louise*, starring Sarandon and Davis as friends who go on the run from the authorities after they murder an attempted rapist, sent ripples of excitement through Hollywood. Its unapologetically female spin on a familiar story of outlaws in the American West made a tidy $45 million at the box office and earned an Oscar for its screenplay, as well as Best Actress nominations for both its stars and a bevy of articles suggesting Hollywood was entering a new era for woman-driven stories. Beyond Hollywood, there was reason to believe the culture was ready for a renaissance of films centered on thriving, independent women. In 1990, the average age of marriage in America rose for the first time to 24. Women were pursuing higher education and joining the workforce in higher numbers than ever; by 1995, the gender gap in education "essentially disappeared for the younger generation," according to a report by the National Center for Education Statistics. In 1992, Hillary Clinton became a more substantial First Lady than the country had seen in some time; during her husband's campaign, Bill stressed Hillary's importance to the ticket and sold his candidacy as a "two for one deal." Once elected, he appointed Janet Reno as the first woman secretary of state. The decade would also see the first woman president of an Ivy League institution (Judith Rodin—Penn) and CEO of a Fortune 100 company (Carly Fiorina—Hewlett-Packard).

With the success of *Thelma and Louise* confirming that audiences were hungry for stories about women in male-dominated settings, and the recent run of successful baseball films that began with *The Natural* still going strong, *A League of Their Own* was an idea whose time had come. Released in the summer of 1992, it generated pre-release buzz not just from its uncovering of a mostly forgotten historical event but also from its exciting roster of talent in front of and behind the camera. The story of the All-American Girls Professional Baseball League was first optioned for a film by director Penny Marshall, coming off her box-office smash *Big* and the Oscar-nominated *Awakenings*. Screenwriters Lowell Ganz and Babaloo Mandel, who had just had their biggest hit with the Billy Crystal–starring *City Slickers*, were commissioned to write it. The casting process was a little more involved. With so many meaningful parts for women in the script, the audition process was mayhem. "Every woman in Hollywood was reading for this movie," Lori Petty, who plays Kit, said in an oral history on the film. "It was a strong female movie, which, you know, we don't have now, and we didn't have in 1991 either. I mean, Marla Maples auditioned, for Christ's sake."

Two thousand actresses reportedly showed up to the initial audition, held on the fields of University of Southern California under the watchful eye of USC baseball coach Rod Dedeaux. In addition to Maples, performers as varied as comedian Paula Poundstone and model-turned-actress Brooke Shields were on the field, taking batting practice and getting dirty on the infield. In order to do justice to the real-life trailblazers (and perhaps knowing that male baseball fans would be looking for any excuse to discredit the film), the producers focused exclusively on women who could hold their own on a ballfield. Tea Leoni tried out and ended up being cast in a non-speaking role as a member of the Racine Belles, where all she did was play. Marisa Tomei sent an audition tape—produced during the filming of *My Cousin Vinny*—that included a display of her baseball skills, but Marshall decided she just wasn't believable as a ballplayer. "There were some great actors there that couldn't play," Marshall told Rosie O'Donnell, when reminiscing about the film on her talk show. "One came in ballet slippers, and you can't... come on."

It's worth noting the double standard. For many years, male stars were cast in baseball films without demonstrating any ability to play the game. Gary Cooper had to learn how to swing a bat, and even then, the filmmakers needed to employ archival footage and stunt doubles just to complete the illusion. Anthony Perkins could barely play catch. The women of *A League of Their Own*, on the other hand, had to prove they could credibly compete on a baseball field before even being considered for a role.

But Marshall's commitment to high-level athleticism paid off. The action on the field in *A League of Their Own* is just spectacular, particularly in the film's try-out scene at Wrigley Field, which must have mirrored the offscreen try-outs at USC in featuring a large group of young, athletic women fighting for their big break. When you factor in our lowered expectations—not because they're women, but because they're non-professionals—this montage contains some of the most realistic baseball action in any movie. Dottie's throw to second base from behind the dish is on the money, and the sequence of shortstops fielding ground balls and making snap throws to first could have them confused for major leaguers. Still, the player that impresses me every time I watch it is the anonymous outfielder, who, in tracking a fly ball, picks it up off the bat and then puts her head down and sprints to a spot near the fence, where she makes a leaping grab. An amateur would drift back on the ball and likely watch it sail over their head, but this particular background actor plays like an All-Star.

This baseball realism, however, is merely the foundation for the film's deeper success. *A League of Their Own* seamlessly integrates thrilling on-field action with interpersonal drama better than any other baseball film. Its story of competition and jealousy between two sisters, Dottie and Kit, could really have been told in any setting and still be effective. The characters are drawn with that much care and specificity. As written and performed, it's easy to see how their distinct personalities have developed in opposition to each other; Dottie, the natural beauty, world-class athlete, and devoted wife, has had everything come easy. Kit, her diminutive sister, has developed a fierce competitiveness from having to keep up with her beautiful big sister. When watching them interact, you feel deep familial love, as well as a sense that they will never be able to peacefully coexist.

The casting is immaculate; even when milking a cow and wearing an apron, Davis has the effortless beauty of a supermodel, while Petty, whose schoolgirl haircut was surely designed to hide the fact that she was 28 at the time of shooting, vacillates between wide-eyed enthusiasm and fiery anger, like a kid who was never given room to grow up. Dottie was the perfect role for an ascendant star like Davis, coming off an Oscar win for her supporting role in 1988's *The Accidental Tourist* and the success of *Thelma and Louise*. Petty's career was also on the rise. Although she wasn't on the same star trajectory as Davis, her roles leading up to *A League of Their Own* paved the way for her performance as Kit. The year prior, she starred in *Point Break* as the lone woman in a group of macho male surfers, including Keanu Reeves and Patrick Swayze. Petty was developing a reputation for playing athletes and tomboys, while holding her own against major stars.

Another actor whom the film caught at precisely the right time is Tom Hanks, whose natural charisma and balance of comedic and dramatic chops enriches the character of Jimmy Dugan, the drunkard ex-major leaguer who reluctantly agrees to manage the Peaches. Dugan is a surrogate for skeptical male viewers who will be nodding along when he shouts, "I haven't got ballplayers, I've got girls!" Of course, they will also likely find themselves in lockstep with Dugan when he is won over by the players' grit, resilience, baseball knowledge, and skill. It might seem strange in retrospect to see Hanks in a supporting role, but at the time he needed the film as much as it needed him. He was coming off an unfairly-maligned pair of comic flops—*The 'Burbs* and *Joe vs. the Volcano*—and one fairly-maligned one, the legendary 1990 disaster *Bonfire of the Vanities*. His swerve into serious acting with *Philadelphia* and *Forrest Gump* was still a year away. *A League of Their Own* bridges the gap. Hanks proves adept at the physical comedy, particularly in his half-conscious smooch with Miss Cuthbert and his hilarious attempts to stifle his anger while relaying the importance of hitting the cutoff man to right fielder Evelyn (Bitty Schram), but his dramatic work is just as crucial in establishing the film's tone and themes. The seriousness with which he delivers the news of the death of Betty's husband shows how Jimmy has come to respect the women who play for him. In the crushing scene, he drops his sarcastic facade and embraces her in a fatherly hug.

His quiet heart-to-hearts with Davis, both on the bus and in the driveway before she leaves the team before the big game, are in many ways the most important scenes in the film. Dottie's transformation from seeing baseball as a lark—something she's doing for her sister, or as an opportunity to have fun before she settles down for the real work of popping out babies—to a crucial part of her identity reflects the film's central assertion that creating space for women to do the things they're passionate about, including raising a family, has value. Hanks' supporting (in the truest sense of the word) performance plays a large part in dramatizing that idea.

It seems wrong, however, to spend too much time on Hanks, when the film's soul, ethos, and commercial success hinges on its deep roster of women. One of the best decisions made by the filmmakers was to reject the old, male conventions of baseball cinema and instead create new archetypes more tethered to the female experience. *Blue Skies Again* tried to insert a woman into a man's world. *A League of Their Own* shows us a baseball league of, ya know, their own. In other baseball movies, there's the cocky pitcher and the grizzled catcher. There's the Christian guy. The womanizer. The superstitious guy. The one who's into voodoo. If *A League of Their Own* had simply imposed those templates onto the Peaches, it would only have been a men's story dressed up in a woman's uniform.

Marshall, the first woman to direct a sports movie since 1951 (when Ida Lupino helmed the tennis drama *Hard, Fast and Beautiful!*), honored the players of the AAGPBL by creating characters that reflect the experiences of women in that time period, while never sacrificing the universality that makes them relatable in 1991. There's a promiscuous one, "All the Way Mae," played effectively by Madonna, although part of me still wonders what Marisa Tomei would have done with the role. There's a beauty queen (Ellen Sue Gotlander, played by Freddie Simpson) and a harried mom (Evelyn Gardner, played by Bitty Schram). These are tropes, not three-dimensional characters, but there is one for every young girl to emulate. Jessica Mendoza, an Olympian softball player and the first woman to serve as an analyst for nationally televised baseball games, grew up revering the film for this very reason. "I can't remember the first time I watched it because I watched it so many times. Literally, hundreds and hundreds of times." To Mendoza, who spoke about the film's influence on her on the *This Movie Changed Me* podcast, the depth and diversity of the Peaches' roster was revelatory. "I learned that being a woman isn't defined by one thing. A lot of times in media and motion pictures, women are portrayed as beautiful, a specific body type, very humble, very kind, and very sweet. It's similar across the board. When I saw *A League of Their Own*, I learned that a woman can be a Doris with a bigger body. She can be 'All the Way Mae,' and say, 'I'm going to be rebellious, and I like boys, and I'm gonna kiss them when I want, even during a baseball game.' We're complicated, and we don't belong in one box."

There's one unfortunate exception to the film's otherwise unimpeachable feminism. Her name is Marla Hooch. In an early newsreel sequence, each Peach gets a close-up, while the announcer rattles off her hobbies and relationship status as if she's a *Playboy* centerfold. When he gets to Marla, she is filmed in a wide shot so we can barely make out her face. "What a hitter!" he says. Viewed generously, the visual gag could be considered commentary on how the league favored women who were conventionally attractive, except the rest of the film doesn't treat Marla much better. In the sequence set at finishing school, the instructor gets a big laugh at her expense. "What do you recommend?" her assistant asks, while the two are assessing the players' faces and offering grooming tips. "A lot of night games," she cracks.

The biggest wound the film inflicts on Marla, oddly enough, is in the happy ending it contrives for her. She meets and falls for Nelson (Alan Wilder) at a roadhouse. The two begin courting over romantic letters and quickly decide to get married. The next thing we see is Marla driving off with Nelson, waving goodbye to her teammates, and promising to return next season. This is cruelty disguised as kindness. When Dottie decides to leave just before the World Series to return to Oregon with her husband, the film criticizes her for it. She redeems herself by returning. But the film suggests Marla is so lucky to have found a husband that it's fine for her to leave in the middle of the season. "She loves to play," her father tells the scout in her first scene. The film ignores what she loves and gives her what she's supposed to want, suggesting that, for homely women, getting married is the ultimate goal.

It's the lone blemish on a film that otherwise shines in its nuanced portrayal of its women, who are captured doing something many young female viewers had never seen women do onscreen: standing up for themselves. Once these players get a taste of equality, they don't let it go. An entire generation was taking notes. Writing for *The Cut* on the occasion of Marshall's death in 2018, Seyward Darby said, "*A League of Their Own* was my unwitting introduction to feminism, a word I didn't have in my fourth-grade vocabulary. The notion of women unapologetically doing things they weren't supposed to do was revelatory. Here were dirty, sweaty women playing their hearts out in skirts foisted upon them by the patriarchy—another word I didn't know but would in time." She went on: "They were talented, passionate, and demonstrative." They acted sad when they felt sad, angry when they felt angry, even lustful when they felt lustful. I wanted to be friends with them. I wanted to *be* them."

Although the core images of women playing baseball were surely enough to inspire young girls everywhere, the film's effectiveness as a drama is what elevates it as a baseball film. Its iconic climax, when the ongoing feud between Dottie and Kit reaches its heart-stopping conclusion, is formed by all we know about the characters and their history. Kit has been traded to Racine, a roster move orchestrated by Ira Lowenstein to keep Dottie from leaving the league altogether, after she and Kit have a major blowout. Now Racine and Rockford are facing each other in the World Series. Dottie's husband (Bill Pullman) has returned from war, and the two were on the road to Oregon, but Dottie convinces him to return at the last minute, finally listening to the side of herself that wants to be more than a wife and a mother. She has a lifetime of domestication ahead of her, but today she's a ballplayer.

It's a close game. In the top of the ninth inning, Racine is up by a run, one out away from a championship. Dottie strides to the plate. Kit is on the mound. As they face each other, the score by Hans Zimmer introduces a lone trumpet that recalls famed composer Ennio Morricone's scores for Spaghetti westerns. It's a stand-off that draws on classic male tropes, but the moment's power comes from its femininity. The attention to the characters' emotional lives—with a few exceptions, largely non-existent in male baseball movies—pays off in an unbearable tension, and it's entirely believable when, after Dottie gives Rockford the lead with a hard-hit single up on the middle, Kit has an absolute meltdown in the dugout, crying into her glove and shaking with emotion.

Now it's the bottom of the ninth, and Racine is down to their last out. Kit strides to the plate with a runner on first. It will either be her redemption or a knockout punch from which she may never recover. It feels like her life is on the line. Dottie barely even looks at her. She knows her sister's weaknesses. "High fastballs," she tells pitcher Ellen Sue in a mound conference. "Can't hit 'em, can't lay off 'em." Kit swings through the first two but sends the third into the right-field gap, scoring one run and tying the game, and it looks like Kit will be in for a stand-up triple and we'll be going to extra innings, but wait, hey now, she's not stopping, she is not stopping, she's going to try to score! The throw is in, and here comes Kit, she barrels into Hinson, and...

"Hinson dropped the ball! Hinson dropped the ball!"

So says the play-by-play announcer, thus initiating one of the most important unsolved mysteries in movie history. Arguing about movies is good sport, and perhaps it's more fun to debate this one than to solve it. Each side has a strong case. Those who believe Dottie dropped the ball intentionally will point to the film's early scene in which the older Dottie, on her way to the Hall of Fame, encourages her grandson to go easy on his younger brother in their driveway basketball game, perhaps intimating that she did the same thing several decades prior against her sister. Others will note the costume design in the scene after the big game when Dottie bumps into Kit outside the clubhouse. Kit is still in her yellow Racine uniform, while Dottie is in street clothes, wearing a blouse in the exact same shade. It's almost as if she was secretly playing for Racine.

The counterargument, of course, is every single thing that happened in the game up to that moment. Dottie decided on her own to come back and play, and she displayed a killer instinct for all nine innings. Just moments before the collision at home plate, she gave her pitcher crucial information to get her sister out. To be clear, if Kit struck out there, it would have crushed her spirit, and maybe even ruined her life. Dottie didn't care. She wanted to win. It's very hard to believe she changed her mind while Kit was running the bases, although sometimes we don't know what we really believe until we're forced to decide, like when a full-grown woman carrying 20 years of suppressed rage is barreling down the third-base line at you. It's the first time in the film—since they raced each other to the barn in an early scene—that the two of them are facing off. In the end, what Dottie tells her afterward might very well be the closest we get to the truth: "You wanted it more than me." The simplicity of that statement covers all kinds of conscious and subconscious motivations.

The endless debate over whether Dottie dropped the ball on purpose has helped keep *A League of Their Own* alive in the public discourse. For that reason, it matters. The truth, however, is that there is no right answer because we're asking the wrong question. It's not important whether she intended to drop the ball. What matters is why the film needs her to. Throughout the film, Dottie is conflicted between being a housewife or a ballplayer. To some degree, it's the conflict within all the players, and the film rightly passes no judgment either way. Marla and Dottie leave the team for their husbands. Other characters stay with baseball for as long as they can, and being a ballplayer becomes their identity. In his perceptive review, Roger Ebert credits this nonjudgmental approach to its woman director: "A man might have assumed that these women knew how all-important baseball was. Marshall shows her women characters in a tug-of-war between new images and old values, and so her movie is about transition—about how it felt as a woman suddenly to have new roles and freedom."

When Dottie drops the ball, it indicates to the viewer that she will not choose baseball. Despite her love of the game, she will not abandon her dreams of motherhood for it. Nearly a century later, we know that women can be professionals and wives and mothers all at once, but at this moment of new images and old values, Dottie can't see that. She feels like she must choose one or the other—perhaps watching Evelyn try to blend the two by bringing her monstrous child Stilwell to work dissuaded her from attempting to have it all. When the ball slides out of her hand, she is showing us who she is and what she cares about, intentionally or not. It allows her to return home, and for Kit to stay and continue forging her new identity. Did Dottie drop the ball on purpose? It doesn't matter. She had to drop the ball—to literally let go of baseball—or the movie doesn't make sense.

Despite its thoughtful portrayal of the ongoing dilemma for women in the workplace, its showcasing of talented actresses, and the incredible excitement it generated in young girls, *A League of Their Own* didn't bring about the immediate revolution in female-led stories that many hoped it would. It was beloved by audiences (with a $107 million domestic gross, it was the seventh-biggest hit of the year) but wasn't accepted by the largely male gatekeepers. It didn't make a dent at the Oscars. The Academy went nuts for *Field of Dreams* a few years prior, but they couldn't find a single place to honor *A League of Their Own.* Instead, it made do with a lone Golden Globe nomination (Davis for Best Actor—Musical or Comedy) and a trio of nominations at the MTV Movie Awards, which, with their focus on young viewers, sometimes do a better job of identifying the cultural artifacts that live on in our collective imagination. In 1993, MTV nominated *A League of Their Own* for Best Female Performance (Geena Davis), Best Breakthrough Performance (Rosie O'Donnell), and Best Kiss for the comic smooch between Hanks and Pauline Brailsford, who plays the team chaperone.

For years, it was rarely mentioned in public discussions of the best baseball movies, but somewhere in the mid-2010s, this began to change. Women journalists and athletes, like Jessica Mendoza, who were inspired by the film as children, began championing it in the press. The #MeToo revolution encouraged media outlets specializing in both sports and pop culture to hire more women and, in many cases, actually listen to them. *USA Today* placed it at 24th in their 2015 ranking of film's greatest sports films. That's a decent showing, but it had further to climb. In 2019, *Vulture* ranked it the ninth-best sports movie of all time, just between *Slap Shot* and *Ali*. In 2020, *Chicago Tribune* slotted it in at fourth. Even *Men's Health* found room for it in the top ten list they published that same year. It's hard to imagine stronger evidence that *A League of Their Own* has been accepted into the baseball canon.

Its real legacy, however, is on the silver screen. Hollywood is an industry of imitators, and it's easy to see how *A League of Their Own* gave studio executives the confidence to take a chance on other projects about female athletes, like *Bend it Like Beckham,* the roller-derby comedy *Whip It,* or *Love and Basketball*, about a young athlete's journey to the WNBA. Here in the first quarter of the 21st century, there are more women in front of and behind the camera than ever before. Hollywood has been making "women's pictures" since the beginning, albeit with very large gaps in the timeline, but the commercial success and the enduring legacy of *A League of Their Own* in a genre once defined solely by its maleness has permanently redefined what a movie—not just a sports movie, and certainly not only a baseball movie—can be.

Bathroom Break No. 2
Is *The Naked Gun* a Baseball Movie?
An Investigation

What is a baseball movie? It's a question I should probably have a good answer for, but it's harder to figure out than you might think. We could measure it by the amount of actual baseball played in the movie, but then *Field of Dreams* probably wouldn't count. We could go by whether the filmed baseball actually moves the plot forward, but we'd have to ditch *Pride of the Yankees*, in which Lou Gehrig's exploits are a given and no game has an outcome that matters. We could just cast a wide net and count any film that revolves around baseball at all, even those without significant baseball action, but then we'd have to include *Night Game,* a 1989 thriller about a cop chasing a serial killer who kills sex workers only on days that a certain Houston Astro is pitching. I'm not prepared to do that.

The Naked Gun: From the Files of Police Squad! proves a fascinating case. Baseball is barely even mentioned for the first hour. The plot certainly doesn't revolve around it. And yet the entire final third takes place during a game between the California Angels and Seattle Mariners. Lieutenant Frank Drebin (Leslie Nielsen) has learned that the Queen of England is to be assassinated at an Angels game by a brainwashed player (this part of the film is a loose spoof of

177

The Manchurian Candidate), so he devises a plan to sneak onto the field to check the players for weapons during the game. Initially, he takes the place of Enrico Pallazzo, an Italian opera singer set to sing the national anthem. After bumbling through the song ("And the rockets' red glare…bunch of bombs in the air"), he switches costumes, disguising himself as the home plate umpire, and sets about frisking every player he can get near.

Shot at Dodger Stadium, it's a bravura comic set piece, in which director David Zucker displaying a solid understanding of the game. To mock something well, you have to love it, and *The Naked Gun* loves every part of baseball. A scoreboard blooper reel escalates from comical mishaps to absurd tragedies in which one player gets run over by a car on the field, another gets mauled by a tiger, and an outfielder's head falls off while tracking a fly ball. Drebin checks the pitcher for illegal substances and finds a power sander in his pocket and a jar of Vaseline under his hat—then lets him off with a warning. He dusts the dirt off home plate with a Dustbuster and then a vacuum. The film even spoofs the phenomenon of the ever-expanding broadcast booth, with Mel Allen, Curt Gowdy, Tim McCarver, Jim Palmer, Dick Vitale, Dick Enberg, and, presumably to provide a psychological analysis of the players, Dr. Joyce Brothers, all seated in front of microphones.

It all builds to an ingenious sequence in which Drebin is forced to use his power as home plate umpire to prolong the inning. He knows the assassination is due to occur during the seventh inning stretch, so he pulls out all the stops to keep the third out from occurring. He calls balls on obvious strikes, and when that fails and the batter swings and pops one up at the plate, Drebin throws two handfuls of balls into the air, confusing the catcher, who cowers as they rain down on him. The play goes on, though, and Drebin has to run out to second base to continue the disruption. He gets involved in a rundown, eventually tossing the ball back and forth with the runner, while the fielder gets between them and tries to catch it. Even The Bad News Bears never played this badly.

The centrality of the umpire makes *The Naked Gun* a special case. Rarely does an umpire figure prominently into a baseball film, despite their importance to the game as both arbitrators of the play and villains in the minds of the fans. An exception is 1950's *Kill the Umpire*, featuring William Bendix (fresh off his starring turn in *The Babe Ruth Story*) as an idiot fan who loses several jobs over his obsession with baseball. He has a hatred for umpires, but after having been out of work for some time, he takes a job as one to support his family. Once he becomes an umpire, he learns, hey, it's not so easy! *Kill the Umpire* is a broad, unremarkable film, but at least it's more realistic than having Bendix play a teenaged Babe Ruth.

Other than that, umpires mostly stay out of baseball films. Even when they do appear, they somehow recede into the background. We all remember Crash Davis arguing a call at home plate with the umpire, who throws him out after Crash calls him a word that crosses the line. I have no idea if the call was correct, but we're predisposed to agree with Crash, because he's a player; the players are our heroes, which makes the umpires the villains. The same goes for the first base umpire in *Little Big League*, who gets called all kinds of dirty words by a 12-year-old manager on a power trip yet somehow comes off like the bigger jerk. Umpires are never the protagonist, and we're trained to side with the protagonist. In *A League of Their Own*, one gets told he looks like "a penis with a little hat on." Again, it's rude, and the umpire was only trying to help by encouraging Jimmy Dugan to be nice to the women on his team, but somehow we come out of it thinking the ump deserved the insult.

That's why *The Naked Gun* is so revelatory: It makes the umpire—a mostly reviled figure throughout baseball history—a relatable protagonist. For me, the highlight of the entire sequence comes when Drebin first steps behind the plate to call balls and strikes. Entirely unprepared, he pauses a long beat after the first pitch whizzes into the strike zone, then tentatively puts his hand up and says meekly, "Strike?" The crowd roars its approval. On the next pitch, he amps up his strike call ("Steeeeerike two!") and turns around to bow to the crowd. Drunk on power, he calls the third strike before the pitch even passes through the zone and breaks into a moonwalk to celebrate.

If you're reading this book, you probably dreamed of being a ballplayer when you were young, but maybe you fantasized about being an umpire once or twice, too. I always loved how every umpire had their own style, and I liked to imagine what my strike and strikeout calls would be. For those of us who never had a shot at the major leagues, being an umpire somehow seemed attainable and a meaningful way to be part of the game. Although the good ones stay anonymous, they find a way to put their stamp on the sport all the same.

Is this earnest focus on the umpire enough to classify *The Naked Gun* as a baseball movie? It still feels like a stretch. The film could exist without its baseball. The game is a setting for its comedy rather than a fundamental element of its story, but then again everything in a good spoof is just a set-up for laughs. If *The Naked Gun* were a feature-length spoof of a baseball movie, it would obviously merit inclusion. But it's not. It's a spoof of gritty '70s cop movies like *The French Connection* or *The Seven-Ups*, just as *Airplane!* was a spoof of the disaster movies of the '70s and *Scary Movie* parodied the horror movie renaissance of the '90s.

So while we can't call it a baseball movie, it certainly deserves credit for its intelligence, its humor, and its appreciation of a figure that fans and filmmakers have either reviled or ignored for as long as baseball has existed. Long live *The Naked Gun*, and long live the umpire, as long as he's secretly Enrico Pallazzo.

· PART IV ·

The Boomers Have Kids

Chapter 12

The Sandlot (1993)

THE SANDLOT IS AN HOUR AND FORTY-ONE MINUTES LONG, BUT THE film—and maybe the entire baseball genre—peaks around 43 minutes in. It's Independence Day, and while the rest of this Southern California suburb is celebrating the birth of America with BBQ and beer, Benny "The Jet" Rodriguez is rushing through a crowded suburban street to knock on the door of the house of his new friend Smalls. Benny tells him to grab his glove. They're going to play a night game. Their makeshift field doesn't have lights, but on this one evening, the fireworks light up the sky enough for them to play. The excitement is palpable. Smalls tells us in voice-over that they all played their best at night because the ambience made them feel like big leaguers.

So they go to the field, and they play. Director David Mickey Evans (who also wrote the film) drops the dialogue, the voiceover, and even the sounds of the game, and instead fills the soundtrack with Ray Charles' soaring rendition of "America the Beautiful." From there, it drifts into sheer poetry. With the blooming fireworks glancing off his face, Benny cranks one into the night sky. The fielders all turn to gaze at his mighty blast, and as they do, the ball gets lost in the color and sound, and it's not clear anymore if they're amazed by Benny's hit or the majesty of the fireworks or maybe the entire American experience. As if there were a difference.

With nostalgia, patriotism, and baseball itself merging for one shining moment, this scene is enough to justify *The Sandlot*'s place in the canon, but the film's meaning outside of this one moment deserves a deeper dive. It's a work of uncritical nostalgia, a sepia-tinted memory of a childhood that never quite existed, although we wish it did. Its gaze is irresistible and pernicious. Just a year after *A League of Their Own* uncovered a forgotten chapter in America's history to explain its present moment, *The Sandlot* peers into our past for a different reason altogether: to avoid the present.

Released in the spring of 1993, the film was followed by a parade of other baseball films for kids, including *Rookie of the Year,* the Disney remake of *Angels in the Outfield,* and *Little Big League.* It was the beginning of the end of the genre's most prolific era. The boom that began in 1984, when *The Natural* overturned Hollywood's stubborn thinking that baseball movies for adults were box-office poison, would soon sputter out, brought down by a very real dip in the quality of the films (Does anyone remember 1996's *Ed,* about the ballplaying chimp? No? Okay, good.) and perhaps a broader disillusionment in the game brought on by the 1994 MLB players' strike.

Of these films, *The Sandlot* is remembered the most fondly, and not only by the fans. Ask any major leaguer born between 1980 and 2010 for their favorite movie, and they will invariably mention *The Sandlot* in an offhand way that suggests its omnipresence in their imagination. And don't mistake their nonchalance for apathy. Evidence of their sincerity is all over major league ballparks. In 2013, when Evans and two stars of the film, Chauncey Leopardi and Patrick Renna, stepped onto the field at Fenway Park to watch batting practice, David Ortiz ran over to them and gave them a big hug. "You guys are my heroes," he exclaimed.

Two major league teams have actually recreated scenes from the movie for posterity, with the players mimicking the cast to an impressive degree (admittedly, the acting bar is low for ballplayers). The 2015 Yankees took time away from spring training to act out the scene in which Smalls, played by fiery outfielder Brett Gardner, discovers that the signature on the ball he stole from his stepfather's mantle belongs to Babe Ruth. Dellin

Betances, Jacoby Ellsbury, CC Sabathia, and Didi Gregorius fill out the roster as the other Sandlot kids.

The 2018 Brewers produced a beat-for-beat recreation of the moment when Ham hits the ball over the fence and Smalls gets his first glimpse of The Beast. The casting is solid, and the acting isn't terrible. Jeremy Jeffress makes a very believable DeNunez, Stephen Vogt hams it up as Hamilton, and Brett Phillips is just as wide-eyed and eager as Smalls. Christian Yelich is a dead ringer for Benny. In the video's most delightful moment, a Bichon Frise mix named Hank—a dog who wandered into the Brewers spring training facility in 2014 and became a de facto mascot for the team—plays The Beast.

Bottom line: Everyone loves *The Sandlot*. With the focus on children rather than established major leaguers, it's easy for viewers of any age or skill level to relate. And years later, they still do. The cast reunited in 2018 for a sold-out, four-month tour of major and minor league stadiums to promote the film's 25th anniversary. Cast members rotated in and out of the events, but Renna, who played Hamilton "Ham" Porter, seemed to be at all of them. In the early days of the Covid pandemic in 2020, Los Angeles Dodger Justin Turner organized a virtual cast reunion to raise money for his charitable foundation. Turner also convinced a few of his fellow major leaguers, including Mike Moustakas, Dee Gordon, and Andre Ethier, to join in. Clearly, the legacy of *The Sandlot* is stronger than ever, perhaps Major League Baseball, with its annual controversies and never-ending labor negotiations, has drifted further yet from the game that we knew and loved as kids.

Its legacy was born of modest beginnings. *The Sandlot* did okay in its theatrical run, earning $32 million, but it really thrived on DVD and on cable. In a sense, it was designed to endure. It's the kind of movie you love as a kid and then, when you grow up, get excited about showing to your own kids because it represents the childhood you wish for them. With nostalgia its primary subject, *The Sandlot* might very well live forever. A glorification of postwar America, it would have felt more at home in the 1980s, alongside *The Natural* and *Back to the Future*, than in the early 1990s, when politicians, film producers, and marketing executives, feeling the pull of the digital age, started looking forward to the next century rather than back. *The Sandlot* offered one last rosy view of a particular past, using voiceover narration by Evans himself to set the scene as a grown-up remembering his childhood, much like actor Daniel Stern's narrator in the hit ABC sitcom *The Wonder Years*, or maybe Ralphie from *A Christmas Story*, both paeans to the postwar era.

Evans was born in Wilkes-Barre, Pennsylvania, in 1962, the same year that *The Sandlot* takes place. He was technically too young to remember the era it's set in, but with its perpetually sunny skies, brightly lit soda shoppes, and manicured front lawns, *The Sandlot* seems influenced by other movies about the era rather than Evans' lived memories. His reply when asked if the film was based on his own life is telling:

"Walt Disney finished Disneyland in 1955. It took him one year and a day to finish construction of the park. They said it couldn't be done. And he was walking a bunch of dignitaries down Main Street, U.S.A., and a guy was looking at the great 1800s and 1900s shops and said to Walt, 'Boy, Walt, you really nailed it. This is exactly the way it was.' And Disney said to the guy, 'No, it's the way it should have been.' Now, *The Sandlot* is not my childhood, but it's the way that I wanted my childhood to have been."

Evans moved to Los Angeles to study film in 1980 and never went back. It's fascinating to think of *The Sandlot* as a collision of his own childhood memories and the exigencies of the Hollywood propaganda machine, resulting in a concentrated nostalgia that's both immensely pleasing and slightly troubling. *The Sandlot* looks back at 1962—the year before Kennedy was shot, and two years before the Civil Rights Act was signed into law, a disturbing corollary to how *The Natural* was set moments before baseball integrated—and sees a simpler, safer time. It's a world in which children could roam free in their neighborhood without supervision. At the beginning of the film, Smalls' mother (Karen Allen) encourages him to get out of his room, go make some friends, and "get into trouble." He takes her words to heart, and alongside his teammates, spends the summer getting banned from the public pool, terrorizing an old man and nearly killing his dog, and ruining some sort of end-of-summer event involving a very large cake.

The most startling moment, at least viewed through modern eyes, is when Benny comes to Smalls' home on that July 4th, and Smalls simply yells, "Mom, I'm going out!" Without waiting for a response, he grabs his glove and chases Benny down the street. If you accept the world of the film, nothing feels strange about it. There's no danger in this town. No crime, no abductions. On this night in particular, everyone is out celebrating, and there seems to be safety in numbers.

It's an alluring fantasy, but it's hard to divorce its mood from the mood of the country when the film was made, when many parents were no longer comfortable letting their children roam free in their town. America wasn't exactly a lawless wasteland in the early '90s, but if you paid attention to the discourse, you might think it was. By 1993, parents were more than a decade into "stranger danger" culture, a phenomenon set off by the abduction of Etan Patz, a six-year-old taken somewhere between his home and the school bus stop in 1979. The Patz disappearance was covered nightly on the news and provoked a national panic about the abduction of children, leading to the creation of a Reagan administration task force on the issue. It was around this time that they started putting photos of kids on the back of milk cartons. In reality, abductions by strangers didn't spike at all during this period, and the increase in reported kidnappings was largely due to custody disputes. The concerns over child abductions, however, were a political crystallization of other moral panic issues, such as urban crime spilling out into the suburbs, the increase in working women, and more widespread acceptance of homosexuality. Politicians used it to promote a pre-feminist agenda; the primary recommendations of Reagan's task force revolved around lowering divorce rates and reuniting nuclear families. His focus—and some would say, fear mongering—on crime and child abduction supported his central political idea to return America to its postwar boom. That's the mood that *The Sandlot* faithfully recreates.

But who was welcome in that postwar boom? There was little room there for women or people of color, and *The Sandlot*, whether knowingly or not, recreates that dynamic, too. There are only two women in *The Sandlot*: a supportive mother and an object of lust. It's true that Smalls' mom, played by the accomplished actor Karen Allen, is one of the first characters we see in *The Sandlot*, but her only real role in the story is to facilitate the relationship between Smalls and his stepfather, played blankly by Denis Leary. Once Smalls finds his chosen family at the sandlot, her time in the film is over. Although *The Sandlot 2*, a direct-to-video sequel, would introduce female characters to battle the boys for control of the titular ballfield, there are no girl players in the original. In fact, the idea would be anathema to these guys, as we learn that being told you "play ball like a girl" is a stop-everything, record-scratch insult that's akin to slapping someone with a pair of leather gloves. An argument could be made that this scene simply reflects how most 12-year-old boys actually think, and that being told you play like a girl really was the ultimate admonishment in 1962. But as Evans himself said, this isn't the world. It's the world as he wishes it were, which makes the film's soft misogyny harder to swallow.

Then there's the strange case of teenaged lifeguard Wendy Peffercorn, who suffers what would undoubtedly be considered sexual assault by a minor (not *of* a minor) when Squints (Chauncey Leopardi) dives into the deep end of the public pool, despite not knowing how to swim, so that Wendy can save his life and he can finally get some physical contact. She drags him out of the pool and works to resuscitate him, and we quickly discover he's faking the whole thing. He grabs her by the back of the head and kisses her for a few seconds before she can resist. There's a lot to unpack here. Squints is portrayed as being driven to this dangerous stunt after years of pining for Wendy—"I can't take it anymore," he whines—but he barely looks old enough for puberty. Are we really supposed to believe this child has gone mad from unfulfilled lust?

Of course, if Squints pulled this stunt as a teenager or adult in our era, it would be taken far more seriously. There would be lawyers and counselors and, if it were caught on someone's cell phone, the whole scene would be uploaded to Twitter and debated until the end of time (or at least a day). Even if he did it as a child in 1962, I have to think there would be a slightly bigger consequence than being kicked out of the pool area. At the very least, it's likely that Wendy would not shake it off so easily. In the film, she likes it. She smiles at him before he walks away, and adult Smalls tells us in narration that she did the same thing every time Squints walked by from then on. Oh, and at the end of the film, we learn that they got married. Again, this isn't the world. It's the world the filmmaker wishes it were. It's a world in which a woman is so flattered by a little boy tricking her into kissing him that she marries him.

If the film's portrayal of women reinforces its framing as a young male fantasy, its depiction of race is a little more complicated. First, the good: It's admirable that Evans not only created a Latino character to play in his group of nine, but actually made him the best player in the group. Benny is one of those kids who is a star from the first time they set foot on a diamond, and he becomes a legend over the course of *The Sandlot*, not just for stealing that ball back from Hercules but for stealing home in a clutch situation while a member of the Los Angeles Dodgers (for what it's worth, a questionable decision for an aging speedster who has "lost a step or two").

Evans grew up in a majority Latino community, and all the kids in the film were inspired by real people he knew. Benny may have been a composite, but the centering of a Latino player is important, as it both reflects and affects the game's changing demographic. It was in 1987 that the Los Angeles Dodgers became the first franchise to open a baseball academy in the Dominican Republic, creating a pipeline for young Dominican players to get to the majors. Eventually, every other team would do the same. It took a few years, but the impact was dramatic. In 1986, Latino players made up 11.6 percent of major league rosters. By 1996, it was over 20 percent and still growing. For young Latino baseball fans in America, Benny must have been an aspirational figure. He's a role model, not only the best player on the team but also a genuinely good guy. He's kind to Smalls from the start, which is more than you can say for the other players. In a way, Benny is the future of baseball—it was fewer than two months after the film's release that another Rodriguez, first name Alex, was the first pick in the MLB draft—and Evans deserves credit for refusing to ignore these changes happening in the game.

Unfortunately, *The Sandlot* has a maddening blind spot when it comes to Black players. The problem isn't the roster. There is one Black player on the team, although naming him DeNunez implies he might be of Latin origin (Brandon Adams, the actor who plays him, identifies as Black). More frustrating is the scene that unfolds with James Earl Jones toward the end of the film. When the kids finally get the ball back from Hercules, they unwittingly trap the great beast beneath a fence. Fearing that he is injured, they save him and bring him back to his house. They've been told a mean old man lives there, but instead they find Mr. Mertle (Jones), an ebullient blind recluse with a room full of priceless baseball memorabilia. From what we can tell, Mr. Mertle doesn't get out much, but he seems eager to chat. Smalls and Benny learn his story when they see a photo of him in uniform standing next to Babe Ruth himself.

SMALLS: You knew Babe Ruth?

MERTLE: George? I sure did. And he knew me. He was almost as great a hitter as I was. I would've broken his record, but….

It's easy to imagine the next line being, "I wasn't allowed to play in the majors," or "I was stuck in the Negro Leagues." Instead, Smalls fills in the end of Mertle's sentence: "You went blind," and Mertle explains how he lost his vision when he took a fastball to the head. With three words, *The Sandlot* erases segregation in baseball from its world. We're meant to believe that a Black player could have played alongside Babe Ruth in the 1920s and 1930s, when in reality players like Satchel Paige, Pop Lloyd, and Josh Gibson (who Jones is clearly meant as a stand-in for) were confined to the Negro Leagues. Incredibly, the photo shown of James Earl Jones next to Babe Ruth was actually a shot of Ruth and White slugger Jimmie Foxx. They just photoshopped Jones' head onto it. That's as close to a literal erasure of segregation as you're likely to find.

It would have been so simple for *The Sandlot* to use this opportunity to incorporate the Negro Leagues into its story and educate young fans on the real history of baseball. Mr. Mertle could have taught Smalls and Benny about segregation, and how Babe Ruth's record should not be considered sacred since he never had to play against any Black athletes. Or he could have told him that he had to play with the Babe on barnstorming teams in the off-season—that part is true—because Black players weren't allowed in the majors. It would have smartly undercut the film's blissful nostalgia by reminding these youngsters of the risks of letting our love of baseball blind us to more important realities, and nicely framed the life and career of Benny Rodriguez as a victory in baseball's ongoing struggle to reckon with its Whiteness.

The Sandlot isn't ultimately interested in any of that. It's interested in the world as David Mickey Evans and the film's millions of fans wish it were, not the world as it is. Sure, it's a fantasy for children, but what we choose to fantasize about reveals much about who we are. It's no coincidence that this film, more than any other, is the one that Major League Baseball glorifies. This is the one they encourage their players to recreate scenes from, and the one pro teams hold bobblehead nights and reunions for. They have chosen as their sacred myth a film made in the 1990s about the early 1960s. Is it any wonder they are still struggling to grow the sport? As the smart people at MLB headquarters brainstorm ways to get more women, people of color, and young fans to embrace the game, they might try celebrating a more inclusive film.

Chapter 13

Rookie of the Year (1993)

ATHLETIC EXCELLENCE IS A GIVEN IN MOST BASEBALL MOVIES. IN THE FILMS of the postwar era, scouts searched the great plains, purple mountains, and city sandlots for the next great talent, and they found it in baseball heroes like Lou Gehrig, Monty Stratton, and Dizzy Dean. Later, *Fear Strikes Out, Damn Yankees*, and *Bang the Drum Slowly* portrayed greatness on the field, even as they punctured American exceptionalism off it. In the '80s, Roy Hobbs was a god, and Nuke LaLoosh could have been one if he wasn't such an idiot.

But the kids of the '90s flat-out couldn't play. Smalls from *The Sandlot* didn't know how to have a catch, while Henry Rowengartner from *Rookie of the Year* and Billy Heywood from *Little Big League* were the worst players on their Little League teams. For them, and the uncoordinated adults in the audience who identified with them, the fantasy of being a great athlete was too far-fetched to even dream of. Instead, our avatars were kids who sucked at every level of play and needed divine intervention just to make it to the field. Most baseball films deal in myth. These deal in outright miracles.

Some people are born athletes, so it stands to reason that others are born into a life of strikeouts and errors, but the kids' baseball movies of the 1990s aren't content to chalk it up to the law of averages. Instead, they all offer the same explanation for their heroes' ineptitude: They were raised by single mothers. Smalls, Henry, and Billy all suffered the same misfortune of losing their fathers at a young age, and in lieu of proper male role models, they found their idols on the diamond. It didn't help them play better, though. Without a father to teach them the fundamentals of the game, they were still hopeless cases.

There were a lot of us like that. I was born in 1980, raised by a single mother, and with a father who was not consistently in my life. After a year of fleeting tee ball dominance, I proved myself to be a terrible athlete. I never quite grasped the mechanics of the game. Once the pitchers started throwing with any velocity, I struck out in every at-bat. In the field, I choked on easy plays, forgetting to keep my eye on the ball, preparing to throw to first before the grounder was in my glove. I sped things up when I should have slowed them down, and I froze when a quick reaction time was needed. I can't blame my unorthodox family situation for this. My mother encouraged my love of baseball, my grandfather took me to games, and my sister and I played wiffle ball in the backyard every day in the summertime. But when it came to really learning how to play, I found there was little substitute for a father who knew the game.

I needed the movies, specifically these movies. The kids' baseball films of this era inherently posit baseball as a cure for an epidemic of "latchkey kids," a popular term in the '70s and '80s to describe children who came home every day to empty houses because their mothers, following the victories of second-wave feminism, had gone to college and entered the workforce. The politics of this narrative trope are muddled. There's something encouraging about normalizing single mothers, especially in *Rookie of the Year*, where Henry's mother invents a tale about his estranged father being a great pitcher, only to ultimately reveal that she was the athlete in the family. "I wanted you to have someone to look up to," she tells him to explain the lie. "I already do," he replies earnestly. Cue the waterworks.

On the other hand, these films see the latchkey kid as a curable condition. Their insistence on pairing single women with grizzled ball-players suggests the family is incomplete without a man. Even the most pro-woman baseball films typically have some semblance of misogyny baked in—it's one of the unfortunate foundations of the genre. *Bull Durham* ended with the independent Annie standing by Crash as a supportive wife, while *A League of Their Own* gets its biggest laughs from mocking the unladylike appearance of Marla Hooch. Similarly, *Rookie of the Year*'s pairing of Mary, a strong, independent woman, with Gary Busey of all people just seems unnecessary. It feels like a relic from the postwar era when Americans were told through the media that no woman could exist without a man, and every baseball film was expected to uphold the primacy of the nuclear family.

The focus of this family is young Henry Rowengartner (Thomas Ian Nicholas), who loves baseball but is absolutely terrible at it. Even on his Little League team, also called the Cubs, he's a benchwarmer who only plays when the right fielder, the second-worst player on the team, suffers an asthma attack. Once there, he makes the most boneheaded play you'll ever see. He drifts back on a fly ball, falls down, and, when his cap shifts on his head and obscures his vision, searches around blindly for the ball instead of simply pulling his cap up. Eventually he finds it—but throws it in the wrong direction over the fence. Cubs lose.

We know in this moment we're in for something closer to a Saturday morning cartoon than a realistic portrait of baseball—even kids' baseball— but things take a turn for the truly fantastical when Henry breaks his arm and weeks later discovers that the tendons have healed too tight (or something), and he now has the ability to throw a 100 mph fastball without even trying. Medical fact-checkers should stay away. This is just a device to get Henry onto a major league field. In the 1954 film *Roogie's Bump*, a clear inspiration for *Rookie of the Year*, the kid gets visited by the ghost of an old player who simply transfers the gift of a rocket arm over to the young boy. That boy, also fatherless, is signed by the Brooklyn Dodgers after stunning the crowd with a laser from the crowd to catcher Roy Campanella (playing himself). In *Rookie of the Year*, the action is transported to Chicago so that Henry can help a different lovable loser.

As of 1993, when *Rookie of the Year* was released, the Cubs had not won a pennant in 48 years and had not won the World Series since 1908, as Cliff Murdoch (John Candy), the Cubs play-by-play announcer, tells us. They were a historically inept franchise, although their fans still came out to watch them play every day. Depicting the stadium as nearly empty in early summer, and suggesting the owners would have to forfeit the franchise if attendance does not improve is one of the film's least persuasive leaps of imagination. In the 2011 book *Scorecasting: The Hidden Influences Behind How Sports are Played and Games are Won*, authors Tobias J. Moskowitz and L. Jon Wertheim demonstrated through statistical analysis that Cubs attendance is historically "the least sensitive to performance in all of baseball," meaning that the fans show up in almost equal numbers whether the team is in first place or last.

Rookie of the Year surely provoked mixed feelings in Cubs fans, who finally got their own baseball movie that, unlike many films about pro teams, was actually shot at their home stadium. It's just too bad they had to see themselves degraded as fair-weather fans in a film that suggests they can only win a World Series through an actual medical miracle. The Cubs have embraced *Rookie of the Year*, though, bringing Nicholas back to the stadium to throw out the first pitch in the 2015 National League Championship Series against the Mets, and holding a 30th anniversary event for the film in 2023.

Perhaps its flaws are easier to ignore because the film is clearly designed for children, who are unlikely to pick up on them. *Rookie of the Year* was actually beloved by burgeoning young pitchers. "That movie came out on my birthday when I turned 10," said Brandon McCarthy, who played for seven teams during his 13-year major league career. "It was one of those perfect kid movies when I was already obsessed with baseball. Being that young and having that magic happen to him. It stuck with me for the rest of my life. Every time I woke up and my arm was really stiff, I thought, 'Oh my god, I might throw 103 today,' but it turned out I was just hurt and had to miss the next six weeks."

Former relief pitcher Jerry Blevins, who played for the A's, Mets, Braves, and Nationals, had a similar experience. "I broke my arm twice as a kid, and unfortunately the tendons healed up normally," he told me. "What Hollywood BS that movie is." Still, the film was a major influence on the baseball culture of his youth. "In Little League, every kid who got to first base would do 'pitcher's got a big butt' at the pitcher. We used to quote every line from that movie, and I still remember most of them." Watching as an adult, the character of Henry Rowengartner is pretty grating—we really don't need to hear him shouting "Give him the cheese, the hot, stinky Limburger" once, let alone twice—but when he's on the field, the film knows what to do with him, making fine comedy out of his youthful naivete. Particularly enjoyable is his reaction upon giving up a towering homer in his first big-league appearance. Most pitchers would kick the dirt and curse. Henry, young and guileless, exclaims, "Wow!" and watches in pure amazement as the ball soars through the air. A similar moment occurs when he looks down the bench at a bunch of surly teammates giving him the collective stink-eye, and instead of cowering in the corner, he responds with a jubilant, "Hey!" The kid is truly just happy to be there, as we all would be.

The success of a baseball film, however, is measured at least in part by its realism, and *Rookie of the Year* demands you to turn that part of your brain off. First up are the performances, a real mixed bag of broad comic portrayals and honest, thoughtful ones. In the former column, there's actor-director Daniel Stern, who portrays Brickma, the team's woefully underskilled pitching coach, with a performance so broad it can barely fit in the stadium. He yelps, he twitches, he mimes an extended fly-swatting routine to signal to a pitcher in the bullpen to come into the game. Similarly outsized performances are given by two usually dependable character actors: Dan Hedaya, playing the team's soon-to-be-owner who whimpers like a dog when chastised by his boss, and Bruce Altman as Mary's boyfriend, who seems like a reasonable guy until he snaps when Henry threatens to skip a photo shoot he set up. "He's my son," Henry's mother reminds him. "He's my client!" Altman shouts back with cartoonish indignance, before she punches him in the face and throws him down the steps. It's a just punishment for the worst line reading in the film.

The unqualified winners in the cast are Busey and Amy Morton, who, as Chet "Rocket" Steadman and Mary Rowengartner, are thrown together in a romantic subplot that's entirely unnecessary, but fare better in developing strong, believable chemistry with the young Nicholas. Busey, known more for his erratic behavior offscreen than his acting, creates a warm, albeit shallow portrait of a grizzled veteran, and while his pitching isn't particularly realistic, he adequately evokes the weariness and determination of a once-great player facing the end of his career. He also has the best mustache in a baseball film this side of Tom Selleck in *Mr. Baseball*. Morton, an accomplished stage actress, handles both the film's comic and dramatic moments with ease. Her blend of terror and anger when Henry is sent up to bat, culminating in a seemingly unscripted bang of her head against a light fixture, is pitch-perfect, and her glee at having punted her boyfriend down the steps—"Maybe I should have killed him!"—is a refreshing note of dark comedy in a film that otherwise stays squarely in a safe, well-lit space.

Much of the film's inconsistency must be laid at the feet of Daniel Stern, who in addition to playing Brickma, also directed. It's the first (and last) directorial effort for the accomplished character actor. Perhaps a more experienced filmmaker could have merged these disparate tones into a coherent whole, but Stern simply throws everything at the wall to see what sticks. Not enough does. Writing in the *Los Angeles Times*, Michael Wilmington pinpointed the problem:

"There's a movie-making knack we might call 'The Gift for the Plausible Absurd.' Simply put, it's the quality that enables some filmmakers to make us believe in giant lovelorn apes, adorable stranded extraterrestrials, the Yellow Brick Road to the Emerald City, and talking mules, dogs, cats, and caterpillars. Canny pros can take this baloney and make us both swallow and love it. That's the quality *Rookie of the Year* really needs. And doesn't have."

He was talking about the filmmaking, but his critique would equally apply to the film's baseball. *Rookie of the Year* is quite simply the most inaccurate baseball movie ever made. Maybe even more inaccurate than *Ed*, which featured a chimpanzee playing third base. We've already covered the shameful fallacy that the Cubs can't draw a crowd, but what happens on the baseball field is equally perplexing. For example: Do the Cubs not have a middle reliever? When Rowengartner's arm goes dead in the final game, wouldn't even a middling bullpen arm be better than a child who can't throw at all? Or one of their other starters? Why does the team's manager behave as if Henry and Steadman are his only options?

The film also has a, let's say, strange understanding of the major league playoff structure. We're told that the final game will decide the division, yet the announcer also muses that the winner will go on to the World Series. How does that work? *Rookie of the Year* was made a year before the Wild Card era began, but even then, there would still have been a National League Championship Series to get through, no? It's also worth wondering how a team that lost its only two good pitchers in the film's climactic game—Henry to a dead arm and Steadman to what appears to be a torn rotator cuff—goes on to win the World Series. It might be plausible if the film demonstrated how Henry's youthful exuberance made the rest of the players better in one of those classic baseball movie montages. But *Rookie of the Year* inexplicably shows us no such thing, so when Henry flashes his World Series ring in the film's final shot, it provides more questions than answers.

There are a few more procedural inaccuracies to note. Moments before the final game, the manager tells Steadman he's pitching that day. That's not how it works. He'd need time to ramp up and throw a bullpen session a couple of days before, especially with a dicey arm. Regardless, Steadman pitches six strong innings, and Henry comes in. Then we get a montage of Henry striking out nine guys (I counted) before he gets to the ninth inning when he loses arm strength. Question: How do you strike out nine guys in two innings? Answer: You don't. Finally, there's the hidden ball trick in the ninth. When Henry hands the ball off to the first baseman, he appears to be standing on the rubber on the pitching mound without the ball, which coaxes the runner to take his lead. Of course, standing on the rubber without the ball is considered a balk for this very reason. To achieve a proper hidden ball trick, you can't touch the rubber, and a smart runner would wait to take his lead until that happens, which is why they're so difficult to pull off. So that play should have been a balk, and the runner should have been awarded second base. For what it's worth, there is little evidence Henry understands the nuance of that rule. He's not only unskilled at baseball. He knows nothing about it.

I could go on, but I won't. Defenders of *Rookie of the Year* would say a film designed clearly for children doesn't need to be accurate and must only appeal to their sense of play and delight. Or they'll say a movie built around an important cultural phenomenon—the latchkey kid, the single mother, and the new American family—is inherently worthwhile. Fair point, but on the other hand, children aren't idiots.

Despite its intrinsic silliness, *Rookie of the Year* marks an important turning point for the baseball movie: the beginning of the end. After 10 years of baseball cinema that pushed the genre into new areas of artistry and authenticity, studio executives started to get greedy, looking for any baseball-related pitch they could put into production as quickly as possible and turn a tidy profit. A kid who endures a freak accident and gets signed by the Cubs? You can almost hear them muttering, "We'll worry about the script later."

Rookie of the Year is ultimately more of a concept than a film, and that's typically enough for children. It doesn't have to be. If you want to read about a much smarter baseball film made from basically the same story elements, simply turn to the next page.

Chapter 14

Little Big League (1994)

Little Big League is about a 12-year-old child who becomes owner and then manager of the major league Minnesota Twins. It also might be the most realistic baseball movie ever made. *Rookie of the Year* told a tale about a kid who gets to the major leagues, but they made everything around him so silly and cartoonish that it ruined the fun. It wasn't exciting or even interesting that he was there because everything else on the screen was just as ridiculous. You need a dash of realism to make absurdism compelling. *Little Big League* gets this. It builds a ridiculous flight of fancy on a solid foundation of baseball knowledge.

The irony is that *Little Big League* got overshadowed by the inferior *Rookie of the Year*, with its vaguely similar concept and much higher box-office gross. Both are about pre-teens who get thrown into the major leagues, where they teach a bumbling group of underachieving professionals how to win by rediscovering their inner child. But while *Rookie of the Year* is defined largely by its cartoonish characterization and total baseball inaccuracy, *Little Big League* scores big by paying attention to the smallest detail. It's a film that did its homework first so it could go out and play. It employs a full roster of active and retired major leaguers to make the on-field action realistic. Not only did the filmmakers expertly replicate the present, but they also somehow predicted the future of the game.

Little Big League was "moneyball" before *Moneyball*. Casual baseball fans became aware of sabermetrics (or advanced analytics, or whatever you want to call it) after the 2003 release of Michael Lewis' bestselling book, a chronicle of how Oakland A's general manager Billy Beane put together a winning team on the cheap by upending conventional wisdom and prioritizing different skills. The next year, the Boston Red Sox applied the same principles to a team with a higher payroll—moneyball plus money—and won the World Series. The word was out, and soon every team in the game followed suit. Still, criticism persisted from old-school baseball types who didn't like how sabermetrics shifted the power from those who played the game (players and managers) to people with economics degrees who had never set foot on a major league ballfield. These new baseball gods were young and smart and probably not very good at playing baseball, but they knew how to get the most out of their players. In other words, they were a lot like *Little Big League*'s Billy Heywood (Luke Edwards), the adolescent son of a single mother who knows everything about the game but can't make a play to save his life.

In the film's opening scene, Billy meekly grounds out to end a Little League game, thwarting his team's attempted comeback, but he alone knows he let the pitcher off the hook by swinging at the first pitch. When a freak play occurs in the field and three runners end up on the same base, the coaches and umpire defer to Billy to tell them the correct call. Certainly part of the reason Billy knows so much about the game is that his grandfather (Jason Robards) owns the Minnesota Twins. Yes, before the fantasy of becoming manager even comes true, Billy already leads a charmed existence. He gets to sit in the owner's box and hang out in the clubhouse after the game. The players know him by name. What else could a kid want? It's a mixed blessing when his grandfather dies and leaves him the team. "I'd rather have my grandfather," he says through tears, but mercifully, the film blows past his grief to get to the fun stuff.

As new team owner, Heywood's first decision is to fire tyrannical manager George O'Farrell (Dennis Farina), who had been hired by Billy's grandfather to help discipline the young, underachieving roster. O'Farrell is a familiar type. In earlier baseball movies, like *Bull Durham* or *The Natural,* the manager is portrayed as a gruff, stern father figure whose job is to scream and yell at the players to keep them in line. To be clear, this was also baseball's idea of what made a good manager offscreen. This was still the era that revered Earl Weaver, Jim Leyland, and Billy Martin, who pleased fans by screaming at umpires, cursing at reporters, and generally looking miserable all the time.

Little Big League takes a hard stand against the screaming manager— probably because it's a kids movie, and screaming managers are just mean—long before MLB did. These days, it's hard to find a manager with a reputation as a disciplinarian. Instead, most teams opt for a "players manager," who is typically closer in age to the players and displays a softer touch with their stars. Billy Heywood may have been the prototype. When Billy sees O'Farrell yelling at his players, he politely asks him to stop. O'Farrell pushes back, telling him, "Your grandfather hired me to shake their cage, so that's exactly what I'm gonna do." The younger, wiser Billy notes: "But it's not working." When Billy fires O'Farrell and appoints himself manager, he makes friends with the players. He's more like today's Aaron Boone or Alex Cora than Weaver or Leyland. He tries to make it fun, and it's only when things are going badly for Billy—on the field and in his personal life—that he falls into bad habits like yelling at umps and scowling at players.

Before he can take the reins, however, he has some convincing to do. This brings us to The Scene, as it should henceforth be known for both its prescience and eloquence. After Billy announces his decision to general manager Arthur Goslin (Kevin Dunn) and bench coach Mac Macnally (John Ashton), they raise serious objections, which the youngster overcomes through what we now would call sabermetric thinking. Mac tells him that to manage the game properly you have to understand "situations and tendencies." Billy challenges Mac to come up with a situation that he can't figure out.

So Mac invents a situation and asks Billy to deduce the proper strategy, but before he answers, Billy has some questions. He needs to know the score, the inning, who's catching, who's rested in the bullpen, who's up in the next inning for the opposing team, and whether the Twins are home or away. He's an information gatherer, not a manager who goes with his gut, and with every new piece of information that Billy requests, Mac understands more of what Billy brings to the table. You can see it in Mac's eyes, and how his cadence changes. It's a great performance by Ashton, already a legendary character actor at this point for his work in *Beverly Hills Cop* and *Midnight Run*. In just a few minutes, he conveys the whole evolution of baseball that would take place in the coming years.

When Billy finally gives his answer, however, Mac initially reverts to old-school thinking and rejects his decision. The kid is not deterred. Confident in his approach, he calmly but firmly replies, "No," and goes on to explain exactly why he would let All-Star Lou Collins (Timothy Busfield) swing away in the eighth inning of a tie game with a runner on first and one out. Mac initially thought a sacrifice bunt was the right play, but Billy rightly determines—first through a series of questions and then with a decision based on rational thought—the play that gives his team the best chance for success.

"If we do A, they'll do B, which leads to C," Rany Jazayerli told me. "That's the essence of analytics. Intelligent decision-making based on the data, not just based on a set of inflexible rules." Jazayerli is the co-creator of *Baseball Prospectus*, a publication founded in 1996 that analyzes major leaguers based on sabermetrics. In the 1990s, Rany and his small group of cohorts worshiped at the altar of Bill James, an independent statistician who also influenced Billy Beane, and they spent many hours strategizing how to get their revolutionary approach to baseball's decision-makers. He and his friends were marginalized and mocked for their rejection of hard-earned baseball wisdom. Eventually, their approach took over the sport. "Teams used clichés like 'always bunt' or 'only use your closer at the end of the game,'" said Rany. "There were all these kinds of pronouncements from on high that the sport followed. Conventional wisdom was sacred. You could not question the book or the unwritten rules."

When Rany saw The Scene in the theater, it was a revelation. "I was in college, and we were already writing [about sabermetrics] on newsgroups online. That scene came out at the perfect time, and it made me feel like, 'I'm not alone.' Even if he doesn't necessarily understand the numbers, he understands that just because you have a different idea of how the sport is played, it doesn't mean you're wrong. Even if you're young, even if you've never worked for a major league team. Sometimes the best ideas come from outside the industry. It was quietly a very important moment for me." Several of Jazayerli's colleagues went on to work for major league teams and helped foment a statistical revolution in the game (Jazayerli was offered such a position but declined). It took time, however, which Jazayerli says is the one thing *Little Big League* gets wrong. "The most unrealistic thing about that scene in 1994 is that, when he was done, the coach asked, 'What do you need me for?' He and the general manager were convinced immediately. That's the fairy tale part, not the thing about a kid managing. It took 20 seconds, but in real life, it took 20 years."

Although the logic in *Little Big League* was ahead of its time, it never feels jarring because the film's groundbreaking elements rest on an otherwise familiar underdog sports story. It's basically *The Bad News Bears*, but with the kid as the manager and the adults as the players. It also features some of the most authentic baseball action put on film. Director Andrew Scheinman hired as many real-life or former ballplayers as he could. Not Busfield; he doesn't quite have the stature to be plausible as a slugging first baseman, but at least he has a nice lefty swing. (Busfield, who is naturally right-handed, worked hard on it.) Also on the Twins' roster are two former major leaguers. Brad Lesley, who pitched in 54 games over four seasons in the early '80s, plays "Blackout" Gatling, the broad, intimidating reliever, and Kevin Elster, the slick-fielding shortstop for the Mets who actually filmed *Little Big League* in his year off from baseball before returning to play six more seasons with the Yankees, Phillies, Rangers, Pirates, and Dodgers. Elster was a good-looking guy and hoped *Little Big League* would be his entree into Hollywood, but he never proved as adept with acting as he was with ground balls.

The cast also includes Scott Patterson, soon to be known as Luke Danes in *Gilmore Girls*, as the greedy starting pitcher Mike McGrevey, one of the few players on the Twins who resists young Billy's charms. Patterson pitched for seven seasons in the minor leagues before pivoting to acting, and he was originally cast in the film as Lou before Busfield (a bigger star at the time due to his run on TV's *thirtysomething*) took the role. Patterson accepted the smaller role as McGrevey, and it pays off in a key scene. McGrevey has been tanking games in an effort to get traded, but Billy finally gets through to him, reminding him in a dugout exchange that McGrevey is only hurting his value as a free agent with his shenanigans. The pitcher immediately turns it on and strikes out the side in the next inning. Patterson, with his authentic pitching motion, sells the scene perfectly.

The filmmakers also enlisted nearly a full roster of stars to play themselves in the baseball scenes. Some are dialogue-free cameos, like Paul O'Neill, Rafael Palmeiro, and Carlos Baerga. Wally Joyner gets one line ("Can't we ever get you out?"). Mickey Tettleton gets two. Neither proved themselves worthy of future acting work.

The two most fascinating cameos, however, come in the film's climactic game, when the Twins play the Mariners in a one-game playoff to decide who will move on to the postseason. Ken Griffey, Jr. serves a key role, hitting a bomb to give the Mariners the lead and then getting picked off during Billy's elaborate spin on the classic "hidden ball trick." It's a noble move by Griffey, Jr. that really supports the film. He shows off his arrogance when he arrives at first base after a walk and a pick-off attempt. "Just for that, I'm taking second, I'm taking third. I might even take home." His hubris is punished when he falls for the trick and is tagged out at second by Elster, whose wink mirrors the one Griffey gave to the Twins dugout after his home run. Kudos to Griffey for allowing himself to be the butt of the joke, although the brilliant catch he makes to end the game—and the Twins' season—in the next inning surely helped soothe his ego.

In a film of great baseball prescience, its greatest prediction came later in that very inning when Randy Johnson, the Mariners flame-throwing starter, is brought in as the closer to face Lou Collins. Summoning an ace from the bullpen was a truly rare occurrence at this point in baseball, not like these days when playoff teams routinely use starters as relievers in the postseason. Conventional wisdom at the time was that pitchers perform best when used in a consistent role. Regardless, the writers of *Little Big League*, in a display of sabermetric thinking, questioned the unwritten rule and came up with something new. Johnson was an intimidator, a 6'10" southpaw with a high-90s fastball and a wipeout slider. What forward-thinking manager wouldn't use him in a crucial situation against the opponent's best left-handed hitter?

Mariners manager Lou Piniella, who appears in the film as himself, did the exact same thing in real life the next season. In the decisive fifth game of the 1995 American League Division Series against the Yankees, Piniella brought in Johnson with runners on first and second in the ninth inning of a tie game. The big southpaw promptly retired the side, and then struck out the side in the 10th, before giving up a go-ahead run in the 11th (he still got the "win," a semi-meaningless statistic, when the Mariners rallied for two in the bottom of the 11th). Whether Piniella was actually inspired by the events of *Little Big League* is unknown. What's clear is that the use of aces as relief pitchers in the postseason is just another thing it predicted about the future of baseball.

Of course, a high baseball IQ wouldn't mean much if the film wasn't such a good time. *Little Big League* is up there with *The Bad News Bears* and *Major League* among the funniest baseball movies, and for that, much of the credit should go to Scheinman, who deftly navigates the challenges of creating a kids movie for adults. It's Scheinman's lone directorial effort, but he has an impressive résumé as a co-founder and executive at Castle Rock Entertainment, the Rob Reiner–founded production company behind *The Princess Bride, When Harry Met Sally,* and *A Few Good Men*. More notably, he was also an executive producer on *Seinfeld*, whose influence on *Little Big League* is evident in its vignettes of sharp observational humor. There's the running bit in which Mac can't figure out the answer to a riddle posed to him by the backup catcher—you know, the one about a cowboy who rode into town on Friday, stayed three days, and rode out on Friday. Or the moment before the climactic game, when the players interrupt their pregame rituals to help Billy with his math homework. It's a word problem about two people painting a house, which causes Blackout to wonder, "Why doesn't he get a house that's already painted?"

The stand-up sensibility really stands out in the scenes between Billy and his two age-appropriate friends played by Billy L. Sullivan and Miles Fuelner. Whenever the three of them are together, the conversation devolves into discussions, as *Seinfeld* would famously describe it, "about nothing," such as whether it still counts as fishing if you never catch anything, or the practical realities of Batman eating fast food. This last one especially follows the deranged logic of *Seinfeld*, as it ends with Fuelner's character musing, "I'd hate to be the guy behind the Batmobile in the drive-thru. When Batman steps on the gas, and those flames come out..." We can finish the thought for him. Despite the juvenile subject matter—and *Seinfeld* itself had its share of that—it's a fairly sophisticated comic exchange.

These little touches are irrelevant to the plot, which at times makes *Little Big League* feel absurdist and almost radical in form, compared to the play-it-down-the-middle kids' sports movies of its era. It's a clever decision. The kids come across as a little more intellectually mature than you would expect, which makes the idea of one of them fitting into a major league clubhouse, where the maturity level is admittedly not high, a bit easier to swallow. In fact, a case could be made that Billy is decidedly smarter than someone like Lonnie (Joseph Lattimore), who is amazed at how smart the kids are in Venezuela because, even at a young age, they all speak fluent Spanish. "They speak Spanish in Venezuela," Lou gently responds, causing Lonnie to exclaim, "I know, that's my point!"

With its baseball bonafides and smart comedy, why is *Little Big League* not considered among the best baseball films? It's not like the film doesn't have its supporters. John Gordon, the real-world Twins announcer who played a thinly veiled version of himself in the film, said that "the actual baseball footage that they got was probably some of the best baseball footage that has ever been produced in baseball films." In the critical community, once again we go to Roger Ebert, who agreed that "it's one of those rare baseball movies that has a real feel for the game, instead of using it as a backdrop for bizarre characters." But the film was mostly shrugged aside by critics and managed only a miniscule $12 million box-office haul. Part of this had to be bad timing. It had been ten years and about thirty baseball films since *The Natural.* Audiences may have simply grown tired of the genre. *Little Big League* also had the misfortune of coming out at the tail end of the kids baseball movie boom; *The Sandlot, Rookie of the Year,* and *Angels in the Outfield* had all been released in the same 18-month period.

It's also worth wondering if the very things that made *Little Big League* unique made it difficult for audiences to wrap their minds around. "*Rookie of the Year* was a kids' fantasy fulfillment," argues Jazayerli, "but *Little Big League* was a weird mishmash of a kids' fantasy with a very mature way of looking at the sport itself. The Venn diagram of that audience is very small, but I was smack dab in the middle of it." *Little Big League* was simultaneously ahead of its time and behind it, which would both explain its poor reception at the time and its slow growth in popularity. In recent years, *Time* magazine, *The Athletic,* and the *Kansas City Star* have all published anniversary pieces celebrating the film's achievements.

And yet the film's artistic success and commercial failure portended a coming storm. Six weeks after *Little Big League* was released, baseball had its first strike in nine years. The previous strike in 1985 led to exactly zero canceled games, but in 1994, the season was scrapped after August 12, and, for the first time since 1904, there was no World Series. The ramifications were far-reaching. Baseball attendance and viewership dropped significantly in 1995, and the sour taste stayed in many fans' mouths until 1998, when it was chemically sweetened by the dual pursuit of the single-season home run record by Mark McGwire and Sammy

Sosa. Most baseball people believe that one reason the league looked the other way on steroids was that they were desperate to win back the fans they had lost during the strike.

By June 29, when the film was released, most everyone knew a strike was imminent, and it's possible that baseball fans weren't in the mood for a baseball movie lark. They wouldn't be for a while afterward either. The next few years represented the baseball movie's dying gasp. *Major League II, The Scout,* and *The Fan* all have their moments; the latter's toxic portrayal of the fan-player relationship, using a Barry Bonds surrogate played by Wesley Snipes, clearly reflected the bitterness of the strike era and maybe even the coming toxicity of the steroid era. But none of them were hits.

For Love of the Game, a Kevin Costner vehicle that's absolutely beloved by former players for its realistic glimpse into the mind of a ballplayer on the field, came out in 1999 and made $35 million, but with its $50 million budget, it was a financial failure. Cable TV proved a soft landing spot for baseball films; 1996's *Soul of the Game,* a nifty bit of fan fiction about the Negro Leagues, and 2000's *61*,* which chronicled the Mantle–Maris pursuit of Babe Ruth's single-season home run record, are both worthy entries in the canon. In 2002, Disney's *The Rookie,* the true story of Jim Morris, a 35-year-old high school baseball coach who made it to the major leagues, offered a temporary return to prominence for baseball cinema; it grossed $80 million. But the film has no legacy today, and it's easy to see why. It feels too calculated to truly inspire, and it tells us nothing of the world. Its baseball magic, while based on truth, rings hollow.

As it turns out, it would take a technological revolution to make the baseball movie relevant again. Somewhere between 1994 and now, the world fundamentally changed. The internet reconfigured our lives, and those who could master data and algorithms took over leadership of the universe. These are people like Billy Heywood, who couldn't play the game but knew how to run it. In reality, he would have used his perch atop the Minnesota Twins organization to hire Bill James long before the Red Sox did, and he would have certainly beat Billy Beane to the moneyball era. It's too bad we never got to see it. *Little Big League* didn't do well enough to earn even a direct-to-DVD sequel. It was too early to its ideas, but that's baseball. You have to lose before you can win, and sometimes the seasons where you watch a great team come together and go on a winning streak but fall short of its lofty goals are the ones you love the most.

Seventh-Inning Stretch
An Interview with Richard Linklater

Writer-director Richard Linklater was the starting left fielder and No. 3 hitter for Sam Houston State University when he was diagnosed with an infection of the heart tissue. It led to an arrhythmia (that has since corrected itself) and a decree from his doctor that he needed to give up baseball. The timing was fortuitous. Linklater had just begun taking a theater class and writing plays. His mind was already drifting away from baseball. He'd be standing in the outfield thinking about Dostoevsky when he should have been focused on the game.

Forty-something years later, it's clear he made the right choice. Linklater has directed twenty-two feature films, including box-office hits (*School of Rock*), cult classics (*Dazed and Confused*), Oscar nominees (*Boyhood*), and critical darlings (*Before Sunrise* and its sequels). His work helped launch the careers of Ben Affleck, Matthew McConaughey, and Glen Powell. He's also the preeminent baseball filmmaker of all time, even if he doesn't think of himself that way.

Richard Linklater: It's bizarre that I even qualify for this book, but I was thinking about it, and I guess I have touched on baseball in five movies.

Noah Gittell: I counted six.

Linklater: The documentary. In *Boyhood*, they go to an Astros game. In *Dazed*, he's a pitcher. And for leading roles, it's *Everybody Wants Some!!*, *Bears*...

Gittell: There's baseball in *Apollo 10½*.

Linklater: Oh, of course. At the Astrodome. So there you go. Well, obviously, it's been a big backdrop to my life.

Gittell: Is that why baseball is in so many of your films—because it's part of your life—or is there something about putting the sport on film that really interests you artistically?

Linklater: Baseball does permeate my life, but there is something special about filmed baseball. You can potentially do a better job with it than other sports. I've contemplated a football movie before, and it's just hard to fake it on screen. It's a choreography of 22 people. In basketball, you've got 10 people, and it's hard to capture the way they move. In baseball, you have these individual acts: pitching, hitting, fielding. You can break it down and still maintain the flow of the game.

Gittell: I think a lot about the pace of baseball. The time between pitches, or at least the time there used to be between pitches. Like the scene in *Dazed*. You stretch the moment before that strikeout for a long time, and we really feel the weight and the drama of that moment.

Linklater: I milk it! I think that was the first time I put baseball on film. It was so much fun. There are a lot of wonderful details with baseball, and it has more of a history to draw from. When I go to film a baseball sequence, I have so many baseball films in my head, good or bad versions of how I would want to do it. There are just more than other sports. Baseball got there first, and it stayed there. It was recorded and historically archived so early. I grew up watching it. Come baseball season, they'd always be on TV, the *Million Dollar Movie*, and I looked forward to watching them every year.

Gittell: Which ones in particular?

Linklater: Some of them are corny, but you like them, anyway. We're very forgiving of baseball movies. *The Babe Ruth Story* or *Pride of the Yankees.* I kind of like the gimmicky ones, like *It Happens Every Spring* or *Angels in the Outfield.* That's the thing about baseball. You can go in so many directions with it. You can make an ensemble film with a team. You can tell a story about one player and his dilemma. You can make an adult drama or a broad comedy. There's a lot of latitude. You can play it raunchy or straight.

Gittell: I was surprised to read you weren't a huge fan of the original *Bad News Bears* when it first came out. Were you just the wrong age?

Linklater: I was the wrong age. I was a freshman in high school playing on the varsity baseball team. I was a serious baseball player at this point. Why would I watch a bunch of 12-year-olds who aren't very good? I was trying to be a cool high school kid and not watch a kids movie, even though I knew it was raunchy and funny. I saw it on cable in the '80s, and of course, I liked it, but I didn't have the reverence for it that younger people did. I remember when I was doing the remake, younger filmmakers were like, "How could you?" They thought it was sacred ground, and I was just like, "Ya know, it's just a good baseball movie."

Gittell: One of the reasons I was surprised to hear you weren't obsessed with it is because it really feels like a Linklater movie. It came out the same year *Dazed* is set, and it looks like they exist in the same universe.

Linklater: They do! It's the same kind of neighborhood-y baseball vibe, and I was trying to capture that. And don't get me wrong. I never saw it and rejected it. I just didn't see it when it first came out. I do love the movie.

Gittell: Okay, you're on the record now. You don't hate *The Bad News Bears.*

Linklater: No, how could you? In fact, when we were doing *The School of Rock*, we referenced *The Bad News Bears* quite a bit since it's also about this group of outsiders who get together and almost win a championship.

Gittell: The original *Bad News Bears* has a lot of baseball in it, which some of these movies don't. Was that part of what appealed to you about doing a remake?

Linklater: Absolutely. I had touched on baseball before, but this probably has the highest percentage of baseball in it than any other movie. It's super high. I appreciated that, and there were so many opportunities to bring authentic baseball. Even though the level of expertise among the players is low, you can still be authentic within their skillset. I took that as a big challenge. I didn't want any stunt people. I got kids who could play. Sammi Kane Kraft, the pitcher, she could really throw. We just took it really seriously as a baseball movie, which is the most fun way to do it. Doing a sequel to a beloved movie, you're kind of dead in the water to begin with. You accept that going in, and then you give it hell.

Gittell: You pointed out once that most movies are made by people who have never played sports.

Linklater: That's true.

Gittell: You obviously have played a lot of sports. What do you think you bring to a baseball movie, as someone who has played this game at a pretty high level, that people who haven't played can't access?

Linklater: You can always tell. When I saw *Bull Durham*, I could tell, "This guy played ball." I didn't need to read a profile of Ron Shelton. I just knew. That inner monologue? That's very real. Someone who didn't play wouldn't even know that. No screenwriter can imagine that. It can only come from your experience. Now, there have been a lot of good baseball movies made by people who didn't play, but often they have these goofy things that throw real players off. You accept the artifice of the whole thing, but you also see stuff and think, "No one who ever made it to the major leagues would be that incompetent." It's not Little League ball. You don't look the other way and get hit in the nuts with the ball. Do you know how good you have to be to be in the majors? No. They're not amateurs. Everyone has a right to get hyperbolic and have fun. There can be a slapstick element. I can enjoy it but also realize that it's not even pretending to be real.

Gittell: I do feel when I watch your movies there's a mission in there to portray not just the action realistically but also the mindset of the athlete. In so many movies, the athlete is depicted in such a one-dimensional way, but your athletes are interested in other things besides sports. Are you trying to bring a certain authenticity to the genre?

Linklater: That is specific to baseball. Having played high school football in Texas and then baseball, I marveled at the differences in the sports. In football, you can die. You can be killed if you're not dialed in and totally focused. There's an intensity in the locker room. There's no room for conversations and jokes. You can have fun and enjoy it, but there's a focus. Even the benchwarmers aren't talking shit. The coaches demand it. In baseball, on the other hand, there's a lot of guys sitting around who have no chance of playing. The starting pitcher who threw yesterday, they're just bench jockeys. They're bored. And baseball players can be witty. You have time to mess with each other. If your team's up at bat, most of the team is just sitting on the bench. There's a lot of time to fill, and they often fill it with humor.

Gittell: You've done a lot of things in your career, but one thing you're known for are these films where people are hanging out and talking. Do you think that style comes from your time in baseball, or did you gravitate toward baseball because you like sitting around and talking?

Linklater: That's a good question. A chicken-and-egg kind of thing. I did always appreciate that about baseball. In *Everybody*

Wants Some!!, the stakes are low. They're practicing. The coach isn't even on the field. The guys are dialed in, but there's room for long-running gags and conversations. Glen Powell talking about probabilistic stuff and superstition. Personally, I don't believe in any of that stuff, but if I get near a baseball field, suddenly I'm superstitious. It's believable that they could be having that conversation on the bench. There's always a guy on every team who sees himself as the team intellectual. He reads more books and acts smarter than everyone. The other guys sort of make fun of him, but usually he's fun to be around. Usually not the best player. And it would never happen on a football or a basketball bench.

Gittell: I put the call out to former and current players to talk about baseball movies for this book, and for some reason, only pitchers responded. I asked a few of them why they thought that was. And they said, well, it's because we have so much time on the bench that we become better conversationalists.

Linklater: I was a position player, but I'm the only one who'll say this: Pitchers are smarter overall. A very good pitcher had to tell me this, and he's right: The best hitters aren't that smart. They can't be. You can't overthink it. See ball, hit ball. Greg Maddux could have been a surgeon. Steve Carlton was always smarter than everyone. Even the fireballers like Nolan Ryan, Bob Gibson, or Roger Clemens, they're tough guys, but you always feel like they're two moves ahead of you. They're a little more calculating because they have to be. Hitters only react. They don't initiate the move. Pitchers are definitely more contemplative. Most of those team intellectuals are pitchers. Only left-handed weirdo pitchers.

Gittell: I heard you say you didn't consider *Everybody Wants Some!!* to be a baseball movie because there's so little baseball in it, but to me as a non-player, a great baseball movie shows me the things that I can't see on TV. The locker room, the team meetings, the first practice of the year. *Everybody Wants Some!!* definitely did that for me.

Linklater: In the end, I do consider it a baseball movie, even though the time on the field is very limited. But what you get with that movie is the mentality. The camaraderie, the brotherhood. Particularly at a college level, where you're all living together. You're teammates, and you're roommates. You're in each other's lives to a huge degree. Pros all travel together, but they don't live together. College is unique that way, and there are no other college baseball movies, as far as I know. I was really trying to show the mentality, the utterly ridiculous arch-competitiveness that reigns at that age. It's laughable, but it's also very telling. That's what winning teams are like. There's at least one guy there is who kinda nuts and refuses to lose.

Gittell: I love the deal with McReynolds, how he won't make friends with the pitcher because he might see them in pro ball, and he doesn't want to give them an edge.

Linklater: I don't know if anyone really said that in college because pro ball is so far away. But I've heard of Barry Bonds and guys like that, once they were in the minor leagues, they didn't want to be friends with pitchers. I thought that was pretty funny, and it's a real thing.

Gittell: We've got to talk about *Boyhood*, where Ethan Hawke, the single dad, takes his kids to the Astros game, talks about Roger Clemens, and witnesses a walk-off homer. How much of that was scripted?

Linklater: The dialogue was scripted. He's talking about Clemens, and how he was so dominant in those years with the Astros. But you can't script the baseball. I got the rights from the club to shoot only for a few innings. It was really minimal. I had a limited area. Two cameras, one in the press box and one in the stands. I was thinking that whatever happened, I would just work with it. But it's one of the more fortuitous moments I ever had. I just thought, "Let's point the camera to left field and hope something happens." It was in our last inning, and Jason Lane hits a home run right down the middle where the camera was pointed. I couldn't believe it.

Gittell: I'm sure you were jumping up and down along with the crowd.

Linklater: Actually, I was sitting in front of the camera so I could turn around and talk to the actors. But when he hit the ball, those are my hands on the screen that go up. I was acting, though. Those were acting hands. Of course, I made it a walk-off home run in the editing. Years later, someone who was at the game came up to me and said, "That wasn't actually a walk-off home run. That happened in the seventh inning."

Gittell: I thought the Clemens stuff was an interesting time capsule. Ethan Hawke's character is raving about how Clemens is beating Father Time and striking out guys half his age. It's the theme of the movie, aging and the passage of time. But Clemens' reputation has also changed so much over the years. It must have felt like one thing when you shot it, and another thing when you were editing it all together so many years later.

Linklater: It sure did. When the Mitchell Report came out, I had already filmed the baseball stuff, and I saw the list of names of guys who had allegedly used steroids—one of which is David Ortiz, who is happily in the Hall of Fame now, no more or less guilty than Roger—-but yeah, my heart kinda sank as I wondered what it would do to my movie. Film critics, people who like *Boyhood*, they don't really know that much about baseball, though.

Gittell: I know you were an Astros fan, but I also read that after you quit playing, you kind of quit paying attention for a while. Where are you now in your fandom?

Linklater: I had a 20-year gap. From 20 to 40. I had a non-athletic binge. Really, I missed entire eras of sports. I was making up for lost time. Watching movies. My life was the arts. I really didn't think much about it at all. I think that when the players are suddenly your age, they're less interesting. They're your contemporaries. Once I was older than all the players, I could start being a fan again. I even lost track of guys I had played with or against. I didn't even know how their careers went. Years later, I got a Baseball Encyclopedia, and started looking up guys I had played against to see how their careers were.

Gittell: Who was one of the better guys you played against?

Linklater: McReynolds is loosely based on a guy I played with named Glenn Wilson. He was a first-round draft pick and spent a lot of time with the Phillies. He had a long career. He had this incredible arm and was always throwing guys out. He was a great hitter, so much better than the rest of us. The guys who were great ballplayers, you could tell right away they had major league talent. And then you look them up, and they only played half a season or something. It just shows how tough and unpredictable it all is.

Gittell: Was it at all painful in those years from 20 to 40 to watch baseball? Was there some sense that you could have still been playing?

Linklater: It was never that. I had no regrets. I never looked back. At some point along the way, I realized I didn't have the mentality to be a major leaguer anyway. I might have the desire, but there's a difference between having desire and some ability, and having that X factor that makes a major leaguer. I thought too much to be a great hitter. I tended to overthink, which only gets you in trouble. Have you ever read that David Foster Wallace essay, "How Tracy Austin Broke My Heart?" He was a pretty good tennis player, but he analyzes very clearly what kept him from greatness. He thought too much. And he analyzed what a banal interview Tracy Austin was, and he was disappointed, until he realized, of course, that's what makes her great.

Gittell: The sport is their language. It's how they communicate.

Linklater: And they don't have to explain it because they've always been really good at it. That's why the best players don't always make the best managers. They're so naturally gifted at it.

And I kinda say the same thing about movie stars. You have to have a mentality for it. You can either hit a 92-mph slider or you can't. If you can't, you can't be here. You wanna be in a musical? Do you have this octave range? If you can't, you can't be here. Can you put a whole film together in your head? Because if you can't, you can't be a filmmaker. I always drew some solace from the realization that I didn't have the mentality to be a professional athlete. I had it to be a filmmaker.

Gittell: That leads me to *Inning by Inning*. When you look at your friend Augie Garrido, the longtime baseball coach at University of Texas, were you interested in him in the ways he was like you, or the ways he was different from you?

Linklater: What I appreciated about Augie was that baseball was his life. He channeled the world through baseball, but he didn't think it was particularly important. He enjoyed those ironies. He'd say, you have to be totally focused, but you have to be loose. You have to be all these things at the same time. Augie had a winning, positive, productive mentality. He created that. He took the greatest hits of his own coaches and incorporated them. I do the same thing. I think it's why many actors go on to be good directors. If you work with a lot of directors, and you pay attention, you can see what makes yourself better or not better.

I just found Augie interesting as an individual, and I asked him on a whim, "Hey, can I put a mic on you and follow you around this year?" He said, "Yeah, whatever." I'm not a documentary filmmaker, but it just seemed like there was something there I could learn. I did eventually ask myself, "How is this like what I do?" I even apologized in advance to him and let him know that every film is a certain amount of self-portrait. I'm not trying to tip the scales. I'm trying to capture his life, but there's an inherent bias in the things that I find interesting. You can't help but personalize it.

Augie sort of got in trouble because I included that one scene where he loses it on the team. It went viral, and it's part of his legacy that is really unfortunate. I talked to one of his players who told me Augie did that once a year at most. But I saw it, and I was like, "There's something good about that." Now I do it once every film, where you demonstrably get a little pissed off because people aren't trying their hardest. That's what a leader has to do every now and then. Show that it matters.

Gittell: There was no one in that room who cared more than him.

Linklater: The leader has to care the most. If the leader doesn't care much, that trickles down pretty quickly. You've got to know your leader cares because you don't want to let them down. It was interesting talking with his former players and seeing what lessons they took from Augie. It was definitely positive. I don't read self-help books. I don't care about any of that shit. I don't want to do anything that artificially makes you feel good about the world. I'm not that kind of positive-reinforcement person. It's just corny to me. What I appreciated about Augie is that his lessons were hard-earned life lessons. You can't just glom it on to something. You have to live it and be it. I don't know. I just liked the dude.

Gittell: *Inning by Inning* premiered on ESPN, and *Everybody Wants Some!!* is the last baseball movie to get a big mainstream release.

Linklater: Is it really?

Gittell: It is actually the longest period without a studio baseball movie being released since 1973.

Linklater: Whoa!

Gittell: There are a lot of straight-to-streaming baseball films being made, but none have gotten a significant theatrical release. I wonder if you have any insight into what makes these movies so difficult to get made.

Linklater: I read this article once. Somewhere along the way, some Hollywood executive was considering the global markets, and how films do and don't travel around the world, and he said,

"The world doesn't want to see our baseball movies." He really had it in for them. And he seemed right the way he laid it out. Like it's economic suicide to make a baseball movie. He was trying to give the industry a wake-up call. "No more baseball movies!"

Gittell: I think people have been saying that since the beginning of cinema.

Linklater: But they have shelf lives, don't they? Baseball is kinda like Hollywood that way. It's been dying forever. It lost out to football a long time ago. Like Hollywood losing out to TV. The demise is always right around the corner. But it keeps reinventing itself and perpetuating itself, somehow, someway. Baseball is sort of a perpetual motion machine. It gets passed on from generation to generation. You take the baton and pass it to the next. Kinda beautiful that way. Movies and baseball.

· PART V ·

The Expansion Era

Chapter 15

Moneyball (2011) and *Trouble with the Curve* (2012)

In late September 2011, legendary political strategist Joe Trippi went to a double feature. Afterward, he shared his thoughts on social media: "Of the two movies—*Moneyball* and *Ides of March*—turns out the baseball movie is more like the Dean campaign." The films came out within two weeks of each other that autumn. One was about politics, and the other was about baseball. Or were they? *The Ides of March* was written by Beau Willimon, an intern on the 2004 Howard Dean presidential campaign that revolutionized American politics by capitalizing on the internet's potential for fundraising and grassroots organizing. After leading in the polls for weeks, Dean came in third in the first-in-the-nation Iowa caucuses, yelled awkwardly during his post-caucus concession speech (forever known in political lore as "the scream"), and was pilloried by the media for the supposed gaffe. In the end, John Kerry won the nomination, and Dean had to settle for being named chair of the Democratic National Committee. His legacy, however, was in how other campaigns adopted his strategies. Four years later, a candidate named Barack Obama used the same grassroots techniques, adding to them a generational talent for oration and an irresistible personal story, and rode them all the way to the White House.

Or to put it another way: "The first one through the door always gets bloodied." Those are the words of John Henry, owner of the Boston Red Sox, in *Moneyball*, talking about Billy Beane (Brad Pitt), who revolutionized baseball in much the same way Dean and Trippi, his national campaign manager, transformed politics: by utilizing the power of data to gain an advantage over better-funded opposition. Beane never got to the World Series, and Dean never got to White House, but imitation is the sincerest form of flattery. The Red Sox adopted Beane's moneyball approach, added money to it, and won a World Series in 2004.

Trippi, a lifelong baseball fan, explained the connection between *Moneyball* and the Dean campaign. "We had to find a completely different way to compete, and without the normal resources. To dive into the digital space and data, and use that to outcompete the bigger, better guys. When we started, we only had $98,000, but we were able to play with the big boys because we were ahead of them on digital," he says. "If John Kerry was the Yankees, we were the A's."

Based on the 2003 bestseller by Michael Lewis, *Moneyball* came at a fallow time for the baseball movie. The boom of the '80s and '90s had run its course, and while the genre still produced an occasional box-office hit, most baseball films of this era failed to make an impact with the public. *Summer Catch* was a disaster. *Mr. 3000* is good, but it never found an audience. The less said about *Ed*, in which Matt LeBlanc from *Friends* plays baseball with a chimpanzee—check that, a man in a chimpanzee costume—the better.

I'd stick up for *Fever Pitch*. A reimagining of Nick Hornby's memoir about an obsessive fan of the Arsenal Football Club, the 2005 comedy from co-directors Peter and Bobby Farrelly expertly taps into the misery of loving a losing franchise. They chose the Red Sox because the brothers grew up in New England, but it works just as well for fans of the Mets, Guardians, Mariners, Rockies, Padres, or any fanbase that views themselves as perpetual underdogs. The scenes in which Ben, played by future *Tonight Show* host Jimmy Fallon, comes to grips with his own toxic fandom are poignant and thoughtfully rendered, and if nothing else, *Fever Pitch* deserves credit for its novelty: It's the first baseball film ever to focus entirely on the fans, at least not ones who end up playing on the team or running it.

Although it wasn't a hit, *Fever Pitch* signaled a change in the baseball film, which began looking beyond its typical underdogs—aging catchers, brainless pitchers, infirm superstars, children with special powers— in search of even more marginalized heroes. This expansion could be viewed as part of a broader trend toward authenticity in Hollywood filmmaking, caused by a confluence of factors including the advent of digital filmmaking, which favored hyper-realistic action over sepia-tinted nostalgia; anxiety about the implications of computer-generated imagery that could replace humans on screen; and even the tragic events of 9/11, which for a time rendered Hollywood sentimentalism irrelevant. The romantic comedy was dead. Action films had little use for quippy stars like Stallone and Schwarzenegger, and instead favored stoic heroes and shaky-cam action sequences, like those that made Jason Bourne a global sensation.

These developments left the baseball movies in limbo. How does a genre built on nostalgia survive in an era of anti-romanticism? The answer was *Moneyball*, a film that balances bold, new ideas on old, familiar tropes. *Moneyball* chronicles a revolution in baseball front-office strategy that mirrored similar changes happening in politics, finance, surveillance, and pretty much every other industry. But it's not a revolutionary film. It employs a tried-and-true narrative in which a team of misfits come together under an unorthodox leader, learn to play to their potential, get close to the championship but lose, and find a happy ending in its "wait til next year" denouement. It's the same template the baseball film used since *The Bad News Bears*, except the adult-in-charge is in much better physical shape.

Even before the film was made, Billy Beane saw himself as a character in a baseball movie. When asked in 1999 to present to the Commissioner's Blue Ribbon Panel on Baseball Economics, an internal MLB effort to solve the growing issue of revenue parity, Beane opened his presentation with a slide that described the plot of *Major League*, and compared the A's, who were also reliant on cheap players, to the Indians of that film. Even to these learned men and women, the best way to describe the A's economic conundrum was to cite a baseball film. *Moneyball* was a movie waiting to happen.

As perpetual underdogs since their heyday in the late '80s and early '90s, the story of the A's may have lent itself to a conventional baseball movie, but there was a chance for *Moneyball* to be genuinely groundbreaking. Before Aaron Sorkin came on to write the script and Bennett Miller, recently minted as an Oscar-friendly director with 2005's *Capote*, was chosen to direct, *Moneyball* was set to be made by Steven Soderbergh. An Oscar winner for 2000's *Traffic*, Soderbergh was also known for a fierce independent streak. In between studio projects like *Erin Brockovich* and *Ocean's Eleven*, he made strange, arty films with titles like *Schizopolis, Full Frontal,* and *Bubble*. When Soderbergh was hired to make *Moneyball*, his bosses likely thought they were getting the former, but the script Soderbergh turned in was more avant-garde. Labeled a "semi-documentary approach" by *The Hollywood Reporter*, it was said to have reflected the innovative spirit of its front-office subjects, mixing real-life major leaguers in with the actors, featuring ballplayers speaking directly to camera in testimonials, and, according to one account, sporting "an abundance of baseball details that executives feared risked alienating viewers." As the rewrites got weirder and weirder, the suits got nervous. In the end, the film was scrapped five days before shooting was set to begin, and producers began searching for a new creative team to tackle the project.

With time to work, Sorkin, Miller, and Steven Zaillian (another Oscar-winner who wrote an early draft and was retained through the film's many permutations) rewrote *Moneyball* to be more conventional, introducing colorful characters, keeping the data-driven discussions to a minimum, and concluding with a classic "big game." They condensed the story of how Beane changed baseball into a single season, creating a satisfying narrative of a rogue employee fighting back against an oppressive system. *Moneyball*, as it came out, is not a story about data or even really about baseball. The new rules that Beane propagated—no bunting, no stealing, only swing at your pitch, run up the pitch count, and get deep into the other team's bullpen—only show up on a few white boards and in well-edited montages of Beane and his right-hand man Peter Brand (Jonah Hill) communicating their approach to the A's players. Instead, it rests on Hollywood's most reliable tropes: underdogs, competition, and a David vs. Goliath narrative, with David played by one of the most charismatic movie stars of his generation.

With Beane's cold, calculating demeanor, he's not the most sympathetic character on the page. He treats the players—who fans of the game have long regarded as heroes—like employees. But that's why you get Brad Pitt, who signed on to play Beane early and whose involvement kept the project going even after Soderbergh's version was canceled. It was his snooping around that turned up Bennett Miller, who is notoriously choosy about his projects. Luckily, the director and star found themselves in lockstep creatively. "We will give them the gift of a Hollywood movie starring Brad Pitt that's going to be real entertainment," Miller described it, "but inside it is some cargo that is not really accepted in a vintage way, something that they don't anticipate."

Beneath its broad, commercial appeal, *Moneyball* tinkered with some of the baseball genre's sturdiest tropes. Consider its portrayal of scouts, who served an important function in the postwar baseball film and remained relevant in later works such as *The Natural* and the 1994 Albert Brooks vehicle *The Scout*. Historically, the scout functions as a reliable entry point for audiences. They can't play the game, but they have a unique ability to appreciate it, just like us (or at least, that's how we see ourselves). They are also a keeper of the mysterious wisdom on which baseball mythology rests. What is the difference between a .250 hitter and a .300 hitter? How can you tell if an 18-year-old kid with a big bat can make it in the show? Who can learn to hit a curveball, and who cannot? Only the scout knows.

In *Moneyball*, the scout knows nothing. Early on, Beane sits in a room full of them, several of which are played by real scouts (the presence of non-actors here feels like a holdover from Soderbergh's vision). As they discuss which players to draft, he listens to a rainbow of clichés that so-called "baseball men" have employed for years to express their gut feelings: They say one player has a "baseball body." He's "clean-cut" with a "good face." He has "a beautiful swing" with "a lot of pop off the bat." Another notes that he "throws the club head at the ball, and when he connects, he drives it," which is more of a literal description of the process of hitting a baseball than an analysis of skills. Sorkin's script saves the biggest laugher for last, as two scouts argue over a player's romantic prowess. "His girlfriend is a six," says one. The other responds, "He's the kind of guy who walks into a room, and his dick has already been there for two minutes." Even to those viewers unschooled in the ways of analytics, it reads as an absurd way to make such a business decision.

For Beane, it's a moment of clarity, in which he realizes the A's cannot overcome their economic obstacles using the same outdated methods that other teams are using. "If we try to play like the Yankees in here," he says, "we will lose to the Yankees out there." Grady (Ken Medlock), the head scout, is unimpressed: "That sounds like fortune cookie wisdom to me, Billy." He's a key figure in the film, the one scout who refuses to play by Beane's rules. Medlock is a secret star of the baseball film genre, a former player who became an actor and appeared as a scout in 1991's *Talent for the Game*, a player in 1985's *Brewster's Millions*, and an umpire in *Mr. Baseball*, *Major League II*, and Richard Linklater's remake of *The Bad News Bears*. He brings an invaluable authenticity to *Moneyball*, with a face that shows its years, and hostility that starts below the surface but explodes in a confrontation with Beane. "This is about you and your shit," he shouts at him. "Some scout got it wrong about you 20 years ago." Although Beane never admits it, the film agrees with Grady. It shows several scenes of young Beane being lavished with praise by scouts and then failing to make it as a professional ballplayer. We might even be tempted to side with Grady, too, if he didn't turn heel after being fired and reveal Beane's plans on a local radio show, bringing intense scrutiny onto Beane as the team endures an early season losing streak. Portraying a scout as not only useless and antiquated but disloyal is a steep and immediate decline from his stature in the genre's seminal films.

The same disrespect is paid to A's manager Art Howe, played with tactical disinterest by Philip Seymour Hoffman. On the page, Howe is little more than an obstacle for Beane to overcome, and while Hoffman ably brings him to life, it's still an unfair portrayal of a baseball lifer who was well-liked by pretty much everyone he met. In reality, Howe was largely supportive of Beane's efforts, but his characterization in the film is a logical way to convey the most meaningful disruption wrought by the moneyball approach: the power struggle between the manager and the front office over the line-up card. Most teams are reluctant to elucidate on the role the front office has in shaping the line-up or any in-game decisions for fear of diminishing the authority of the manager—also, so the manager can take the heat when things go wrong—but it's well-understood that managers have had to relinquish some of their power. Hoffman plays it perfectly, refusing to scream or throw things, instead evoking quiet weariness as a battle strategy. His role as the antagonist, rather than lovable, crusty old-timer whom the team rallies around, is a noteworthy change from managers in baseball cinema's past. It's a dramatic oversimplification of the entire moneyball approach, which hasn't eliminated the need for smart managers or battle-tested scouts, but the dramatic license is worth it. Creating clear-cut conflict is the best way to capture the attention of non-baseball fans, who won't know where the film is stretching or contracting the truth.

The other thing *Moneyball* does differently is, well, its baseball. Very little on-field action is shown in the film. Beane himself doesn't watch the games, so neither do we, and the few moments we do see are filmed unlike any other cinematic baseball action. Many baseball films try to recreate the way the game looks on television, keeping the space between reality and fiction as narrow as possible. *Moneyball* does the opposite, draping its in-game action in high-contrast dramatic lighting, with bright lights hitting the players and heavy shadows behind them. It's hard to describe what exactly it evokes—not quite German expressionism, although close.

Its look is reminiscent of the climactic scene of *The Natural*, but it feels modern instead of ancient. Mostly it just feels new. Which is exactly how the film's events felt. At the time, neither the league, the players, nor the general public knew quite what to make of what the A's were doing. But they could feel the difference, and watching the film, so can we.

In these scenes, we see a lot of pitches being taken and a few walks. Almost all of them occur in montages, but without the typical pop song to tap into your nostalgia. Instead, we get "The Streak," a pulsating bit of score from composer Mychael Danna, and, in the film's climactic moment when Scott Hatteberg (Chris Pratt) hits a walk-off homer to extend the A's win streak to 20, the stirring ambient track "The Mighty Rio Grande" from post-rock group This Will Destroy You. John Fogerty's "Centerfield" it is not, but the approach worked. The song became so iconic that it is now often used in fan-created videos of their favorite real-life moments. When Bryce Harper of the Phillies hit his series-clinching home run in the 2022 National League Championship Series, the YouTube video overlaying his heroics with the *Moneyball* theme was up within hours. *Moneyball* is now the film to which offscreen baseball aspires.

The film's legacy with players is a little rockier. Hall of Famer Jeff Bagwell called *Moneyball* "a farce" for its erasure of the more traditional baseball elements that made the 2002 A's a winner. "They had the three best pitchers in baseball," he said, referring to starters Tim Hudson, Mark Mulder, and Barry Zito, whose names are never mentioned in the film. "You could've stuck anybody out there. My 15-year-old son's team could have been out there with those three pitchers." Other players have noted the relative absence of Miguel Tejada, who is portrayed in the book as a free-swinger who couldn't adjust to Beane's directive to take more pitches and walk more. In the movie, he is played by former major league shortstop Royce Clayton and has but one line of dialogue. In reality, Tejada won the American League MVP in 2002 and had walk-off hits in two separate games during the team's winning streak. Let's also not forget

Eric Chavez, who hit 34 home runs that year and played Gold Glove defense at third base. He also goes unmentioned.

Other players take issue with the whole concept of a film built around Beane, who may be a hero to the business world but is regarded with more skepticism by baseball's labor element. Trevor Hildenberger, who ping-ponged between the majors and the minors for 12 years and played a key role in the unionization of baseball's minor leagues, questions the film's sympathies. "I think what irks me about *Moneyball* is that it celebrates paying players less than they're worth," he says. "The audience is aligned with the billionaire owner and the front office, whose goal is fielding a competitive team without spending the same money as other more popular teams. Instead of paying market value for known production or talent in free agency, they try to find diamonds in the rough who create surplus value because they are in arbitration or pre-arbitration, when players' salary is tied to service time in the major leagues rather than actual production on the field." It's hard to argue with Hildenberger's interpretation, especially as fans, in the years since the film's release, have become more engrossed in news of players' salaries and contract negotiations. Either as a reflection of this shift or an instigator of it, *Moneyball* has something to do with that. "It's not celebrating the players performing at the peak of their craft," he went on. "Instead, it celebrates front-office personnel saving their bosses some money. Saving money should not be the main goal of fielding a baseball team." For many baseball owners, however, that's precisely the goal, and the success of teams like the A's, or more recently, the Tampa Bay Rays, is frequently cited by penny-pinching teams as justification for not spending money in free agency.

The film's influence was felt not just on the field but also in Hollywood boardrooms. After its success (the film grossed $111 million and was nominated for six Oscars, including Best Picture), the sports movie virtually abandoned play on the field and turned its focus toward the White guys in suits. In 2014, Jon Hamm starred in *Million Dollar Arm* as an agent who tries to turn cricket players into professional baseball players in an effort to save his flailing career, while Kevin Costner returned to the sports movie as a rogue NFL general manager in *Draft Day*. Writing in *The Atlantic*, Hampton Stevens cited the rise of fantasy sports as the cause for the new type of sports movie that *Moneyball* embodied. "As fans, we were once armchair quarterbacks or coaches," he wrote. "We now have also become armchair GMs and agents. Fans often spend as much time discussing salary caps and contract disputes as they do completion percentages or a batting average." Hollywood is also a copycat industry, and the success of *Moneyball* clearly paved the way for these other "front-office" sports films.

While the film was an unqualified success in Hollywood, debates continue to rage about whether the strategy it mythologized was good for baseball. Moneyball definitively led to less actual game action. More walks, fewer bunts, and fewer stolen bases added up to fewer balls put in play and, according to some, less excitement. Just a few years after the film was released, baseball started brainstorming new rules to counteract the changes that moneyball spawned: a pitch clock to speed the game up (walks are slow), larger bases to encourage stealing, and minimizing defensive shifts to encourage batters to swing away. Time will tell if these changes mute the negative impact of moneyball on the sport's entertainment value, but either way *Moneyball* cannot be blamed for the decline of the baseball movie. The genre's ability to respond to itself, reflecting America's cultural changes, would not be hindered. In fact, the year after *Moneyball* was released, another film came along that seemed to respond directly to it.

Clint Eastwood has been old for a long time. In 1992, he directed and starred in *Unforgiven*, a western about an aging gunslinger trying to make amends for the violence and cruelty of his younger days. Eastwood was 62 when the film was released, and many critics wondered if it was his swan song. Oops. Since then, he has acted in 14 movies and, incredibly, directed 23 feature films, many of which center his advancing age in their narratives. Taken as a whole, his late-career filmography can be read as a defense or even a celebration of the old-fashioned values on which he built his film persona. His alpha-masculinity. His reliance on instinct. His willingness to use violence to protect the innocent. In *Gran Torino*, he saves his neighbors, a family of Korean immigrants, from gang violence and street thugs. He's Dirty Harry but old. *Sully*, which he directed but did not star in, frames the heroism of captain Chesley Sullenberger—who famously crash-landed a commercial airliner in the Hudson River without losing a passenger and then was criticized by the Federal Aviation Administration for his actions—as a victory for wise, gray-haired men of action over data-driven pencil pushers.

Which brings us to *Trouble with the Curve*, which Eastwood starred in and did not direct, but which nonetheless bears the hallmarks of the late-period Eastwood movie. It was the directorial debut of Robert Lorenz, Eastwood's longtime producer, so it's fair to assume the star had significant influence over the final product. Much like *Sully*, it's a passionate defense of age-earned wisdom against those who think decisions can be made solely on algorithms, equations, and computers. It was released in 2012, too close to *Moneyball* to be considered an intentional response to it; at minimum, movies take several years to be made from greenlight to release date. Instead, it's likely a response to the concept of "moneyball" itself, and it fits perfectly within Eastwood's filmography overflowing with stories of grizzled older men triumphing over the modern world.

The central conflict in *Trouble with the Curve* is between Gus Lobel (Eastwood), a longtime Atlanta Braves scout who runs entirely on baseball instinct, and Phillip Sanderson (Matthew Lillard), an ambitious front-office type who believes he can analyze a player on data alone. Their competing theories are tested as the Braves consider which player to take with the second overall pick in the upcoming amateur draft. Sanderson wants to select slugger Bo Gentry (Joe Massingill) without even seeing him in person. "I don't need to see him play," he says. "These programs are an essential tool to evaluate today's talent." A few scenes later, Gus retorts, "Anybody who uses a computer doesn't know a damn thing about this game." It kind of sounds like they both should be fired.

Nevertheless, the script by Randy Brown stacks the deck in Gus' favor, reminding us in awkwardly scripted exposition that he once signed real-life Braves stars Dale Murphy, Chipper Jones, and Tom Glavine, and awarding him a rich backstory to allow us to forgive his grumpiness. He is a widower with a beautiful, accomplished daughter (Amy Adams). He has a close friend in the front office (John Goodman), with whom he has maintained a long, loyal relationship. He's kind and generous to the other scouts he sees on the road. When he runs into a former prospect he once scouted (Justin Timberlake) but who later flamed out due to arm injuries, he treats him like an old friend. It's a key point in the broader narrative. To Gus, players aren't numbers on a screen. He sees them as human beings, and that's what makes him good at his job.

The only thing we know about Sanderson, on the other hand, is that he recently bought a boat. He exists only as a foil. We know nothing of his personal life, only his ambition to become a general manager and his willingness to casually push aside a respected veteran like Gus. Played by Matthew Lillard, whose résumé of playing jerks runs from typical philanderers (*The Descendants*) to actual psychopaths (*Scream*), Sanderson is a symbol of everything the film thinks is wrong with the game, and maybe with the world. He is cocky, arrogant, and disloyal, and has no respect for his elders. Worst of all, he's over-reliant on data. "Gus couldn't even turn on a typewriter," Sanderson smirks at one point, "let alone a computer."

Over the next 90 minutes, the filmmakers carefully enact a scenario to prove beyond a reasonable doubt there are things you cannot see on a stat sheet. Gus travels to North Carolina to assess Gentry, an alleged five-tool prospect. Sanderson is salivating over him, but Gus isn't sure. He notices the kid can't hit breaking balls with any authority, even against high school competition. Gus can't see well anymore—he has the early signs of glaucoma—but years of scouting players in person have given him tools that go beyond mere sight. He can hear the sound the ball makes off Gentry's bat, and that's enough for him to recommend to his bosses they look elsewhere in the draft. We know he's right, of course, because he's Clint Eastwood. It all adds up to a victory for humanity over algorithms. To situate it in the world of baseball cinema, it's a celebration of the scout for his ability to identify and nurture human talent. And in case it wasn't abundantly clear, we get this little speech from Gus:

> Scouts, good scouts, are the heart of this game. They decide who's gonna play and if they're lucky, they decide how it's going to be played. A computer, they can't tell if a kid's got instinct or not, if they can hit a cutoff man, or hit behind a runner, or look into a kid's face who has just gone 0-for-4 and be able to come back the next night like nothing's happened.

A clearer rebuke to *Moneyball* would be hard to imagine. In *Moneyball*, it's the front-office guy with a passion for analytics who is played by the movie star, who has a rich backstory, who is down to his last strike with his boss, and who has a daughter with whom he's trying to forge a closer relationship. And it's the scout who is disloyal, arrogant, and stuck in his ways. *Trouble with the Curve* flips this dynamic on its head, creating unshakeable sympathy for the scout and deep antipathy for the analytics guy. In the end, it validates the scout's approach. Gus and his daughter discover a diamond in the rough with a wicked curveball—he's a young man working at the motel they've been staying at throughout the film—and somehow convince the higher-ups to let him face Gentry in a try-out at Turner Field in Atlanta. Of course, their no-name strikes out the lauded prospect. Sanderson gets fired. Clint wins.

Perhaps in part because its views on baseball were out-of-step with its times (or perhaps because it's just not a very good film), *Trouble with the Curve* failed to resonate with audiences the way *Moneyball* did. It grossed only $48 million at the box office, not a terrible haul but the second lowest for any film Eastwood has acted in this century. It also failed to impress the critics or attract any attention at the Oscars, although it was nominated for Best Intergenerational Story at the AARP Movies for Grownups Awards, where it lost to *Silver Linings Playbook*.

The tepid reception of the *Trouble with the Curve*, and the fact it found any audience at all, shows precisely where the baseball movie was headed in the 2010s and beyond. It was a splintered genre. No longer could a baseball film appeal to all viewers. The American public, polarized by political rhetoric, algorithms, and cable news, was too segmented for that. Instead, there would be *Moneyball* for some and *Trouble with the Curve* for others. The national pastime had turned federalist, with each state of fandom getting its own film. This fracturing of the audience would dim the prospects of the baseball film ever returning to its prior glory, when it could dominate the multiplexes and be a no-doubt contender for Best Picture, but it opened the door for new and fascinating stories to be told.

Chapter 16

42 (2013) and *Fences* (2016)

THE STORY OF JACKIE ROBINSON NEVER STAYS DORMANT FOR LONG. As long as racism persists and baseball remains relevant, the tale of the man who broke the sport's color line will continue to be told. It's the origin story of America's postwar dream of racial harmony, a winning argument for democracy, and evidence that our wounds can self-heal. For many years, however, there was only one version. *The Jackie Robinson Story* sufficed. In the years following his death in 1972, however, his myth came roaring back to life in new forms.

The absence is easy to understand, as Robinson became a more complicated figure after leaving baseball. He endorsed Richard Nixon over John F. Kennedy, who won 70 percent of the Black vote in the 1960 presidential election. Later in that decade, Robinson clashed with Black activists, like Malcolm X, who sought a greater revolution than he was willing to embrace. He was always more complicated than Hollywood was willing to admit, but in the '60s and '70s the world got complicated, too, and Robinson's story of racism overcome through passive resistance didn't resonate in the same way.

When Robinson did return, it wasn't to the cinema. First, he came to Broadway. In 1981, a young David Alan Grier starred in *The First*, a musical based on the life of Robinson. Although Grier was praised for his performance and nominated for a Tony Award, the play itself was roundly panned, and it closed after a month of performances. In 1989, *Play to Win* adapted Robinson's story into a one-hour musical aimed at a younger audience. Up until this point, the Robinson myth had been painted only in broad strokes, with one-dimensional heroes and cartoonish villains. Turning it into the theatrical equivalent of an after-school special was a logical move.

In 1990, the cable network TNT aired *The Court-Martial of Jackie Robinson*. A bold reimagining of the Robinson mythology, it focuses almost entirely on his time in the Army, culminating in a tense dramatization of his trial for refusing to adhere to the illegal segregation at Fort Hood. While not a baseball film per se—there is little actual game action in it—the film is noteworthy for its distinct change in tone from the saintly portrayals of Robinson in prior tellings. As played by Andre Braugher, this Robinson is a cauldron of suppressed rage. When challenged with overt racism, he remains outwardly composed, but his lip quivers and his eyes bulge almost imperceptibly. Robinson's eventual explosion at a bus driver is a catharsis of righteous anger. It's a side of Robinson, and in fact of the entire experience of being Black in America, that had rarely been seen in American film to this point. Perhaps that's why it was relegated to cable television, but it deserves to be rediscovered.

Soul of the Game, an HBO original movie that premiered in 1996, featured Robinson (Blair Underwood), alongside Satchel Page (Delroy Lindo) and Josh Gibson (Mykelti Williamson). It's a heavily fictionalized account of life in the Negro Leagues just before baseball desegregated, but fiction can still correct the record. Simply expanding the circle of Black ballplayers from this era who are deemed worthy of dramatization— beyond Robinson to Paige and Gibson—inherently dismantles the pernicious argument that Robinson was exceptional and uniquely suited for the major leagues. It also revises our view of Branch Rickey, the Dodgers owner who schemed for Robinson to break baseball's color line. There's a scene in which New York City mayor Fiorello La Guardia informs Rickey that he's planning on desegregating baseball himself, which motivates Rickey to move ahead quickly with his own plan so that he can receive the credit. In this telling, he's less of a hero and more of an opportunist.

These disparate works brought much-needed depth and shading to our collective portrait of Robinson, but none fundamentally altered it. They simply didn't reach enough people. Neither play was a major success, and both films went straight to cable television, not yet known as a place for prestigious fare. It wasn't until 2013 that Robinson's story would be retold in a manner that reached millions. *42* is best remembered as the world's introduction to Chadwick Boseman. It was also a bonafide hit. Released in April to coincide with the start of the baseball season, the film grossed $27 million on its opening weekend, the most ever for a baseball movie. It ended its run with a worldwide total of $97.5 million, more than doubling its $40 million budget. It is the last hit baseball movie to date.

Watching it today, it's easy to see why the film landed well with audiences. *42* is rousing and rewarding, with a few doses of expertly placed humor to ensure it doesn't collapse beneath its own righteousness. It pairs a rising young actor, Boseman, with an older, established star, Harrison Ford, who plays Rickey. It portrays its baseball with accuracy and verve. The ball pops off the bat, and the fielders make plays with grace and athleticism. Not for one moment does the on-field action seem less than credible.

What frustrates about *42* is how similar it is to *The Jackie Robinson Story*, which came 63 years earlier. Each uses the same timeline and moral framework, focusing on how, in Jackie's first year with the Dodgers, he overcame the objections and abuse of his teammates, his opponents, other owners, and the fans. There are a few welcome tweaks to the formula, although each comes with a caveat. *42* gives Rachel Robinson (Nichole Beharie) more screen time, although really not much more to do. Still, the palpable chemistry between Boseman and Beharie humanizes Rachel to a degree not found in the 1950 film. It also includes Wendell Smith (Andre Holland), one of the sportswriters who burnished Jackie's legend, even as the film largely elides the role he and other journalists had in laying the groundwork for integration, instead simply using his writing as a framing device to narrate the story.

Otherwise, it might as well be a straight remake of *The Jackie Robinson Story*. It follows Jackie from his signing through his first two years in professional baseball, first with the minor-league Montreal Royals and then that famous, tumultuous 1947 season with the Brooklyn Dodgers. It mostly tells the stories we already know. We see the famous scene in Rickey's office, with Ford barking, "I want a player with the guts not to fight back!" We see Jackie booed and threatened by fans and opposing teams. We see him tempted to retaliate with violence before thinking better of it. We see him slowly win over his teammates. Finally, we see him put all his fears and anxieties aside and thrive as a ballplayer, earning the love and respect of baseball fans everywhere, and changing the game forever.

It's still a nice story, but it's unsettling that Hollywood saw no need to revise its perspective. *The Jackie Robinson Story* embraced the idea of Robinson as a preternaturally restrained figure because it was essentially an advertisement for integration; in 1950, only five of the 16 major league teams had Black players on their roster. But *42* was released a few months into the second term of America's first Black president. A new narrative was called for, but *42* offered only the same comfort and relief that many voters took away from Obama's election. With its sepia-toned, simplistic narrative of a Black man overcoming racism with the help of a benevolent White man, it subtly sends the message to White viewers (and voters) that racism in America is a thing of the past. It's an alluring tale, but Robinson deserved more. Politicians may survive by flattering the electorate, but film is a place where public opinion can be gently challenged, and *42* fails to avail itself of that opportunity, instead telling White viewers a story they want to hear—again.

42 might best be classified as a "White savior" film, a term that originated in Rudyard Kipling's 1899 story *The White Man's Burden* but was increasingly used over the years before exploding in popularity in the 2010s. Here's the basic idea: Every film about racial progress offers an unspoken theory for how change is forged, and most of the time, they lean into narratives in which people of color are lifted out of poverty and other poor circumstances through the courage and kindness of White benefactors, as opposed to securing freedom through their own agency, or failing to achieve any justice at all. White savior movies highlight individual racism, dramatize the lives of those who overcome it, and ignore the systems of oppression. 2009's *The Blind Side*, based on the (debated) true story of a White, Southern woman who took in a Black orphan and taught him how to play football, is one. So is 2011's *The Help*, based on a bestselling novel about a White woman who helps Black domestic workers in Mississippi during the Civil Rights Era tell their stories. Unsurprisingly, these films are almost always all written, directed, and produced by White people, and embraced by the largely White Academy of Motion Picture Arts and Sciences. Both *The Blind Side* and *The Help* were nominated for multiple Oscars, including Best Picture.

As the White savior film became a bankable genre, it also faced increased scrutiny due to the newfound focus Obama's campaign and election brought to race in America. In 2015, activist April Reign started the social media campaign #OscarsSoWhite to draw attention to the lack of Black nominees at the Academy Awards, but it also launched a discussion about the kind of films for which Black actors did get nominated, most often ones in which they suffered and were saved by White characters, like the Oscar-winning *12 Years a Slave* (2013). By centering White people in stories of racial progress, these films, it is argued, reinforce the very power structures that perpetuate racism. As author and critic Noah Berlatsky wrote in *The Atlantic* during the Oscar run of *12 Years a Slave,* "when every major film representation of slavery hinges on venerating the noble sacrifices of honorable Whites—well, let's just say that as a challenge to White supremacy, it leaves something to be desired."

It may have been justifiable to center Branch Rickey in 1950 because *The Jackie Robinson Story* was made primarily for pre–Civil Rights Era White audiences, but one would have hoped a Robinson film made in

2013 would find Robinson sufficient as a main character. Maybe the economics precluded this, as having a major movie star like Ford onscreen a whole lot surely pleased the financiers. Perhaps that explains why *42* goes even further than *The Jackie Robinson Story* in its lionization of Rickey, opening on a scene of him explaining his plan to break baseball's color line that essentially frames him as the main character. Ford gives a pleasingly gruff performance, but the film gives Rickey too much credit. In reality, the wealthy owner had very little to lose from his experiment, and the color line was soon to be broken with or without his initiative.

At least it got its casting of Robinson right. Boseman had acted before—in the theater and as a regular on several television series—but *42* marked the first time film audiences were introduced to his grand presence, his confidence that stops just short of arrogance, and the delight in his eyes when faced with a challenge he knows he can meet. These qualities, which were Boseman's trademarks for the rest of his too-brief career, made him a perfect fit for the genteel Robinson depicted in *42*. He would not have been suited for the righteous anger of *The Court-Martial of Jackie Robinson*, and in fact the few scenes when he is asked to summon such defiance fall flat. There's an interaction with the gas station attendant who refuses to let him use the bathroom, and another with an airline employee who bumps him and Rachel from their flight to spring training. In neither one does Robinson's anger leap off the screen. Then there's the moment when a police officer threatens to arrest him on the diamond for breaking local segregation laws. The cop wields his billy club in Robinson's direction, and he responds: "If you use that thing, you'd better hit me square between the eyes," but Boseman's heart isn't in it. His rage isn't palpable except in a brief moment when, after enduring viciously racist abuse from Philadelphia manager Ben Chapman (Alan Tudyk), Robinson enters the tunnel behind the dugout and slams his bat against the wall. Still, even here, the film keeps us at a distance, framing him in shadow with light streaming in from the field behind him. We can't make out his face or his eyes. It's a picture of Christ-like endurance, not human anger. Of course, Rickey works his way into the scene, entering the tunnel to talk Robinson down from his rage.

There was one film that embraced Robinson's anger, although, perhaps uncoincidentally, it never actually got made. Spike Lee wrote a script simply titled *Jackie Robinson* that he planned to make with Denzel Washington in the lead role. It took some time to get the financing; convincing producers that there is an audience for Black-made films has never been easy, even for a director of Lee's stature. By the time it came together, Washington felt he was too old to play the role, and the financiers dropped out.

Lee's version would have been incredible. The script opens in meta-text with an older Robinson at home with Rachel watching *The Jackie Robinson Story* on TV. It acknowledges the myth before ripping it to shreds. Lee's screenplay corrects the missteps of nearly every other telling of the Robinson story. It shows how his call-up to the major leagues decimated the Negro Leagues and its players. There's a haunting scene of Satchel Paige, drunk and despondent when he realizes he's too old to make it to the show. It dramatizes that glorious moment in Montreal, when Robinson was serenaded by the crowd after winning their minor league World Series and was chased by, as Lee describes it in the script, a "mob of love." It makes room to celebrate the Black patrons who showed up to the park that season, keeping as cool in the stands as Robinson did in the field, which, as Lee puts it in the screenplay, "made this experiment a success." It even extends its focus beyond Robinson's first year in the major leagues, showing what it looked like when Robinson wasn't the only Black player on the team. The next year, Roy Campanella and Don Newcombe join him on the Dodgers, where they engage in thoughtful debates about how to continue making change in the league.

And yes, it captures Robinson's rage. For that famous game against Philadelphia, when Chapman stood on the top step of the dugout and hurled racial obscenities at Robinson, Lee's script offers Robinson a moment of liberation. Robinson fantasizes about walking into the dugout and viciously beating Chapman and the other players with his bat. It's all happening in his head, but it's described in gory detail in the script. Reminiscent of the Tarantino movies of the 21st century, like *Inglourious Basterds* or *Django Unchained*, in which rogue heroes get bloody revenge on history's greatest monsters, the short scene is crucial to this more honest, contemporary vision of Robinson. It doesn't shy away from the "angry Black man" stereotype, but instead understands and even embraces his anger. This portrayal is more authentic to Robinson's experience, and it better serves the story, making his iconic restraint seem all the more impressive.

Unfortunately, Hollywood thought the world wasn't ready for a more radical Jackie. Instead, they gave us *42*, which is only looking for saints: Robinson, Rickey, and ultimately American capitalism. That's the not-so-secret message of the film. "Dollars aren't Black and White," Rickey says, when first explaining his plan. "They're green. Every dollar's green." Just a few scenes later, Robinson, offended by a gas station attendant's refusal to let him use the bathroom, threatens to take the team bus and "our 99 gallons of gas somewhere else." The attendant changes his mind, and the viewers get a lesson in the power of the free market to change minds. This is the film's central idea: that racial progress occurs through capitalism, not through protest, boycotts, or political activism. If it wasn't perfectly clear, there's the exchange with a journalist on Robinson's first day of professional baseball: "Is this about politics?" the reporter asks. "It's about getting paid," Robinson responds.

It's an honest portrayal of Robinson, who well understood that impacting people's pocketbooks was the quickest way to change their minds. In his autobiography, he shared a theory for why his teammates warmed to him so quickly. "They realized I was a good ballplayer who could be helpful in earning a few thousand more dollars in World Series money," he wrote. "They hadn't changed because they liked me any better; they had changed because I could help fill their wallets." Nevertheless, the message hits differently in 2013, when we have learned the limits of that approach, than it did in 1950. *42* is built around the idea that once Robinson was accepted into the majors, and he demonstrated his dominance over the White players, baseball's racial problems simply disappeared. Emily Ruth Rutter, author of *Invisible Ball of Dreams: Literary Representations of Baseball behind the Color Line,* feels this framing is designed to reaffirm the status quo. "Baseball profits from this," she said. "The one-percent profits. It lets everyone off the hook to say that Jackie Robinson integrated baseball, and then everything was fine. There wasn't much left to grapple with." In reality, baseball's racial issues were not resolved when Robinson conquered the league. They just got more complicated. "The film doesn't account for how long it actually took to integrate baseball or the fact that baseball's front offices aren't that well integrated today," says Rutter. "Everything that's lingering gets airbrushed, and that's the Hollywood playbook."

The numbers back up Rutter's point. Things did get better for Black players in baseball, but then they got worse. In 1981, 18.7 percent of major league players were Black, an all-time high point that hasn't been reached since. It dropped below 10 percent in 2005 for the first time in almost 45 years. In 2013, the year *42* was released, only 6.7 percent of major leaguers were Black, and the racial disparity extended to the dugout and the front office. As of 2016, there were only two Black managers, four general managers of color, and just 14 percent of team vice-presidents were people of color. Here's a fascinating stat: 67 percent of first-base coaches were people of color in 2010 but only 23 percent of third-base coaches, which is a more important, well-paid position. Robinson understood this. In the final speech of his life, given before a game at the 1972 World Series, he bemoaned the lack of opportunities for Black former players in baseball, specifically in the coaching box. "I am extremely proud and pleased to be here this afternoon," he said, "but must admit that I am going to be tremendously more pleased and [prouder] when I look at that third-base coaching line one day and see a Black face managing in baseball." His stance stemmed from personal experience; as Robinson reached the end of his playing career, he looked for opportunities to work in a front office and found none.

The overall numbers reveal a league culture that was still very much in the throes of a diversity problem that *42* implied through its framing had already been resolved. To be clear, filmmakers are free to tell whatever version of Robinson's story they please, and there is no evidence of the film's writer-director, Brian Helgeland, willfully distorting the facts. "It's not grossly inaccurate," Rutter summarized, "but it had an opportunity to represent complexities, and it forfeited that in its conclusion."

In the years after *42* was released, Hollywood began taking its portrayals of race more seriously and Black filmmakers seized the chance to tell their own stories. The changes were immediately apparent. The #OscarsSoWhite campaign began in 2015; *Moonlight*, a low-budget drama about a young, gay, Black man in Miami, won Best Picture in 2017. The racial satire *Get Out* was a surprise hit at the Oscars in 2018, winning Best Original Screenplay and earning a Best Picture nomination, while *Black Panther*, starring Boseman, was the first film based on a comic book to be nominated for the top prize.

Despite this progress, however, the great racial baseball film has yet to be made. It might even be getting further away, since so few baseball movies are made at all these days. Baseball cinema is expensive to conjure, and in the 2010s the major studios began moving away from anything that wasn't franchise material or surefire Oscar bait, and toward films with global appeal. Traditionally, the baseball movie fits into none of those categories, let alone the racial baseball film. There is one film from this era, however, that reckons honestly and authentically with baseball's race problem, even if it contains almost zero baseball action: *Fences*, the 2016 adaptation of August Wilson's Pulitzer Prize–winning play directed by and starring Denzel Washington.

In the film, Washington plays Troy Maxson, a sanitation worker in 1950s Pittsburgh. A former Negro Leaguer who was too old to make the jump to the majors by the time baseball integrated, Troy has never forgiven the world for the injustices done to him. He claims to have been a Negro Leagues star who hit seven career home runs off of Satchel Paige, but it's unclear how much he has printed his own legend. His bitterness destroys his relationship with his son Cory (Jovan Adepo), a high school athlete who wants to play football in college. When Troy finds out Cory has quit his after-school job so that he can practice with the team, he forbids him from playing. Cory correctly deduces that his father is simply angry that his son might take advantage of opportunities he was once denied, which further enrages Troy. Over the course of the film, Troy's resentment nearly destroys his family, and while his abbreviated baseball career serves as a stand-in for all the atrocities inflicted upon Black Americans, the film never panders to a non-baseball audience. It gets its baseball talk exactly right.

In an early scene, Cory tries to talk with his father about the Pirates' recent winning streak, but Troy complains he can't invest himself in an "all-White team." Cory reminds him about their budding young Latino star, Roberto Clemente. Unable to revel in Clemente's talent, Troy can only point out that the manager isn't giving him enough at-bats. "If they got a White fella sitting on the bench, you can bet your last dollar he can't play," he says, sourly. "Colored guy gotta be twice as good to get on the team." Troy can't enjoy the national game anymore because, when he looks at it, all he sees is the pain it caused him. It's like the baseball he has hanging by a rope off a tree in his backyard. The ball is there for practice, and while we see Cory take a few swings at it, Troy never does. Still, Washington repeatedly shows it to us, hanging there lifelessly, waiting to be reengaged.

Despite his cynicism, Troy's mind is dominated by the game. He speaks in baseball metaphors through the film, lecturing Cory about getting "strike one," after he disobeys his father. He describes his fear of death as a "fastball on the outside corner" that he used to crush in his youth. In a poignant monologue, he compares the Black American experience as akin to being "born with two strikes." Troy is a complicated character. He behaves unforgivably toward his family at times, but the film also empathizes with his plight, intertwined as it is with the promise and the pain of baseball. The game was Troy's salvation—he learned to play in prison—and his damnation. In the end, he dies offscreen, while grinning and holding a bat. Baseball was a dream he couldn't let go of, or a nightmare from which he couldn't wake. Who among us can't relate? The racial baseball films of the 21st century show, through both their losses and their victories, how little had changed and how much more progress was needed.

Chapter 17
Sugar (2008)

BASEBALL CINEMA HAS BEEN ACHINGLY SLOW TO RECOGNIZE THE contributions of Latin American players to the game. For the many films about Jackie Robinson, there has yet to be one about Roberto Clemente, the Puerto Rican icon who dazzled fans with his talents and inspired them with his charity work, before dying in a tragic plane crash while bringing aid to earthquake victims in Nicaragua. MLB honors the man; every year, they give the Roberto Clemente Award to a player for his off-the-field contributions to the community. It's hard to imagine a life better suited for the sort of inspirational baseball drama Hollywood used to regularly produce.

There has also been no film about Esteban Enrique Bellán, the Cuban player who was a star in the early American professional leagues from 1868 to 1873. He wasn't much of a hitter but was renowned for his defense, with the *New York Clipper* labeling him "one of the pluckiest base players." After playing in America for a few years, Bellán returned to Havana and served as a player-manager in the first year of Cuban professional baseball. He is widely credited with contributing to the game's immediate popularity in his homeland. Other names for baseball biopics that jump to mind: Minnie Miñoso, Chico Carrasquel, Orlando Cepeda, Luis Aparicio, Juan Marichal. They were all groundbreaking

Latino stars in the years following Jackie Robinson's breaking of the color line, and none has ever been featured in a baseball film.

Instead, we get supporting Latino characters, each portrayed as an exotic creature with a natural gift for the game, little or no intellectual ability, and mysterious traditions that instill fear and ignorance in their teammates. Pedro Cerrano from *Major League* is the best example. A Cuban immigrant, Cerrano worships Jobu, a fictional Voodoo god invented for the film, and possesses only a single athletic tool: an ability to hit fastballs very far. He is incapable of learning to hit breaking pitches, which is a nifty way of suggesting he is dumber than everyone else on the team. The performance by Dennis Haysbert, whose eyes convey both wisdom and intelligence, elevates the character, but as written it recalls the racial prejudice—used to justify slavery and nearly every other form of racial discrimination—that people of color are physically gifted and intellectually stunted, unable to make full use of their own talents without White supervision. As a final insult, Cerrano finally hits a curveball in the film's climactic game, but only after rejecting his god. ("I say, 'Fuck you, Jobu.' I do it myself.") I'm surprised the sequel didn't open with Cerrano having converted to Christianity, although the arc they do ascribe him is somehow just as insulting; Cerrano has studied meditation under a Buddhist master and returned to the team with the competitive instincts of a daffodil.

1991's *Talent for the Game* starred Edward James Olmos, an Oscar nominee two years prior for *Stand and Deliver*, as a down-on-his-luck scout who, after his car breaks down in the middle of nowhere, discovers a White farm boy with incredible raw pitching talent. Rippling with clichés, it has virtually nothing to say about the experience of Latinos in baseball. Neither does *The Sandlot*, even though it gives Latino baseball fans a hero to root for in Benny the Jet.

The lack of Latino characters in baseball films is more than a casual oversight. It's an outright denial. Baseball's roots in Latin America are almost as deep as they are in the U.S. In the late 1800s, students from Cuba and Venezuela who had been studying in the U.S.—like Esteban

Enrique Bellán—returned to their home country and spread the good news of baseball. Before too long, each country had its own league. As early as 1902, the sport was popular enough in Venezuela that *Base-Ball* magazine was founded to satisfy rabid fans. None of these stories have been told on screen. In fact, only one movie has portrayed the experiences of Latin-born players in professional baseball with any empathy, insight, or curiosity. That movie is *Sugar*, a 2008 independent film that shines light on the journey of a Latin American prospect who comes to America with big dreams and uncovers a more complicated reality. It's a true underdog story about a minor leaguer, and a Latino minor leaguer at that, and, what's more, a Latino minor leaguer who never makes it to the show. It's not based on a true story. It's based on thousands of them.

Told in three acts, the film follows the journey of Miguel "Sugar" Santos (Algenis Perez Soto), a stud pitching prospect from the Dominican Republic. He lives during the week at a major league facility in the DR run by the fictional major league Kansas City Knights. On the weekends, he returns home as a conquering hero. Technically, he hasn't conquered anything yet; he is signed by the Knights but has not been called to the states. Still, the promise of a major league career is as good as gold to him and his friends.

Eventually, Miguel is brought to the U.S. to play for the Knights' Class A team in fictional Bridgeport, Iowa. Here the film morphs into a fascinating blend of baseball movie and immigrant story, with more of the latter than the former. There are only a few scenes of game action, with more time spent in the clubhouse and on the practice field. Mostly, the film lingers on his time between games, as he struggles to adjust to life in America. Co-directors Ryan Fleck and Anna Boden (who also co-wrote the screenplay) precisely capture the isolation of life in a strange and unfamiliar land where Miguel doesn't speak the language. One of the saddest scenes is simply about breakfast: A teammate teaches Miguel how to order French toast at the local diner, but his education on American cuisine stops there, so it's all he ever orders. One day, he gets sick of French toast and tries to order eggs, but when the waitress asks him if he wants them scrambled, over easy, or sunny side-up, he has no choice but to revert to his standard order. "French toast," he sighs. This small scene powerfully encapsulates the loneliness of Miguel's existence. He has no way of expressing his basic wishes, let alone his deeper emotional needs.

It's a bracingly original work that turns the clichés of the baseball film inside out. The conventional arc of a team of castaways learning to put aside their differences and play as a single unit is cast aside. Miguel spends his entire professional career—all of a few months—with the same team, but his teammates come and go with promotions, demotions, and releases. He befriends a bonus baby (Andre Holland, who also played Wendell Smith in *42*) just in time for him to get promoted to Double A. That roster spot is taken by another Dominican, Salvador (Kelvin Leonardo Garcia), who impresses the coaches with his wicked cutter just as Miguel's performance is starting to falter. An injury disrupts his momentum, and when he returns, his fastball is a couple miles per hour slower. Miguel resorts to amphetamines to help him keep pace, but the drugs make him lose command of his pitches and his emotions. When he takes his anger out on a locker room water cooler, he gets chastised and fined by his manager.

Miguel's inability to cope with his inconsistent performance leads to a startling decision: On the morning of a road trip, he abandons the team without warning and takes a bus to New York, where he hopes to connect with a recently released teammate and the strong Dominican community there. Unlike in most Hollywood screenplays, there is no single event that precipitates his decision. No trauma or inciting incident, as screenwriters call it. *Sugar* never explains why Miguel wants to leave, and why he's so reluctant to return to the Dominican Republic. Jarring as it may be, it feels true to Miguel's experience. He has no one to talk with. He has friends on the team but no sense of consistency that would allow him to really open up, and he lacks even the vocabulary to describe his first-ever experience with failure on a baseball field.

Credit Boden and Fleck for not psychoanalyzing Miguel or having him spout some clichéd dialogue about baseball being a game of failure.

Instead, we follow him without judgment as he searches for an authentic life. When he gets to New York, he doesn't find his friend right away, but he does procure a place to live and eventually a job making furniture with a Puerto Rican shop owner. Eventually, he reconnects with his old teammate, who invites him to join a non-professional baseball league made up of other former prospects. It turns out Miguel is happier playing baseball for fun than for a living. It puts the smile back on his face. You can't overstate the depth of this subversion: There has never been another baseball film that portrays quitting as anything other than failure. Typically, these movies celebrate perseverance, gutting through it, putting in the work, and beating the odds. They're about teamwork and sacrifice and how we can accomplish more together than we can as individuals, and a hundred other clichés that are commonplace in sport and film but reveal very little about their characters' lives.

We don't always go to movies for the truth, but sometimes, the truth finds the movie. The story of *Sugar* could have been told at any time—Latin players have been making an impact on baseball since the beginning of the sport—but it's notable that this film premiered just a few days into the Obama presidency. There was an implicit promise in his campaign that the election of a Black president would open doors for other marginalized groups, including immigrants; that his rising tide would lift all boats making their way to American shores. He also made an explicit promise, one that he would break, to make immigration reform a priority in the first year of his presidency. Obama was elected in part on the backs of these promises; his success with Latino voters comprised his unexpectedly large margins of victory in purple states Colorado, New Mexico, and Nevada. He captured a majority of Latino voters in Florida, the first time a Democrat had accomplished such a feat since at least 1988, when exit polls were first conducted there. As a whole, Latino voters believed in him, and he largely disappointed them, failing to pass immigration reform or the DREAM Act (which would have created a pathway to citizenship for children brought to the U.S. illegally), and deporting more undocumented immigrants than any other president.

Sugar was conceived and made before Obama's election, but Miguel ends up an accidental symbol of the immigrant experience in our era, arriving full of enthusiasm for the American Dream, finding challenges he is unprepared for, and eventually resorting to life as an undocumented immigrant in New York City.

Sugar finds hope amidst the rubble of Miguel's career by focusing on his character, rather than his meaning as a symbol. It tells a story about baseball and America that reflects not sunny myths of their greatness but the ups and downs of immigrant life. Said Fleck, "I think it was always clear to both of us that it was not just a baseball movie, and even though I was a fan and could add from my fan knowledge a certain dimension, it was never going to be the typical heroic, home-run-in-the-ninth-inning ending. Whether they end that way or not, that's what a baseball movie is. It's about the game on the field, and for us the game on the field was only as important as how it affected our character." There are times *Sugar* doesn't even feel like a baseball movie, and not just due to the relative lack of game action. Miguel ultimately decides his life is better without the dream of Major League Baseball at all. In this way, it's almost an anti-baseball movie or at least an anti-MLB movie.

It's a true character study, rather than a conventional sports film. Miguel's trials aren't particularly dramatic. We never feel as if he is on the verge of tragedy. There are no major obstacles to overcome, and certainly no big game to be won. He makes his professional debut, has a few good weeks, gets injured, and has trouble rebounding. And then he quits. He isn't released or demoted. The film doesn't make him a victim of racism or systemic oppression. In real life, the team would have likely given him every chance to work out the kinks, but Miguel doesn't want that, and while it's far more common for players to get released than to quit, Boden and Fleck smartly make Miguel the master of his own fate. It gives him agency and self-respect, qualities that minor league players, especially those from overseas, are systematically denied.

"*Sugar* does what MLB is scared to do, which is highlight the journey of the Latino player,' says Dave Zirin, whose article "Say it Ain't So, Big

Leagues" for The Nation in 2005 was among the first to point out the corruption and hypocrisies in baseball's international signing system. "There are so many dynamic Latino players in MLB right now, but the sport doesn't lean into it. You don't see them turning someone like Vlad Guerrero Jr. into the commercial superstar by all rights he should be. I think discussions of the journey from the hardships of Major League Baseball's academy to the big leagues isn't something they want to highlight because it's very different from other sports. To find that one brilliant player, baseball demands forty players who are never going to make it. And they don't want you asking what happens to those other players." In general, baseball has a higher washout rate among prospects than any other sport—no other team has the sophisticated, multi-tier minor league system of baseball—but it's even higher among Latin-born players. Because of the international signing system, teams often have less money invested in their Latino and Hispanic players than the American-born players who come through the amateur draft, and it makes them easier to cut. Players from Latin American countries account for around 30 percent of major league rosters, but 35 percent of roster spots in the minor leagues, which means a lower success rate. More Latin players end up like Sugar than Vladimir Guerrero, Jr.

The fact that MLB has a relatively older and mostly White audience may explain why the league isn't great about marketing its Latino stars—based on a questionable assumption that White fans can't relate to Latinos—but MLB has even bigger reasons for wanting to keep its Latin players two-dimensional and deny them the opportunity to tell their stories. There's corruption to bury. Those baseball academies, like the one Miguel comes from in *Sugar*, have become the subject of intense scrutiny in recent years. The system, in place for decades, relies heavily on Dominican trainers who identify the talent and work with young athletes to prepare them for their showcases for MLB scouts. When they sign, the trainers get a cut of the signing bonuses. There's nothing inherently corrupt or illegal in this system, but for years it has been largely unregulated, creating opportunities for trainers to promise more than they deliver and take larger cuts than are justified.

In recent years, the situation has gotten even worse. A hard cap on international signing money was imposed by MLB in 2017, which led teams to look for ways to cut corners. Franchises have started negotiating unofficial contracts much earlier, reportedly with "players" as young as 12, and then training them at their baseball academies until they reach 16, the minimum age for an official signing. Signing an athlete earlier in their career is always a cost-saver; the further they are from reaching their potential, the more eager they are to lock in a bonus. Trainers have reportedly started working with children at 10 or 11, who are willing to sacrifice their education to devote themselves full time to baseball. You can't blame them, as baseball often represents their best chance at changing the economic fortunes of their family, but as *Sugar* asks, what happens to them if baseball doesn't work out? For most players, it doesn't.

Although the insights of *Sugar* were recognized by some critics—the American Film Institute listed it among the top ten films of 2009—its true legacy lies far away from Hollywood. In the time since *Sugar* was released, the international signing system has come under attack. The lack of regulation into the process was highlighted by Zirin's article in *The Nation*, and the subsequent 2011 documentary *Ballplayer: Pelotero*. Narrated by John Leguizamo, the film takes a similar approach as the acclaimed basketball documentary *Hoop Dreams*, following players with huge talent and uncertain futures as they navigate the intricate international signing process. It exposes the cold, calculating relationship between the major leagues and their human capital, and, in the case of young Miguel Sano, who would go on to have a significant career in the majors, overt corruption. *Ballplayer: Pelotero* documents how the Pittsburgh Pirates collaborated with a Dominican trainer to deflate Sano's signing price by planting rumors that he has lied about his age.

The light shone by *Sugar* and *Ballplayer: Pelotero* on corruption in the international signing system put pressure on MLB to make significant reforms. More articles were written. Internal discussions were had.

Finally, in 2022, it looked like the dam would break. In the new collective bargaining agreement between MLB and the MLB Players Association, an international draft was agreed to in principle that would replace the traditional signing system. If implemented, the draft would bring signing bonuses for Latin-born players closer to what college and high school players in the U.S. receive, and eradicate the process of signing players at outrageously young ages. Some Dominican players raised concerns about the draft, arguing that teams would invest less money in their academies there, which will hurt local economies, but most parties agreed the system would be a positive change for the players. A draft would also reduce PED use among the teenage prospects by making drug testing mandatory.

Most importantly, it would prevent players from being low-balled, as each draft slot would come with a pre-set signing bonus. The corruption on display in *Ballplayer: Pelotero* would be history. Zirin thinks the films had something to do with that. "I do think *Sugar* and *Pelotero* and other journalism has led to the idea of the International Draft being taken seriously," he says. "There was no awareness about the lives of Latin American prospects beyond Horatio Alger stories of people rising from poverty. These films moved us beyond 'rags to riches' narratives and toward an understanding of structural poverty and Major League Baseball's complicity in benefitting from it."

There's an unfortunate, hopefully temporary epilogue to this story: While the International Draft was agreed upon in principle, it was quickly scuttled after the fact. The league and the players' association failed to meet their deadline to finalize the agreement, and as of this writing, the old system remains in place. Maybe the profile of the issue is just too low; outside of those who live and breathe baseball, it's unclear how many people are even aware of the problems with the international signing system. A great movie like *Sugar* has the power to change the narrative and bring the issue to the forefront. The sad irony is that, at least in the short term, a film that challenges the status quo typically fails to find enough of an audience to alter it.

Still, its legacy should not be ignored. When asked how the film was received by Latin American players, Boden speaks glowingly of the film's premiere in Santo Domingo, the capital of the Dominican Republic. "The president came, and all these Dominican baseball superstars were there," she told me. "David Ortiz. Sammy Sosa. It was in the old national theater that holds a thousand people. They brought a bunch of Little Leaguers. There was a great energy while it was screening. People were talking and laughing. And the feedback afterward was so positive, even from those who made it as major leaguers. They were like, 'You got it. That's what it was like.' Even though they hadn't been through that particular kind of failure. They said, 'That thing about the French toast! I remember that!'"

Whether pop culture can create any kind of lasting change offscreen is an open question, but for marginalized people, seeing yourself onscreen is an empowering experience. *Sugar* may have not changed baseball, but it found its audience, and that's a start.

Chapter 18

Faith-Based Baseball Films

DID THE BASEBALL MOVIE DIE? DOES IT NEED A RESURRECTION? *42* WAS the last one that could be considered a hit, and there hasn't been a baseball film with even a significant theatrical release since 2016, when Richard Linklater's wonderful *Everybody Wants Some!!* landed with a thud at the box office. Since then, the straight-to-streaming baseball documentary has become a popular form, but the grand baseball movie—the kind that plays on the big screen and captivates a nation—is nowhere to be found.

Yes, baseball cinema might be on life support, but reports of its death have been greatly exaggerated. It's just hiding in an unfamiliar place. Consider the following titles. *A Mile in his Shoes. One Hit from Home. Full Count. Home Run. Milltown Pride. The Final Season. The Perfect Game. Hitting the Cycle. Running the Bases.* These are baseball films released between 2009 and 2022. If you haven't heard of them, it's only because you are not their target audience. The baseball movie has been born again for faith-based audiences.

Christian filmmaking was not always a niche genre. It's part of the foundation of cinema itself. In 1906, director Alice Guy-Blache made *The Birth, The Life, and The Death of Christ*, a 33-minute biblical drama with gorgeous sets, hundreds of extras, and even special effects portraying Christ rising from the grave. It was a religious blockbuster for its time. *The Ten Commandments* and *Ben-Hur* have both been made and remade several times, including well-known versions in the 1920s and 1950s. These films continue to be produced, and they continue to perform well at the box office because they have a reliable audience. Christians have always been a majority in America, and Hollywood, although founded by Jewish immigrants from Eastern Europe, has historically been eager to cater to them. For a time, it came largely in the form of self-censorship. In the 1920s, Hollywood was so concerned about a looming boycott from the Catholic League over their depictions of violent and sexual content that they created the Production Code, an onerous list of rules for what could and could not be shown on screen to which all studio films adhered. It remained in place until 1968, when it was replaced by the MPAA rating system still used today.

But why cater to Christians through omission when you could make films directly for them? The industry finally saw the full potential of this approach in 2004 when Mel Gibson's *The Passion of the Christ* shocked Hollywood insiders by grossing a whopping $600 million worldwide. The film, which dramatizes Christ's final days, was written, directed, and produced independently by Gibson completely outside of the studio system. It was mostly reviled by critics, and concerns were raised by interested parties about its use of antisemitic tropes. Yet it was the fifth-highest grossing film of the year, fitting snugly between *The Incredibles*, about an animated family with superpowers, and *The Day After Tomorrow*, a parable about a climate change apocalypse.

Secular folks went out of curiosity—Gibson was still a major star at the time—and even the reports of antisemitism likely stoked the public's interest. The main drivers of ticket sales were churches, who bought a huge number of tickets for their congregants. "They started very early, targeting pastors, inviting them to early screenings, and encouraging them to buy blocks of tickets, which is how I saw it," says Alissa Wilkinson, an author and film critic for the *New York Times* who grew up in an evangelical community. "The feeling I remember very clearly is that you're a bad Christian if you don't go see this movie. Jesus suffered for you, and you can't even sit through a two-hour movie just because it's violent?" *The Passion of the Christ* portrays vicious bloodshed, but it was perceived by churchgoers as distinct from the gratuitous violence that Hollywood has long indulged. Many Christians were happy to support a film that dramatized the brutal realities of Christ's sacrifice. As of this writing, it's still the highest-grossing R-rated film in the domestic market.

With profits so large, Hollywood couldn't help but take notice. Over the next decade, as streaming services began to cut into the profits of theatrical releases, faith-based films became a safe bet. Hollywood had long been a villain to the Christian right, who saw them as little more than a secular congregation of heathens and hedonists who promoted poor values to the masses, but in the wake of *Passion*, Hollywood and faith-based filmmakers formed a holy union to get the Christian message out and bring the dollars in. Studios created faith-based subsidiaries to produce low-budget inspirational films. The first project to hit was 2008's *Fireproof*, a drama about a fireman (Kirk Cameron) suffering from marriage problems and a pornography addiction. It was produced by Affirm Film, an arm of Samuel Goldwyn Films, a production company founded in 1978 and run by the descendants of one of the titans of early Hollywood (the same one who greenlit *The Pride of the Yankees*). Micro-marketed to Christian audiences, *Fireproof* grossed $33 million at the box office on a mere $500,000 budget.

Hollywood insiders were also behind 2014's *Heaven is for Real*, a TriStar Picture starring Oscar nominee Greg Kinnear as the father of a boy who suffers a near-death experience and returns from the ordeal with evidence of the afterlife. In that same year, 2014's *God's Not Dead*, about a college professor persecuted for his belief in God, shocked Hollywood insiders by grossing $64 million. *God's Not Dead* was made independently by PureFlix Entertainment, which rode the success of the film to immense power in the faith-based film world. At their peak, PureFlix was releasing five inspirational films a year in theaters. More recently, they have focused on their streaming service ("the No. 1 streaming service for wholesome, faith-based and family-focused entertainment"), which currently has more than 125,000 monthly subscribers.

To the untrained eye, all faith-based films may look the same, but there are actually two distinct categories. How can you spot the difference? I asked filmmaker and actor Luke Barnett, whose experiences growing up in an evangelical home informed his 2020 comedy *Faith Based* about an underemployed actor who makes a faith-based film strictly for the money. "There are people who want to take a sermon and do it in film form, and there are people who want to make movies, but they also happen to be a Christian," he explains. "The latter is always better." The accidentally Christian movies have B-list stars, albeit sometimes in minor roles, and craftsmanship that comes close to the standards set by studio films, or least well-funded independents. They look and feel like normal movies. The sermon-movies have casts and crew drawn entirely from artists working outside the mainstream film industry and sometimes exclusively on faith-based films.

Either way, baseball proved a fitting subject. "When these people think of America," Barnett told me of the evangelical community, "they think of Jesus and baseball." There's an inherent conservatism in these films, a baked-in nostalgia that aligns with America's most traditional sport. Faith-based baseball films promote old-fashioned values like sacrifice and teamwork. They uphold the traditional American family. They tell stories of personal redemption that are often about current or former ballplayers who fall from grace due to unprocessed trauma or substance abuse, but who are able rebuild their lives after giving themselves over to Jesus. We hear these stories on baseball broadcasts all the time. They are baked into our understanding of the game. While these faith-based films may feel hokey compared to the grittier baseball movies of the prior generation, their wholesomeness is rooted in the genre's origins. They're not too far afield from the films of the postwar era, when baseball was seen as a galvanizing and inspiring force to help Americans through challenging times.

Their craft can be shaky, but faith-based filmmakers do their homework, and they draw from the sturdiest conventions of the genre. In 2011's *A Mile in His Shoes*, Dean Cain, who once played Superman on TV and has in recent years devoted himself to rightwing causes, plays a former player and manager of an independent league team who is suffering a crisis of faith following the death of his son. When his car breaks down on a country road, he discovers on a family farm a young man with Asperger's syndrome who is pretty good at hurling apples into a bucket. He puts the guy on the team and coaches him through his immense challenges, and in the process renews his own Christianity. The set-up of a broken-down car and a lucky discovery of a raw and talented player is straight out of *Talent for the Game* and reminiscent of so many others, like *Pride of the Yankees*, *The Stratton Story*, *The Natural* (and even the awful Albert Brooks movie *The Scout*), that open with scouts discovering star players in unlikely places. *Moneyball* may have killed the scout as a heroic figure in mainstream baseball cinema, but he still can shine in the faith-based film industry.

Alcoholism plays a major role in faith-based films, perhaps because it's such a common vice that the Christian filmmakers don't worry that they're titillating their audiences with a new drug, but the trope also has its roots in the original baseball cinema. 1952's *The Winning Team* tells the story of Grover Cleveland Alexander (played by a young buck named Ronald Reagan), a star pitcher who returned from fighting in WWII with shell shock and turned to alcohol to ease his pain. He loses his job in baseball due to his drinking problem, before his wife (Doris Day) nurses him back to sobriety, good health, and a job on a major league roster. Numerous faith-based films follow similar templates, as does the life of real-life president George W. Bush, during whose presidency the faith-based film movement was born. Bush's life story basically is a faith-based baseball movie. In the 1980s, he quit drinking, found God, and ended up leading an ownership group that purchased the Texas Rangers. Even his presidency is intertwined with the game; one of his most galvanizing presidential moments came when he stepped to the mound at Yankee Stadium to throw the first pitch of the World Series just six weeks after the events of 9/11—and threw a perfect strike.

I'd watch that movie. So would the American electorate. In 2000, Bush received 68 percent of the evangelical vote, and after backing a constitutional amendment banning same-sex marriage, a partial-birth abortion ban, and public funding for religious schools and charities—and throwing one very meaningful pitch—he received 78 percent of their vote in 2004. Supported by the right-leaning Fox News, which became the top-rated cable news network in 2002, and an internet culture that increasingly sorted users into echo chambers that reaffirmed their most extreme positions, evangelicals grew more powerful and emboldened, transforming themselves from a vocal minority into a significant force in American culture.

Bush's baseball-related achievements came on the national stage, but few faith-based baseball films are set in the major leagues, preferring to guide their heroes toward less worldly achievements, like family, sobriety, or just a steady job coaching Little League. In *Home Run*, Cory Brand (Scott Elrod) plays an All-Star with rage and alcohol problems. After he injures a young bat boy in a tirade, he is suspended from baseball, and he returns to his hometown, where he coaches a Little League team to rebuild his image. The team just happens to be co-managed by Cory's ex-girlfriend, and his estranged son is on the roster. The ending is preordained. There are few surprises in *Home Run* and relatively little religion, although Cory does attend Christian Recovery, an actual Christian 12-step program where his newfound sobriety is supported by emotional stories from others who have conquered their addiction with God's help.

Home Run is the directorial debut of David Boyd, who was working steadily as a director of photography on series such as *Friday Night Lights* and *The Walking Dead* when he received a call from a producer in Oklahoma asking if he'd like to make a faith-based baseball movie. "A producer from Oklahoma, I thought that was an oxymoron like 'jumbo shrimp' or 'military intelligence,'" he says. "She asked if I would consider directing this movie she had in mind, and also photographing it. That was the attraction. It was a project where I could make some mistakes, always a plus." Boyd, who identifies as non-religious ("I never even thought about it," he says when asked of his religious beliefs), brought a few of his own people from Texas to work on the film, including a gay assistant director he worried might be an issue for the Christian producers. In the end, it turned out to be fine. "The producers were pretty hands off," he says. "They were interested early on that I go to church with them and meet a congregation. I got introduced in a couple services. On the set, we had a little pop-up tent where people could pray. I was too busy to sit down." Boyd had no issue with the religious elements of the production, but he thought his time was better spent working than praying. "In the movie business, it's the same thing, anyway," he grinned.

The collaboration between a thoroughly secular filmmaker from Hollywood and Christian producers from Oklahoma proved surprisingly fruitful. *Home Run* grossed over $2 million, not a *God's Not Dead*–level hit, but not bad for a film with no major stars. Even the secular media liked it. "Considering it's a movie with an avowed mission; considering that mission has to do with addiction and spiritual righteousness; and considering that the story involves a Major League Baseball player coaching a Little League team made up of spunky kids...*Home Run* is actually pretty OK," wrote Tom Long in *The Detroit News*. He added that "director David Boyd has an eye for crisp, lovely compositions. This movie may be preaching to the choir, but at least the preacher has good taste." It's modest praise, but praise nonetheless.

On the other hand, there are movies like 2011's *Milltown Pride*, produced by Unusual Films, a film studio associated with evangelical Bob Jones University. According to its website, the studio was founded in 1950 "with the purpose of producing professional motion pictures with an emphasis on spreading the gospel of Christ." Whether religious or blasphemous, prioritizing message over story or character is a surefire way to make bad art, and *Milltown Pride,* about a ballplayer from a devout family who joins a local mill team and promptly becomes addicted to alcohol, is most certainly bad. The cast is made up almost entirely of students or faculty members at the university, and it shows. The film's cheap digital aesthetic clashes badly with its period setting. Like many lesser inspirational baseball films, it leads with its puritanism, strong-arming the viewer into accepting its simplistic message.

In reviewing the best and worst of this subgenre, it's clear that these films work better when the filmmaker has a personal connection to the material besides their Christian faith. Consider 2009's *The Perfect Game*, which is based on the 1957 Little League World Series, when an unheralded team from Monterrey, Mexico won the whole thing on the strength of a perfect game by pitcher Ángel Macías, the only one such pitching performance in LLWS history to date. The story follows the sports-underdog playbook, but it gently integrates its faith-based message through its rare representation of Latin American baseball. The kids and their coach (Clifton Collins, Jr.) are accompanied on their trip to America to play in the World Series by a local priest (Cheech Marin), but after he is forced to return to Mexico, the team refuses to play unless they can be led in prayer before the game. The White opposing coach jumps at the chance for a forfeit, but a Black groundskeeper (who we later learn is former Negro Leaguer Cool Papa Bell) played by Louis Gossett Jr. helps out, calling on his minister son to come and offer a quick service. It's framed as a victory for Mexican culture (in solidarity with Black Americans) over an unfair system.

The Perfect Game was directed by William Dear, one of the true mainstays of the faith-based baseball film. He also helmed the remake of *Angels in the Outfield* and *A Mile in His Shoes* (as well as a direct-to-video *Sandlot* movie). Dear was raised Protestant and played softball for his church as a kid, but he has no particular love of baseball. "It's really one of the most…I don't want to say 'boring,' because it's the national pastime," he told me, before trailing off. His films—particularly *Angels in the Outfield* and *A Perfect Game*—are better than most faith-based movies because they're motivated by his own emotional connection to the material, not a desire to promote a message or even celebrate the game. Regarding *Angels*, he notes, "My biological dad left when I was young. I think I connected deeply to the idea of the father giving away his son in the film." That film's protagonist is a boy in foster care whose father tells him he'll come back to get him "when the Angels win the pennant." Meanwhile, Dear sees his *A Perfect Game* and his other faith-based films (he's currently developing a Christmas movie highlighting the routine desecration of nativity scenes around the world) as a way of honoring his late mother. "She was such a believer," he says of her. "It was hard for her to see the world become more critical of religion, or at least debating the value of religion. She could never handle that. She didn't understand why people couldn't just believe. I've never said it out loud before, but I think I probably did this to do something more in line with her values."

The sentiment that Christians have become oppressed in America is the driving force behind many faith-based films. Wilkinson has identified it as an "outsize, navel-gazing persecution complex" that deadens storytelling in faith-based films, although Dear's films fare better than that. While he may be motivated by a desire to make Christian values mainstream again, he works in a more universal style of storytelling. *The Perfect Game* is about a team of underdogs that happens to be Catholic, and *Angels in the Outfield* is about a kid who just wants to reunite his family.

For every passable *Home Run* or *The Perfect Game,* however, there are several that might make you wonder if you're watching the worst film ever made. Even in those Christian calamities, the conventions of the baseball film still hold power. If you make it to the climatic game, you'll find yourself grinning all the same when that White, Christian guy crosses home plate or hits the winning home run, and the team crowds around him to cheer his redemption. He has suffered hardships, learned a lesson, maybe fallen in love, and now he gets to celebrate on the field with his chosen family. No matter how bad the film was up until that point, it's a convention that works every single time. In a sense, these films are the ultimate testament to the supreme power of baseball cinema. They work, even when they're terrible.

While these films may seem niche in today's cinematic landscape, there's nothing exceptional about religion in a baseball film, even if the vehicle for them—the faith-based film industry—is new and unfamiliar. We must not forget Jackie Robinson sitting with his preacher as he wrestled with the decision to accept Branch Rickey's offer to play for the Brooklyn Dodgers, or the hagiography of *The Babe Ruth Story*. The original *Angels in the Outfield* would certainly qualify as a Christian film. Spirituality even plays a major role in *The Natural*, which contains enough Christ imagery to qualify Robert Redford for sainthood. And of course, *Field of Dreams* offers a vision of life and the afterlife compelled by mainstream Christian values. "Is this heaven?" Shoeless Joe asks. It's not, but the American heartland is pretty close.

The religiosity in baseball cinema never stood out, in part because both religion and baseball were long considered fundamental components of the American character. It's true that America has become more secularized in the intervening years, with only about 70 percent of Americans identifying as Christian (down from 90 percent in the 1950s), and religion continues to dominate American institutions. Out of the 535 members of the 118th U.S. Congress (2023–24), only a single member identified as "unaffiliated" (another identified as "humanist"). So why have overtly religious films become niche? It's for some of the same reasons that baseball films have become niche. Our culture has become polarized, and Hollywood is not in the business of committing major budgets to a project that could alienate any segment of the population, Christian or otherwise. It's why franchise films based on pre-existing intellectual property dominate the box office now. Global economic forces play an even bigger role, with box-office receipts in China, which forbids Christianity, now crucial to a film's profitability. To appeal to the broadest possible audience, the movie industry plays it safe and invests only in films whose edges are so thoroughly sanded off that only vanilla themes of friendship, family, and teamwork are allowed.

Meanwhile, baseball itself has fallen from its perch atop American culture. It's hard to accurately measure the popularity of a sport—everything from TV ratings to Twitter impressions are relevant data points—but in-game attendance has been steadily declining since 2007. In 2021, a *Washington Post* poll found that only 11 percent of American adults said baseball was their favorite sport (football was the leader by a large margin). It can hardly be considered the national pastime anymore, unless you put the emphasis on "past." In fact, the loudest discussions about baseball these days are typically about its increasing obsolescence and the dramatic steps MLB has been taking—from the banning of defensive shifts to the rule requiring relief pitchers to face a minimum of three batters—to make the game more intense and help it regain its prior glory.

Clearly, the baseball movie needs baseball to survive, but maybe baseball needs cinema just as much. "A thriving national pastime requires good movies to support it," according to Joe Posnanski, an award-winning sports journalist and author of numerous bestselling books. "If you asked a casual fan for the ten greatest moments in baseball history, they'd have Roy Hobbs hitting it into the lights and Kevin Costner playing catch with his dad, or Dottie Hinson dropping the ball. Those moments are more famous in some ways than Kirk Gibson's World Series home run or the Shot Heard 'Round the World. They're a hugely important part of baseball history. We may be in a boom for sports movies right now, but none are about baseball. It's like Hollywood has felt like there's no player in the last 50 years that's worth making a movie about. And that's a problem for baseball."

Maybe the baseball movie isn't dead. Just segmented. Faith-based baseball films continue to be made. Baseball documentaries, at least the kind that go straight to streaming services, seem to be as popular as ever. 2014's *The Battered Bastards of Baseball*, a rousing and hilarious documentary about an independent professional team out of Portland in the 1970s, was almost made into a mainstream baseball movie before falling into turnaround. Documentaries about Yogi Berra, Nolan Ryan, and Reggie Jackson have all performed well on streaming services. Like many other genres that once flourished in theaters, baseball has found a home on the small screen. IFC's *Brockmire*, about an announcer (Hank Azaria) who has a drunken meltdown on the air and works his way back to the major leagues, ran for four seasons from 2017 to 2020. *Pitch*, a network series that imagined the trials of the first woman to make the major leagues, was canceled after a year, but it still has a devoted following. Even *A League of Their Own* was remade as a TV series that delved more deeply into the queer and racial elements of the All-American Girls Professional Baseball League to which the film barely alluded.

It almost feels as if things have come full circle. The baseball movie was an underdog from the beginning. Before *Pride of the Yankees*, no one thought they could make money. That stigma lasted in Hollywood through the postwar era, the '60s, Watergate, and the early Reagan years, before Robert Redford and *The Natural* changed a few minds. But the great thing about baseball is that there is no time limit. If you're still at the plate, you have a chance to win. "Since baseball time is measured only in outs, all you have to do is succeed utterly," wrote sportswriter Roger Angell. "Keep hitting, keep the rally alive, and you have defeated time. You remain forever young." Right now, the baseball movie itself is like a fallen hero trying to regain the glory of its youth. It's a veteran catcher on a team of misfits grinding its way into playoff contention. A gruff manager looking for one last shot at a championship. All it needs is one good training montage, some Hollywood magic, and maybe a smidgen of faith, and the baseball film will be back on the big screen—where it belongs.

Epilogue

Extra Inning

As I put the finishing touches on this book, Major League Baseball has just embarked on a grand experiment to update the game to match the tempo of 21st century life. The slow, grinding rhythms of baseball are being replaced with a faster, more modern pace. A pitch clock is being instituted, along with rules that limit the number of times a batter can call time-out and a pitcher can throw over to first base or step off the rubber, what they now refer to as a "disengagement." It's a fitting descriptor for what baseball is trying to prevent the fans from doing. Although no one in the league offices has said as much, it seems clear that the goal of these new rules is to replicate the pace of the NBA, which has leapfrogged MLB in popularity over the last several decades.

By the time you read this, perhaps the experiment will have been deemed a success, and baseball will be on the rise once more. The question that's less likely to have been answered is what will happen to the baseball movie, which lives in the in-between moments that these rule changes are designed to eliminate. Think of the iconic scenes we wouldn't get if a pitch clock had been in place. Nuke LaLoosh wouldn't have had time to shake off Crash Davis, and Crash wouldn't have been able to mutter under his breath about it and tell the batter what pitch was coming. The competing sign-off between Dottie Hinson and Jimmy Dugan that resulted in Dugan taking control of the Rockford Peaches? That took almost a full minute. Henry Rowengartner tempting the runner at first base to steal by casually dropping the ball and then throwing it straight up in the air? Sorry, kid, that's a pitch clock violation. Go back to Little League.

A faster game means less time to build drama. It makes the batter-pitcher dialectic feel more like a metronome and less like a duel. In classic Westerns, the filmmakers would stretch out those moments before the gunslingers drew their pistols for as long as they could. The baseball movie did that, too, and we were grateful for it. Think of the final at-bat of *For Love of the Game*, in which Billy Chapel (Kevin Costner) is trying to finish off his perfect game. The first pitch is lined foul. There are then 36 glorious seconds from when he receives the ball back from the catcher to the start of his wind-up. That's time for him to do a little self-talk, explain to the audience what he's thinking, and build the tension. Between the second and third pitch? A minute and five seconds. That's not just time. It's space. It allows Costner room to take a long, humbling look at the cheering crowd. It's space for us to consider how the manager, his teammates, and the opposing batter might be feeling. Space for Vin Scully to intone, "Will this be the last pitch of the game? Will it be the last pitch of Billy Chapel's life? Will it be the end of his brilliant major league career?" Without that time, we would not have the chance to properly appreciate those thrilling final moments.

Speaking of thrilling, the other thing happening as I wrap up this book is the 2023 World Baseball Classic. Maybe you've heard of it. The World Baseball Classic is one of the best things to happen to baseball, raising its profile in countries where it has long been a little brother to the game most of the world calls football. It could also be the best thing to happen to the baseball movie. For decades, the knock on the baseball film has been that it has no international audience. *The Natural, Eight Men Out, Major League, Bull Durham*; none even warranted a release outside of the U.S. and Canada. *Field of Dreams* managed to make $20 million overseas, which might speak to the paucity of actual baseball in it. *Moneyball* did about the same when adjusted for inflation, grossing

$34 million in international territories. The lesson is that baseball movies play well overseas when the poster features a major movie star, like Kevin Costner or Brad Pitt, which an industry now hopelessly devoted to superheroes and intellectual property seems to think isn't particularly important.

In the 21st century, the international box office has become even more important in factoring in a film's overall profitability, which is yet another obstacle any baseball movie must overcome in getting greenlit. Maybe the World Baseball Classic made it a little easier. The 2023 iteration scored huge viewing numbers across the globe. The championship game between Japan and the U.S. was the most watched baseball game in history. Countries like Great Britain, Australia, and the Czech Republic are now more invested in baseball than at any prior point in history. If a baseball movie was released in those countries, there would surely be a little more interest than there was before.

So here's my pitch, Hollywood: Make a film set at the WBC. You've got all the ingredients for a great baseball movie and a worldwide hit. You've got young guys who may never make the majors getting their one shot at glory. Older players who may be on the fringes of MLB rosters but are still stars for their home country, like Yoenis Cespedes. Redemption projects like Matt Harvey. Managers who are newly retired players, like Yadier Molina and Mark DeRosa, auditioning for coaching jobs in MLB. You could have mentors and proteges, and a cast of international stars to create a worldwide sensation. It could also create new meaning out of the baseball film by turning it into a symbol for the world, not just of America.

As just one suggestion, a key storyline coming out of the 2023 WBC was the play of Randy Arozarena. The current outfielder for the Tampa Bay Rays was once a top Cuban prospect, reaching his home country's professional league at the age of 18. He still wasn't earning enough to support his family, so he defected from Cuba via raft and made his way to Mexico, where he found success as a ballplayer and was eventually signed by the St. Louis Cardinals. From there, he was traded to the Rays, where he went on a tear in the 2020 World Series that they eventually lost to the Dodgers. In that series, he went 8–22 with three homers; in the whole postseason, he batted .377/.442/.831 with 10 homers, 19 runs, and 14 RBI. It was one of the greatest postseason performances in major league history.

Arozarena didn't truly become a household name, however, until that spring, when it was reported that he personally lobbied Mexican president Andrés Manuel López Obrador (via Instagram!) to make him a citizen so he could play for Mexico, the country that welcomed him, in Arozarena's words, "like a son." Obrador fulfilled his request, and Arozarena shined for Mexico in the WBC, crushing the ball in nearly every at-bat and making incredible catches all over the field, bringing them within a half-inning of making the championship game. It's a classic baseball movie, in which a heroic player galvanizes a team with his play and personal story, only to fall just short of their ultimate goal.

Just as the World Baseball Classic has invigorated interest in the game worldwide, so could the next great baseball movie revitalize interest in one of cinema's most reliable and consistent genres. The baseball movie is a sturdy thing. It has survived for nearly a century, changing with the times while retaining its most redeeming features. Its heroes never die, and its clichés don't get old. It never stays down for long. As we say every April, hope springs eternal—in baseball and at the movies.

Acknowledgments

THIS BOOK IS A COLLISION OF MY TWO LIFELONG PASSIONS, AND IF YOU squint, you could even consider it a memoir. As such, it would not be inappropriate for me to thank every person I've ever met, as they have all helped, in at least some small way, to mold me into the person who wrote this book. In the interest of time, however, I'll acknowledge just a few.

First and foremost is my wife, Breanna, who has had to endure more baseball—and certainly more baseball movies—than she could ever have imagined. She embraced the challenge, mustering an enthusiasm for the subject matter that spanned dozens of movie nights and hundreds of conversations over breakfasts, lunches, dinners, dog walks, and lazy afternoons. She was a willing traveler on the journey, making the trip infinitely more enjoyable, and ensuring I reached my destination without incident. Authors often speak of the agony of writing a book. I never felt that way, and I wonder if it's because I had such an incredible partner.

My foundational passion for writing and for books motivated me on this journey, and for that I must credit my mother, Amy Miller. I love the written word because she loved it first. She is the greatest writer I know, and one of the great readers anyone has ever known. As my own life as a writer has grown and evolved over the years, I have relied on her support, wisdom, and patience at every turn. She is my inspiration, creatively and personally, and she also watched a lot of baseball with me.

Next on the list is Justin Brouckaert, without whom this book would certainly not have happened. They say it only takes one person to believe in a new author, and Justin is my one. I'm so lucky to have found an agent who believes in me and challenges me. Justin made my pitch palatable, and his expertise throughout the process was of incalculable value to this neophyte to the publishing world.

Every writer, if they're lucky, has a network of friends who read their work before it is finalized and offer notes and ideas for revisions. Mine went above and beyond. Many thanks to Daniel Joyaux, Ethan Schwartz, and Will Jovanovich for their diligent reading and thoughtful suggestions. The book would never have reached its potential without their help.

I must also thank Triumph Books for believing in this project, my editor Jesse Jordan for his graceful shepherding of it from manuscript to finished product, and the entire Triumph team for their dedication and skill in getting my words into the world. It's an honor to be part of the Triumph family.

There are several people I interviewed for the book whose words didn't make it into the final draft. Nonetheless, their ideas greatly influenced my thinking on the subject, and I'm grateful for their time and energy. E. Ethelbert Miller, Steve Wulf, Jason Clinkscales, Bob DiBiasio, Eric Gilde: Thank you.

I am also grateful to the employees of The New York Public Library for the Performing Arts and the Woodbury Public Library, who saved me time and money by tracking down clips and books that were essential to my research. A special shout-out to David Makusevich, Woodbury's master of the interlibrary loan. Kids, go to libraries. They're amazing places, where people do favors for you—like lend you books and movies—just because it's the right thing to do.

I also send my gratitude to two friends I've never met and know only through social media but who were kind enough to provide guidance and support to this first-time author: Luke Epplin and Pete Croatto. They've each written a stellar sports book of their own, and I strongly recommend you seek them out.

Thank you to the rest of my friends and family, who inspire and indulge me. And, of course, to my dogs, who give me daily opportunities to express pure, unadulterated love, and without whom none of this would matter, anyway.